DREAMLAND'S
GRADED
MATHEMATICS
PART - 6

By :

TIRTH RAAJ BHANOT

MA (English), MA (Hindi), Hons. (Urdu), BEd.
(Formerly Sr. Teacher Air Force Central School, New Delhi)

Graphics :

KRISHNA MAHARANA

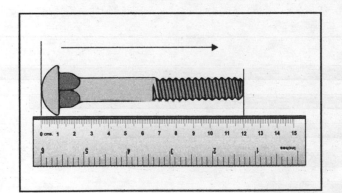

Published By

DREAMLAND PUBLICATIONS

J-128, KIRTI NAGAR, NEW DELHI - 110 015, (INDIA).
Fax : 011-543 8283 Tel : 011 - 512 1050
E-mail: dreamland@vsnl.com
http://www.dreamlandpublications.com

First published in 2000 by

DREAMLAND PUBLICATIONS

J-128, Kirti Nagar, New Delhi - 110 015 (India)

Fax : 011-543 8283, Tel : 011-512 1050

Copyright © 2000 Dreamland Publications

ISBN 81-7301-458-2

Printed at :
Engineering Enterprises

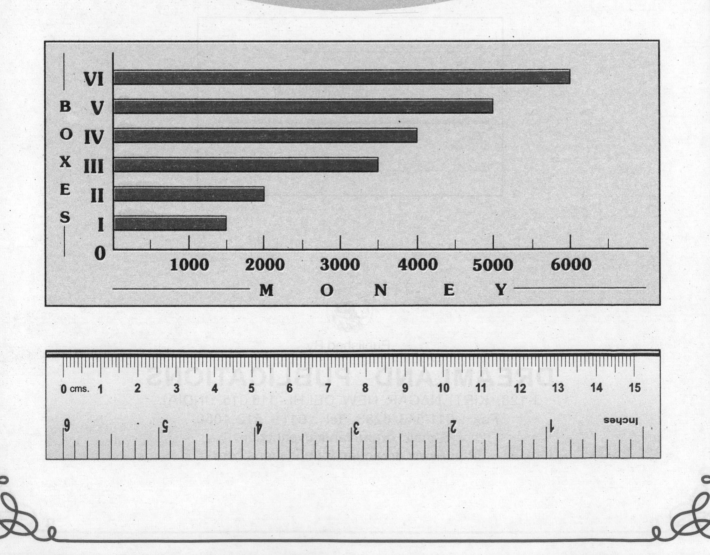

PREFACE

The present series—**GRADED MATHEMATICS**—has been brought out to cater for the needs of the students of Middle Classes in the subject of mathematics. Till recently, this subject was considered to be a bug-bear by students only because of the stereo-typed methods of its teaching. But our treatment of the subject is altogether different and so the present series is certainly a series *with a difference.*

The series has been brought out in conformity with the latest syllabus issued by the NCERT. It encourages the student to develop a mathematical, *i.e.* logical thinking which is so useful in day-to-day life. Liberal use of *diagrams* as well as *illustrations* and the choice of *sums from day-to-day life* are some salient features of the book.

The present volume is meant for class VI. Topics in this book have been given an easy-to-difficult order while exercises contain numerous sums to give ample practice and self-confidence to pupils. Two chief features of the book are a **miscellaneous exercise** at the end of each unit followed by a list of **memorable facts** studied in the unit.

We feel highly delighted to place the series in the hands of the teachers and the pupils hoping positively that it will admirably meet their approval from every angle. Still improvement has its scope in every human effort. So, constructive suggestions for the betterment of the series are highly welcome.

—**T. R. BHANOT**

CONTENTS

Revision of What We Have Learnt **5**

UNIT I — ARITHMETIC   **9-68**
1. Numbers—Natural and Whole 10
2. Operations in Whole Numbers—I 19
3. Operations in Whole Numbers—II 28
4. Factors and Multiples 35
5. Lowest Common Multiple 44
6. Integers—I 49
7. Integers—II 57
MISCELLANEOUS EXERCISES I & MEMORABLE FACTS *65-68*

UNIT II — COMMERCIAL ARITHMETIC   **69-108**
8. Ratio and Proportion 70
9. Unitary Method 81
10. Percentage 85
11. Profit and Loss 92
12. Simple Interest 100
MISCELLANEOUS EXERCISES II & MEMORABLE FACTS *106-108*

UNIT III — ALGEBRA   **109-128**
13. Introduction to Algebra 110
14. Addition and Subtraction 116
15. Linear Equations 121
MISCELLANEOUS EXERCISES III & MEMORABLE FACTS *127-128*

UNIT IV — GEOMETRY   **129-186**
16. Basic Geometrical Concepts 130
17. Line Segments 137
18. Rays and Angles 144
19. Parallel Lines 151
20. Kinds of Angles 157
21. Triangles or Trigons 163
22. Circles 171
23. Practical Geometry—I 175
24. Practical Geometry—II 180
MISCELLANEOUS EXERCISES IV & MEMORABLE FACTS *184-186*

UNIT V — MENSURATION   **187-210**
25. Measurement of Area 188
26. Measurement of Volume 203
MISCELLANEOUS EXERCISES V & MEMORABLE FACTS *209-210*

UNIT VI — STATISTICS   **211-217**
27. Bar Graphs 212
OBJECTIVE TYPE TESTS 218
ANSWERS 223

REVISION OF WHAT WE HAVE LEARNT

A. Write the following numerals in words using the Indian System :

1. 7,41,801
2. 4,16,23,005
3. 4,95,00,003
4. 34,12,009
5. 25,35,00,902
6. 88,08,08,808

B. Write the following as numerals in the Indian System :

7. Ninety-eight crore ninety-seven lakh fifty three thousand seven hundred and eighty-three.

8. Seventy-five crore eight lakh nine thousand eight hundred and forty-three.

9. Thirty-nine crore fifty-nine thousand and eleven.

10. Forty-seven crore ninety-six lakh twenty-six thousand and four hundred.

11. Fifty-five crore seventy-eight lakh nine-hundred and thirty-two.

12. Ninety-three crore ninety-two lakh, nineteen thousand and nine.

C. Write the following as numerals in the International System :

13. Fourteen million ninety-five thousand six hundred and three.

14. One hundred sixty-three million four hundred forty-seven thousand eight hundred and nine.

15. Thirty-five billion seven hundred fifteen million nine hundred twelve thousand four hundred and fifty-three.

16. Nine hundred forty-three million four hundred seventy-six thousand two hundred and thirty-eight.

17. Write the *largest* and the *smallest* numerals that can be formed using the digits 8, 7, 6, 5, 4, 3, 2, 1, 0. Then write them in words.

D. Answer :

18. How many millions are there in a crore ?

19. How many lakhs make a million ?

20. How many thousands are there in a million ?

21. How many digits are there in a million ?

22. How many hundreds are there in a crore ?

23. Write the following numerals in words using the Indian as well as the International system :

  (a) 69431209   (b) 693771502   (c) 765394673
  (d) 556813367   (e) 834174360   (f) 249713685

5

24. Write in Roman numerals :

(a) 19 ~~XIX~~ (b) 242 CCXLI (c) 3369 MMMCCCLXIX (d) 200375

25. Write in Indian numerals :

(a) MLXXVI   (b) MCDLXV   (c) $\overline{CC}$DXIV

26. Which of the following numerals are divisible by 11 ?

(a) 231232   (b) 292575   (c) 8530764

27. Fill up the blanks :

(a) $3 \times 7 + 3 \times 9 = 3 (\ldots + \ldots)$

(b) $2 \times 7 + 3 \times 7 = \ldots (2 + 3)$

(c) $4 \times 9 + 4 \times \ldots = 4(\ldots + 11)$

(d) $a \times b + a \times \ldots = a(\ldots + c)$

28. Solve :

(a) $\dfrac{2 \div 2 + 2}{2 \times 2 - 2} \dfrac{(2 \div 2) \div 2}{2 - 2 \div 2}$ (b) $\dfrac{8}{9} - \left(\dfrac{5}{6} - \dfrac{2}{3} - \dfrac{1}{6}\right)$ of $\dfrac{1}{3}$

(c) $7\dfrac{8}{9} - \left(\dfrac{4}{7} \div \dfrac{1}{7}\right) \div \dfrac{2}{3}$ (d) $\cdot 3 \times \cdot 4 + 1\cdot 2 \times 4 - 2\cdot 4 \div 6$

29. 6 workmen prepare a shed in 40 days. How long will 20 men take to make it ?

30. 12 men can do a job in 7 days. How long will 4 men take to do it ?

31. Find the HCF of 1379 and 2401

32. Find the LCM of 385, 539 and 1540.

33. The LCM of two numbers is 6525 and their HCF is 25. If one number is 225 find the other.

34. A room is 5 metres long and 4 metres wide. Find its area. If it is 3·5 metres high, find the area of its four walls also.

35. The area of the four walls of a room is 63 sq. metre. If its length be 6 metres and height be 3·5 metres, find its width.

36. A lawn 25 metres long and 15 metres wide is bounded by an outside path 2·5 metres wide. What will it cost to pave the path at Rs. 7·50 per square metre ?

37. A wall is made up of bricks. It is 8 metres long, 5 metres high and 23 cm. thick. Each brick used to build it is 23 cm × 10 cm. × 8 cm. How many bricks will be required to make the wall.

6

38. A farmer sowed wheat in five fields and they yielded 36, 38, 42, 44 and 45 bags of wheat respectively. Find the average yield per field.

39. *(a)* What is meant by *per cent* ?

(b) Express $\dfrac{7}{25}$ and ·105 as *per cent*.

40. Out of the total of 428 runs of the Indian innings, Kapil Dev made 107 runs. What per cent of the runs did he make.

41. A person bought a house for Rs. 8000 and sold it for Rs. 6000. Find his gain/loss per cent.

42. The tag-price of a fan was Rs. 600. But a discount of $16\dfrac{2}{3}\%$ was allowed on it. What is its selling price ?

43. Ram borrowed some money from a bank at Rs. 18% per annum and paid Rs. 2950 in all after one year. How much money did Ram borrow ?

44. A widow deposited Rs. 9000 in a bank that gives interest at 11% per annum. After a certain time, her money amounted to Rs. 12300. After how long did it happen ?

45. Define :

(a) adjacent angles
(b) alternate angles
(c) corresponding angles
(d) vertically opposite angles
(e) supplementary angles
(f) complementary angles

46. Name each of the angles :

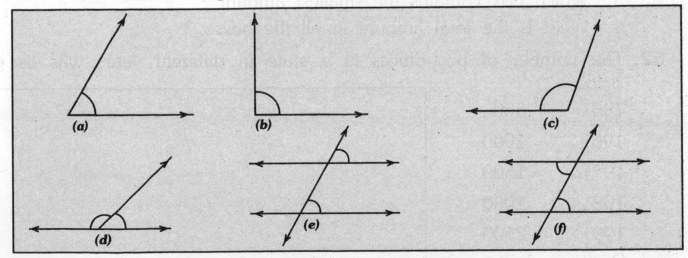

47. Draw angles of 60°, 90°, 120°, 30°, 45°, 135°, 75° and 150° using compasses and a ruler only.

48. (a) Draw an angle of 90° and bisect it.

(b) Draw a line parallel to a given line.

(c) Draw a line perpendicular to a given line from a point outside it.

(d) Draw any angle ABC. Draw angle DEF congruent to it.

49. Define :

(a) an acute angle   (b) an obtuse angle   (c) obtuse triangle

(d) scalene triangle   (e) isosceles triangle   (f) equilateral triangle

50. What are the four properties of a parallelogram ? How many types of parallelograms are there ? Name them.

51. Given below is a bar-graph showing amounts of money found in six boxes. Read the graph and answer the questions given under it :

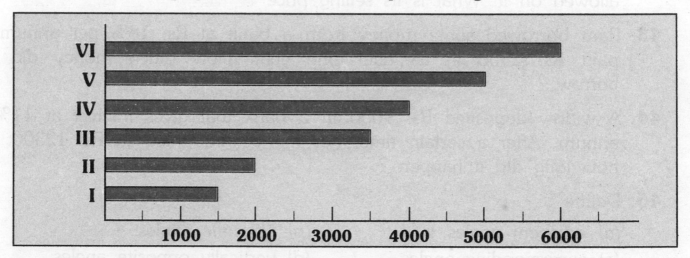

1. What amount is there in each box ?
2. Which box contains the highest amount ?
3. Which box contains the smallest amount ?
4. What is the total amount in all the boxes ?

52. The number of post-offices in a state in different years was as given below :

1951	500
1961	1000
1971	1500
1981	2000
1991	2500

Draw a bar-graph to represent it in the given box.

ARITHMETIC

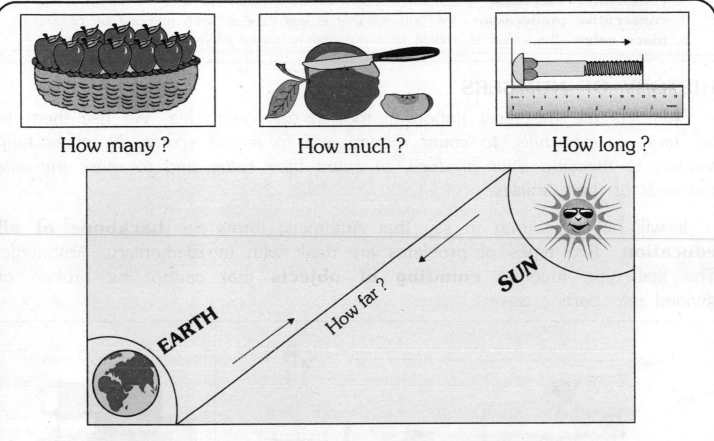

How many ?

How much ?

How long ?

EARTH → How far ? SUN

Arithmetic *is an important branch of mathematics that carries out calculations involving numbers. It helps us find answers to questions such as—How many ?, How much ?, How long ?, How far ?*

IN THIS UNIT—

1. Numbers—Natural and Whole—I
2. Operations with Whole Numbers—I
3. Operations with Whole Numbers—II
4. Factors and Multiples
5. Lowest Common Multiple
6. Integers—I
7. Integers—II

1 NUMBERS—NATURAL AND WHOLE

HISTORY OF NUMBERS

Numbers are the most important tool in day-to-day life. We use them to *tell time, to pay bills, to count money* and to *record scores*. Numbers help farmers to *measure their produce, to count their cattle* and *to mark the sale proceeds* of their articles.

It will not be wrong to say that Arithmetic forms the **backbone of all education**. Two types of problems are dealt with in Elementary. Arithmetic. The first type involves **counting of objects** that cannot be broken or divided into parts ; as—

How many sheep are there in the flock ? ....10..................................

How many books are there in the pile ? ....6..................................

As problems of this type involve counting, we use **natural numbers**—1, 2, 3, 4, 5, 6, 7, 8, 9....... for them. Since the objects to be counted can go to any extent, there is no end to natural numbers indeed. Every natural number has a natural number **to follow it**.

10

Clearly, an *endless number of symbols* are required to indicate the natural numbers. But it is not possible. So, there must be some way-out to solve this problem. It is a matter of pride for us that such a way-out was thought of by scholars in India about 1500 years back.

To begin with, we had a set of numerals called **Brahm Sankhyayen** (divine numbers). The nine symbols used in this set were 1, 2, 3, 4, 5, 6, 7, 8, and 9. With these symbols, most of the numbers could be written however large they might be.

But there was one difficulty with the divine numbers that were in use. Suppose there were five apples with a person and he gave away one apple to each of his five children. How many apples were left with him ?

Evidently, no apple was left with him. There was no symbol to denote this situation of **no apple** or **nothing**.

Aryabhatt was an astronomer who lived in India around 500AD. He had a student named **Bhaskar** who invented the number-system that the world is using today. But at that time, the unit's place *was at the left* instead of *the right* as we have it today. He invented the symbol **0** for **nothing**. He called it **shoonya** which we call **zero** in English.

This system was adopted by the Arabs who called our numbers—**Hindse** (from India). An Arab mathematician, named *Al Khwarizmi*, wrote a book in 825AD. About the middle of the 12th century, this book was translated into Latin and the Indian system of numbers reached Europe. The Europeans called this system of numbers **Hindu-Arabic Numeral System** and this name persists till today.

In early civilizations, different systems of notation developed as under :

	1	2	3	4	5	6	7	8	9	10
Roman	I	II	III	IV	V	VI	VII	VIII	IX	X
Egyptian	I	II	III	IIII	IIIII	IIIIII	IIIIIII	IIIIIIII	IIIIIIIII	∩
Arabic	١	٢	٣	٤	٥	٦	٧	٨	٩	١٠
Indian	१	२	३	४	५	६	७	८	९	१०

The modren form of Hindu-Arabic numerals developed in Europe.

NATURAL NUMBERS

Natural numbers are counting numbers—*one, two, three, four, five, six, seven, eight, nine.....*

They are endless as every natural number is followed by the next natural number greater than it by one.

Whole numbers are *zero, one, two, three, four, five, six, seven, eight, nine.....* It is clear that whole numbers are natural numbers along with the number **zero**.

Symbols used for these basic natural and whole numbers are :

Zero 0	Two 2	Four 4	Six 6	Eight 8
One 1	Three 3	Five 5	Seven 7	Nine 9

These symbols are called **digits**.

NUMBERS AND NUMERALS

The words—**number** and **numeral**—are distinct from each other.

A **number** *is only a concept (idea)* ; as seven, nine, five, twenty.

A **numeral** *is a symbol for a number.* It can differ in different scripts ; as 7, 5, 20, or ७, ५, २० or VII, V, XX, etc.

When we hear or think of a number, its *idea* is formed in the mind. But when we are to write a number, we use *symbols*. Big numbers are written using *groups of symbols*.

REMEMBER—

1. Digits from 1 to 9 are called *natural numbers*.
2. Digits from 0 to 9 are called *whole numbers*.
3. The numerals invented to begin with were called *Brahm Sankhyayen*.
4. Zero was invented by *Bhaskaracharya*.
5. We use the letter **N** to denote natural numbers.
6. We use the letter **W** to denote natural numbers.
7. A number (natural or whole) that exceeds a given number by 1 is called its **consecutive successor**.
8. A number that is less than a given number by only 1 is called its **consecutive predecessor**.

PRACTICE EXERCISES 1

A. Answer :

1. Which is the *lowest natural number* ? 1
2. Which is the *lowest whole number* ? 0
3. Which letter do we use to *denote natural numbers* ? .... N
4. Which letter do we use to *denote whole numbers* ? .... W
5. Which is the *largest natural number* ? *cannot be said* 9
6. Which is the *largest whole number* ? 9

B. Answer *yes* or *no* :

7. Is 0 a natural number ? .... n
8. Is 0 a whole number ? .... Y
9. Is every natural number a whole number too ? .... Y
10. Is every whole number a natural number too ? .... n
11. Is the smallest four-digit number 1000 or 1999 ? 1 000
12. Is the largest four digit number 9000 or 9999 ? 9999

C. Write—

13. all the natural numbers between 4 and 5 : .... none
14. all the whole numbers between 0 and 5 : 0,1,234,5
15. the number of thousands that equal a lakh : 100
16. the number of thousands that equal a million : 1,000
17. the number of lakhs that equal a million : 10
18. the number of lakhs that equal a crore : .... 100 marks
19. the consecutive successor of 0 : 1
20. the consecutive predecessor of 3 : 2
21. the smallest numeral of five digits : 10,000
22. the largest numeral of six digits : 799,999
23. the smallest number of three digits that does not change when its digits are written in reverse order : 101

FACE VALUE AND PLACE VALUE

The **face value** of a digit is equal to it and it always remains the same ; as—the face value of 7 is 7 and of 9 is 9.

But *the* **place value** *of a digit differs with its place in a numeral ; as—*
In the numeral 25, the place value of 5 is 5 but that of 2 is 2×10 = 20
In the numeral 7354—

(a) The *face value* of 4 = 4
   Its *place value* is also 4×1 =4

(b) The *face value* of 5 = 5
   Its *place value* is 5×10 = 50

(c) The *face value* of 3 = 3
   Its *place value* is 3×100 = 300

(d) The *face value* of 7 = 7
   Its *place value* is 7×1000 = 7000

PLACE-VALUE CHARTS

In order to write numerals, we use two types of value-charts as under :

A. PLACE-VALUE CHART IN THE INDIAN SYSTEM

ARABS		CRORES		LAKHS		THOUSANDS		UNITS		
Ten Arab	Arab	Ten Crore	Crore	Ten Lakh	Lakh	Ten Thousand	Thousand	Hundred	Ten	Unit
10000000000	1000000000	100000000	10000000	1000000	100000	10000	1000	100	10	1

B. PLACE VALUE CHART IN THE INTERNATIONAL SYSTEM

BILLIONS			MILLIONS			THOUSANDS			UNITS		
Hundred Billion	Ten Billion	Billion	Hundred Million	Ten Million	Million	Hundred Thousand	Ten Thousand	Thousand	Hundred	Ten	Unit
100000000000	10000000000	1000000000	100000000	10000000	1000000	100000	10000	1000	100	10	1

If we observe both the charts carefully, we shall find that—

(a) **one lakh** is the same as **hundred thousand**.

(b) **ten lakh** is the same as **one million**.

(c) **one crore** is the same as **ten million**.

(d) **ten crore** is the same as **hundred million**.

(e) **one arab** is the same as **one billion**.

THE DIGIT ZERO (0)

We know that the digit **zero** means **nothing**. So,—

(i) **any number multiplied by 0 is equal to 0**.

(ii) **face value of 0 is 0**

(iii) **place value of 0 is also 0 whatever its place in a numeral**.

The reason is that $0 \times 10 = 0$, $0 \times 100 = 0$, $0 \times 1000 = 0$

REMEMBER :

1. 0 is *not a natural number*. The *smallest natural number* is 1.

2. 0 is the *smallest whole number*. It was added before 1 to natural numbers to make the set of whole numbers.

3. The number-symbols—0, 1, 2, 3, 4, 5, 6, 7, 8, 9—are called *digits*.

4. Every digit in a numeral has *two values* :

   (a) Its *face value* is equal to it and *it never changes*.

   (b) Its *place value* depends on its place in a numeral. This value *changes with the change in the digits's place*.

5. A numeral that *exceeds* a given numeral by only 1 is called the *consecutive successor* of the given numeral.

6. A numeral that is *less than* a given numeral by only 1 is called the *consecutive predecessor* of the given numeral.

7. The *face value* and the *place value* of 0 are always the same. Either of them is 0 and it never changes.

8. **0 has no numeral as its consecutive predecessor.**

Let us solve some examples :

Example 1 : What are the *face value* and the *place value* of 7 in the numeral 781532 ?

Solution :   We know that the face value of a digit is always equal to it.

    ∴ Face value of 7 = **7**

    The place value of 7 depends on its place

    It is in *lakh's place, i.e.* 6th from the right

    So, its place value = **700000**

15

Example 2 : **Find the** *difference between the place values* **of two 7's in the numeral 9387612475.**

Solution : One of the 7's is in the *ten's place* while the other is in the *place of ten lakh*.

∴ Place value of 7 in the ten's place = 70

Place value of the other 7 = 7000000

∴ Reqd. difference = 7000000–70

= **6999930** *Ans.*

Example 3 : **Write the numeral 743005 in its expanded notation (form).**

Solution : Place value of 7 = 700000
Place value of 4 = 40000
Place value of 3 = 3000
Place value of 0 = 00
Place value of 0 = 0
Place value of 5 = 5
743005 = 700000+40000+3000 + 0 + 5 *Ans.*

Example 4 : **Write all the numerals that you can make with the digits 7, 5, 2. Which of them are the largest and the smallest.**

We can make numerals with digits 7, 5, 2 as under :

(a) Keeping 2 in the units place, we can make two numerals 752 and 572.

(b) Keeping 5 in the unit's place, we can make two numerals 725 and 275.

(c) Keeping 7 in the unit's place, we can make two numerals 527 and 257.

∴ We can make six numerals in all. They are
752, 725, 572, 527, 275, 257
The largest of these numerals is **752** and the smallest is **257**.

Example 5 : **How many 3-digit numerals are there in all ?**

Solution : Largest 3-digit numeral = 999
Largest 2-digit numeral = 99
Total number of 3-digit numerals = 999 – 99 = **900** Ans.

Examples 6 : Write the smallest numeral of six digits having 3 different digits.

Solution : The three smallest digits are 0, 1, 2.
Smallest numeral of six digits = 100000
This numeral is made up of two digits 1, 0
To keep this numeral smallest we should write 2 in the unit's place.
∴ Required number = **100002** *Ans.*

Example 7 : Write—
(a) **the consecutive successor of 84657**
(b) **the consecutive predecessor of 76345**

Solution : Consecutive successor of 84657 = 84657 + 1 = **84658**
Consecutive predecessor of 76345 = 76345 – 1 = **76344**

PRACTICE EXERCISES 2

A. Answer :
1. What does the digit zero stand for ? .... 0 (nothing)
2. What is the face value of the digit 0 ? 0
3. What is the place value of the digit 0 ? 0
4. Which numeral is the consecutive successor of 0 ? 1
5. Which numeral is the consecutive predecessor of 0 ? .... none
6. What are symbols 0, 1, 2, 3, 4, 5, 6, 7, 8, 9, called ? .... whole #'s/digits
7. How many symbols are used to write numerals ? 10
8. How many symbols are used to write whole numbers ? 10

B. Write the numeral for each of the following :
(a) 9. Ninety-three thousand and fifty-seven   93,057
10. Eight lakh thirty-two thousand four hundred and six   8,32,406
11. Twenty-eight lakh eight thousand nine hundred and six 28,08,906
12. Seven crore fifteen lakh two thousand and seventy 47,15,02,070
13. Forty-five crore twelve lakh thirteen thousand two hundred and one 45,12,13,201
14. Five arab six lakh seven thousand eight hundred and nine 5,00,06,07,809
15. Forty seven arab twenty-three lakh eight thousand and two   47,00,23,08,002

17

(b) **16.** Seven million three hundred and three thousand, nine hundred and eleven 7,303,911

17. One hundred and eight million, seventy-two thousand one hundred and one 108,072,101

18. Five billion, fifty-seven million, ninety-five thousand four hundred and four 5,057,095,404

19. Thirty-two billion, eleven million, forty-two thousand six hundred and twelve 32,011,042,612

20. One hundred and three billion, four hundred and twelve million, seven hundred and nine thousand eight hundred and seventeen 103,412,709,817

C. Write each numeral as a number-name in the Indian System as well as in the International System.

21. 40857 **22.** 5702803 **23.** 943720695

24. 120905034 **25.** 92755325808 **26.** 45630070819

D. Write—

27. the place value of each digit in the number 85349219.
80000000, 5000000, 300000, 40000, 9000, 200, 10, 9

28. the place value of both 5's in the number 398751457. 50000 & 50

29. the numeral 6999932 in its expanded notation.
6000000+900000+90000+9000+900+30+2

30. 700000 + 50000 + 4000 + 000 + 10 + 6 as a numeral.
754016

E. 31. How many six-digit numerals are there in all ? 999999 99999 900000 900000

32. Write all the 3-digit numerals that you can make using the digits 7, 3, 8. 738, 783, 387, 378, 837, 873

33. Write the smallest numeral of five digits with the three lowest digits. 10000 10002

34. Write the consecutive predecessors of 58654 and 637452 58653 637451

35. Write the consecutive successors of 65578 and 758334 65579 758335

36. Write the smallest numeral of 3 digits that does not change when its digits are written in reverse order. 101

37. Write the smallest numeral of three digits that does not change when its digits may be written in any order. 111

38. Write the largest 2-digit numeral that does not change when its digits change places. 99

39. Write the largest and the smallest numerals of six digit. 999999 & 111111

40. How many five-digit numerals are there in all ? 99999 9999 90000

Graded Maths-Part-6

2 OPERATIONS IN WHOLE NUMBERS—I

> *KNOW THESE TERMS :*
> 1. **basic operations**—addition, subtraction, multiplication, division
> 2. **addends**—two or more quantities that are added together
> 3. **minuend**—quantity from which another quantity is subtracted
> 4. **subtrahend**—quantity that is subtracted from a minuend
> 5. **multiplicand**—quantity that is multiplied by another quantity
> 6. **multiplier**—quantity that multiplies a multiplicand
> 7. **product**—numeral obtained after multiplying two numerals together

Four basic operations used to solve Arithmetical problems are :

1. *Addition*   2. *Subtraction*   3. *Multiplication*   4. *Division*

(a) If the problem is of *finding the total* of two or more quantities, the operation used for it is called **addition**. Remember that the quantities that are added together are called **addends.** Their total is called **sum**.

(b) The operation just opposite to addition is called **subtraction**. It tells *how many are left behind* if a few things are taken away from a larger number of things. Remember that—

  1. *the quantity from which another quantity is subtracted is called* **minuend**.
  2. *the quantity subtracted from the minuend is called* **subtrahend**.
  3. *the result of the operation of subtraction is called* **remainder**.

(c) **Multiplication** is a short method of repeated addition indeed. Multiplication facts are called *multiplication tables* also. Remember that—

  1. *the quantity multiplied by another quantity is called* **multiplicand**.
  2. *the quantity that multiplies the multiplicand is called* **multiplier**.
  3. *the result of the operation of multiplication is called* **product**. $1 \times 2 = 2$

(d) **Division** is a short method of repeated subtraction indeed. It separates a group of things into smaller equal parts. Remember that—

  1. *the quantity divided by another quantity is called* **dividend**.
  2. *the quantity that divides the dividend is called* **divisor**.
  3. *the result of the operation of division is called* **quotient**.

Let us now study the properties of these operations. These properties are quite simple. Yet they are very useful in further study of Arithmetic. In this chapter, we shall study the properties of addition, subtraction and multiplication.

PROPERTIES OF ADDITION

PROPERTY 1

We know that 6 is a whole number

Also, we know that 8 is a whole number

When we add 6 and 8, we get $6 + 8 = 14$

Now, 14 is also a whole number.

So, when a whole number is added to another whole number, their sum is also a whole number. In other words,

if a and b are two whole numbers and $a + b = c$, then c is also a whole number.

This property of whole numbers is called *closure property of addition.*

PROPERTY 2

We know that $\qquad 8 + 4 = 12$

Also, we know that $\quad 4 + 8 = 12$

So, if we are to add two whole numbers, the addends can be written in any order. In other words,

if a and b are any two whole numbers, then $a + b = b + a$

This property of whole numbers is called *commutative property of addition.*

PROPERTY 3

We know that 0 means *nothing*

So, $0 + 0 = 0 \qquad\qquad 0 + 1 = 1 + 0 = 1$

$0 + 2 = 2 + 0 = 2 \qquad 0 + 3 = 3 + 0 = 3$

So, if 0 is added to any whole number, it does not change the value of that whole number and the sum is equal to the number itself. In other words,

if a is any whole number, then $a + 0 = 0 + a = a$

This property of whole numbers is called *additive property of zero.*

PROPERTY 4

We know that $5 + 4 + 6 = 15$

Also, we know that $(5+4) + 6 = 9 + 6 = 15$

Again, we know that $5 + (4+6) = 5 + 10 = 15$

Still again, we know that $(5+6) + 4 = 11 + 4 = 15$

Clearly, *if we want to find the sum of any three whole numbers, we can find the sum of any two of them and then add the third whole number to this sum.* In other words,

if a, b, c **are three whole numbers and** $a + b + c = d$, **then**
$(a+b) + c = a+(b+c) = (c+a) + b = d$

This property of whole numbers is called the *associative law of addition.*

Example 1 : Find the sum of 363, 178 and 352.

Solution   : 363 + 178 + 352
              = (178+352) + 363
              = 530 + 363 = **893** *Ans.*

Example 2 : Find the sum of 103, 217, 186 and 274.

Solution   : 103 + 217 + 186 + 274
              = (103+217) + (186+274)
              = 320 + 460 = **780** *Ans.*

Example 3 : Find the sum of 54321, 26529 and 19250.

Solution   : The numbers are quite large
              We shall add them after writing under one another.

54321 + 26529	54321
= 80850	+ 26529
Again 80850 + 19250	80850
= **100100** *Ans.*	+ 19250
	100100

PRACTICE EXERCISES 3

A. Fill up each blank :

1. 79 + 121 = ...121... + 79   **2.** 43 + 159 = ...159... + 43

3. (68+32) + 150 = ...68... + (32+150) = ...32... + (68 + 150)

4. 135 + 0 = 0 + ...135.. = ...135   **5.** 0 + ...175.. = 175

6. (378 + ...122..) + 150 = 378 + (122+150) = 122 + (...150.. + ..378..)

B. Answer *yes* or *no* :

7. Is the sum of two even numbers even or odd ?   ...E...

8. Is the sum of two odd numbers odd or even ?   ...E...

9. Is the sum of two whole numbers a whole number ? ......Y......

10. Is the sum of an *even* and an *odd* numbers even or odd ? ......o......

C. Find the sum by suitable grouping :

11. 33, 41, 159, 267   **12.** 464, 336, 250   **13.** 753, 547, 740 $=2040$

$(33+267)+(41+159)=500$ $(464+336)+250=1050$ $(753+547)+740=$

14. 633, 367, 940   **15.** 657, 343, 251, 749   **16.** 546, 704, 625, 425

$(633+367)+940=1940$ $(657+343)+(251+749)=2000$ $(546+704)+(625+425)$
$=2,300$

17. Add up 35732, 49668 and 14600 $=100000$

D.18. We know that 0 + 0 = 0. Is there any other whole number also that does the same ? No

PROPERTIES OF SUBTRACTION

PROPERTY 1

We know that a smaller whole number can be subtracted from a larger whole number. But a larger whole number cannot be subtracted from a smaller whole number ; as—

(a) 9 – 5 = 4   (b) 15 – 7 = 8 ⎤ *These subtractions*
(c) 4 – 0 = 4   (d) 5 – 3 = 2 ⎦ *are possible.*

But

(a) 5 – 9 = ?   (b) 7 – 15 = ? ⎤ *These subtractions are*
(c) 0 – 4 = ?   (d) 3 – 5 = ? ⎦ *not possible.*

None of these subtractions is possible. Clearly, subtraction of whole numbers is possible in two conditions :

1. If one number is larger than the other.

2. If both the numbers are equal.

In other words,

if a and b are two whole numbers and $a - b = c$ which is also a whole number, then either $a > b$ or $a = b$.

PROPERTY 2

We have seen that 9 – 5 = 4

But we have also seen that 5 – 9 = ? (subtraction is not possible.)

So, we can say that—

if a and b are any two distinct whole numbers, then $a - b$ is not equal to $b - a$

PROPERTY 3

We know that 5 – 0 = 5 but 0 – 5 = ? (subtraction is not possible)

So, 0 subtracted from any other whole number gives the whole number as the result. But any other whole number subtracted from 0 does not give such a result. In other words,

if a is a whole number, then $a – 0 = a$ but $0 – a \neq a$.

PROPERTY 4

Let us take three whole numbers 7, 5 and 4

If we subtract 5 from 7, we get **2**

And if we subtract this 2 from 4 we get **2** ⎤ $c – (a – b)$

But if we subtract 4 from 5, we get **1**

And if we subtract this 1 from 7, we get **6** ⎦ $a – (b – c)$

So, we can say—

if a b and c are three whole numbers, then $a – (b – c)$ is not equal to $c – (a – b)$.

PRACTICE EXERCISES 4

A. Solve :

1. 684 – 354 _330_   **2.** 3656 – 1969 _1687_   **3.** 31210 – 19573 _11637_

4. 573 – 239 _334_   ⑤ 7839 – 1899 _5940_   **6.** 989231 – 565413 _423818_

B. Carry out the following subtractions :

7.
```
  1 0 3 1 0 1 7
–   6 7 6 7 6 5
  ─────────────
    3 5 4 2 5 2
```

8.
```
  7 8 2 7 6 3
– 4 3 1 5 6 0
  ───────────
  3 5 1 2 0 3
```

9.
```
  1 0 0 0 0 0
–   8 7 9 7 8
  ───────────
  1 2 0 2 2
```

C. Replace each * by the correct digit :

10.
```
  9 2 6 6
– 5 * 9 * 7
  ─────────
  3 2 * 9
```

11.
```
    7 2 5 8
– | * * 6 2 9
  ───────────
    5 6 * 2 * 9
```

12.
```
  9 * 6 6
– 3 4 * 3
  ───────
  5 * 6 3
```

13.
```
    6 8 9 7 5
– 2 * 2 * 2 * 8 * 5
  ─────────────────
  4 * 6 6 9 0
```

14.
```
    7 6 8 9 4 3 2
– * 8 * 8 6 4 9
  ───────────────
  6 7 9 * 0 * 7 * 8 * 3
```

15.
```
    2 5 0 0 0 0 0
– 1 * 0 * 5 * 4 3 * 2
  ───────────────────
  1 * 4 4 5 6 7 * 8
```

D. 16. Find the difference between the largest number of seven digits and the smallest number of six digits.

```
  9 9 9 9 9 9 9
  1 0 0 0 0 0
  ───────────
  9 8 9 9 9 9 9
```

9,899,999

23

17. I deposited Rs. 46158 in my bank account. After about a month, I had to withdraw Rs. 21786 from my account. How much money was left behind in my account ? 24372

18. The population of Delhi was 9370475 in 1990. It increased to be 9420614 in 1991. How much did it increase in a year ? 50139

19. Out of the total population 9370475 of Delhi in 1990, the number of males was 5120733. Find the number of females. 4249742

PROPERTIES OF MULTIPLICATION

PROPERTY 1

We know that 7 is a whole number

Also, we know that 6 is a whole number

Now—

If we multiply 7 by 6, we get $7 \times 6 = 42$ which is a whole number too. Similarly $8 \times 7 = 56$ which is also a whole number.

So, it is clear that *if we multiply a whole number by another whole number, the product is also a whole number*. In other words,

if *a*, *b* are two whole numbers and $a \times b = c$, **then *c* is also a whole number**.

PROPERTY 2

We know that $3 \times 8 = 24$ and also $8 \times 3 = 24$

$7 \times 0 = 0$ and also $0 \times 7 = 0$

$12 \times 3 = 36$ and also $3 \times 12 = 36$

So, it is clear that *two whole numbers may be multiplied together in any order, the product is the same*. In other words,

if *a* and *b* are two whole numbers, then $a \times b = b \times a$.

PROPERTY 3

This property concerns **zero** (0). It states that *if any whole number is multiplied by 0, the product is always 0*. In other words,

if *a* is a whole number, then $a \times 0 = 0 \times a = 0$.

PROPERTY 4

This property concerns **one** (**1**). It states that *if any whole number is multiplied by 1, the product is always the number itself.* In other words,

if a is whole number, then $a \times 1 = 1 \times a = a$.

PROPERTY 5

This property concerns the multiplication of three or more numbers. To find the product of three numbers, we first multiply any two of them. Then we multiply their product by the third number ; as—

$$5 \times 6 \times 7 = (5 \times 6) \times 7 = 30 \times 7 = 210$$
$$= 5 \times (6 \times 7) = 5 \times 42 = 210$$
$$= 6 \times (5 \times 7) = 6 \times 35 = 210$$

If a, b and c are three whole number, then—
$$a \times b \times c = (a \times b) \times c = a \times (b \times c) = (c \times a) \times b$$

PROPERTY 6

We know that—

(a) $12 \times 16 = 192$

or $12 \times (9 + 7) = 192$

or $(12 \times 9) + (12 \times 7) = 108 + 84 = 192$

$\therefore$ **$12 \times 16 = 12 \times (9 + 7) = (12 \times 9) + (12 \times 7)$**

(b) $12 \times 4 = 48$

or $12 \times (7 - 3) = 48$

or $(12 \times 7) - (12 \times 3) = 84 - 36 = 48$

$\therefore$ **$12 \times 4 = 12 \times (7 - 3) = (12 \times 7) - (12 \times 3)$**

This property is called the **Distributive Law of Multiplication.** According to it—

(a) **if a, b and c are any three whole numbers, then**
$a \times (b+c) = (a \times b) + (a \times c)$

(b) **if a, b and c any three whole numbers, then**
$a \times (b-c) = (a \times b) - (a \times c)$

Example 1 : Find the product of 385 $\times$ 108.

Solution   : $385 \times 108 = 385 \times (100 + 8)$
$$= (385 \times 100) + (385 \times 8)$$
$$= 38500 + 3080 = \textbf{41580} \text{ Ans.}$$

25

Example 2 : **Find the product of 385 × 92.**

Solution : $385 \times 92 = 385 \times (100 - 8)$

$\qquad = (385 \times 100) - (385 \times 8)$

$\qquad = 38500 - 3080 = \mathbf{35420}$ Ans.

Example 3 : **Find the value of 875 × 91 + 875 × 9.**

Solution : $875 \times 91 + 875 \times 9$

$\qquad = 875 \times (91 + 9) = 875 \times 100 = \mathbf{87500}$ Ans.

Example 4 : **Find the value of 516 × 108 – 516 × 8.**

Solution : $516 \times 108 - 516 \times 8$

$\qquad = 516 \times (108 - 8) = 516 \times 100 = \mathbf{51600}$ Ans.

Example 5 : **Find the value of 3849 × 689 + 14 × 3849 – 3849 × 3.**

Solution : $3849 \times 689 + 14 \times 3849 - 3849 \times 3$

$\qquad = (3849 \times 689) + (3849 \times 14) - (3849 \times 3)$

$\qquad = 3849 \times (689 + 14 - 3) = 3849 \times (689 + 11)$

$\qquad = 3849 \times 700 = 384900 \times 7 = \mathbf{2694300}$ Ans.

Example 6 : **Simplify : 28 + 27 – 8 × (15 ÷ 3) – 5**

Solution : $28 + 27 - 8 \times (15 \div 3) - 5$

$\qquad = 28 + 27 - (8 \times 5) - 5$

$\qquad = 28 + 27 - 40 - 5$

$\qquad = 55 - 45 = \mathbf{10}$ Ans.

PRACTICE EXERCISES 5

A. Fill up each blank :

1. $16378 \times 1 = \underline{16378}$

2. $9037 \times 0 = \underline{0}$

3. $16 \times 172 = 172 \times \underline{16}$

4. $8 \times 125 \times 1654 = \underline{1654000}$

5. $37251 \times 25 \times 16 = \underline{14900400}$

6. $10 \times 10 \times \underline{100} = 10000$

7. $55 \times 37 = 55 \times \underline{35} + 55 \times \underline{2}$

8. $55 \times 37 = 55 \times \underline{40} - 55 \times \underline{3}$

9. $16 \times 44 = 16 \times \underline{40} + 16 \times \underline{4}$

10. $16 \times 44 = 16 \times 50 - 16 \times \underline{6}$

B. Find the product of :

11. $4 \times 1877 \times 25$ 12. $8 \times 748 \times 25$ 13. $8 \times 506 \times 125$

14. $876 \times 1250 \times 8$ 15. $985 \times 60 \times 5$ 16. $5 \times 655 \times 20$

C. Solve using the distributive law :

17. 33944×409 18. 59134×812 19. 81349×495

20. 23107×611 21. 10007×499 22. 896×159

D. Simplify :

23. $665 \times 47 + 665 + 53$

24. $463 \times 62 + 463 \times 38$

25. $279 \times 35 + 279 \times 45 + 279 \times 20$

26. $736 \times 65 + 736 \times 47 - 736 \times 12$

27. $28730 \times 28730 - 28730 \times 28730 + 3200$

28. $489 \times 27 + 489 \times 2 - 489 \times 9$

29. $3 \times 483 \times 17 - 48 \times 483 - 3 \times 483$

30. $540 \times 692 - 180 \times 3 \times 692$

E. 31. Find the product of the largest number of four digits and the smallest number of three digits.

32. The monthly fee charged from a student in a school is Rs. 100. If there are 545 students in all, how much fee is collected every year ?

33. Fill up the missing digits :

(a) The product of two whole numbers is 1. Find the numbers.

(b) A whole number multiplied by itself gives the product 0. Find the whole number.

(c) $0 \times 0 = 0$. Is their any other whole number that multiplied by itself gives the product equal to itself ? If yes, write it.

3 OPERATIONS IN WHOLE NUMBERS—II

We studied the operations of *addition, subtraction* and *multiplication* involving whole numbers in the previous chapter. In this chapter, we shall study the operation of **division** with whole numbers. We know that division is another name for *repeated subtraction* and it is the *inverse of multiplication*. Let us study the properties of the operation called *division*.

PROPERTIES OF DIVISION

PROPERTY 1

We know that $35 \div 7 = 5$ and $36 \div 6 = 6$
But—
$30 \div 4 = ?$ $32 \div 7 = ?$ $72 \div 5 = ?$

So, it is clear that if a whole number is divided by another whole number, the result is not always a whole number. In other words,

if a and b are two whole numbers, then $a \div b$ is not always a whole number.

PROPERTY 2

We know that division is another name for repeated subtraction. For example, 6 can be subtracted from 36 six times as shown in front.

So, we say that $36 \div 6 = 6$

Let us see if this operation also holds good in the case of **zero** or not.

Suppose we want to divide 3 by 0

We see that we may subtract 0 from 3 any number of times, we get 3 every time. In other words, we can never reach 0. **So, division of a whole number by 0 remains undefined**.

$$
\begin{array}{r}
36 \\
-\ 6 \\
\hline
30 \\
-\ 6 \\
\hline
24 \\
-\ 6 \\
\hline
18 \\
-\ 6 \\
\hline
12 \\
-\ 6 \\
\hline
6 \\
-\ 6 \\
\hline
0
\end{array}
\qquad
\begin{array}{r}
3 \\
-0 \\
\hline
3 \\
-0 \\
\hline
3 \\
-0 \\
\hline
3
\end{array}
$$

PROPERTY 3

Let us divide 0 by 3.
Clearly we should find a number that, when multiplied by 3, should give 0.
There cannot be any such whole number *other than 0*. In other words,
if a is a whole number other than 0, then $0 \div a = 0$.

PROPERTY 4

Let us divide 3 by 1.
We see that we can subtract 1 three times from 3 as shown in front.

$$
\begin{array}{r}
3 \\
-\ 1 \\
\hline
2 \\
-\ 1 \\
\hline
1 \\
-\ 1 \\
\hline
0
\end{array}
$$

Clearly $3 \div 1 = 3$

So, *if a whole number is divided by 1, the quotient is the number itself. Also, if a whole number is divided by itself, the quotient is 1.* In other words,

if a is a whole number other than 0, *then*

$a \div 1 = a$ **and** $a \div a = 1$

PROPERTY 5

Let us divide 13 by 5
We can subtract 5 from 13 **twice** and we get 3 as **remainder** as well.
We know that 13 is the *dividend*.

5 is the *divisor*.
2 is the *quotient*.
3 is the *remainder*.

$$
\left.
\begin{array}{r}
13 \\
-\ 5 \\
\hline
8 \\
-\ 5 \\
\hline
3
\end{array}
\right\} \textbf{2 times}
$$

In the above example, we see that—

$13 = 5 \times 2 + 3$

or **Dividend = Divisor $\times$ Quotient + Remainder**

So, we can say that—

if a is the dividend, d the divisor, q the quotient and r the remainder, then $a = d \times q + r$

This rule for division is called *Division Algorithm*.

Example : Divide 96324 by 245 and check the result by division algorithm.

Solution : By actual division, we find that when 96324 is divided by 245, we get—

Quotient   = 393
Remainder = 39
By Division Algorithm
(Divisor × Quotient) + Remainder = Dividend
or (245 × 393) + 39 = Dividend
or 96285 + 39   = Dividend
                = **96324** which is correct

$$
245 \overline{)
\begin{array}{l}
393 \\
96324 \\
735 \\
\hline
2282 \\
2205 \\
\hline
774 \\
735 \\
\hline
39
\end{array}}
$$

PRACTICE EXERCISES 6

A. Perform the division and check your answer :

1. 6552 ÷ 56   **2.** 2305 ÷ 28   **3.** 56670 ÷ 146

4. 56780 ÷ 235   **5.** 11055 ÷ 500   **6.** 99076 ÷ 200

7. 77178 ÷ 215   **8.** 11378 ÷ 337   **9.** 795026 ÷ 745

10. 813735 ÷ 729   **11.** 93755 ÷ 400   **12.** 4512648 ÷ 712

B. Complete each sum :

	Divisor	Quotient	Remainder	Dividend
13.	129	357	....	46047
14.	206	....	126	53068
15.	816	745	6	....

C. Find the value of :

16. 725 ÷ 1.   **17.** 0 ÷ 932   **18.** 379 ÷ 379

19. (729 ÷ 27) ÷ 27   **20.** 117 ÷ 0   **21.** (624 + 520) ÷ 52

22. 234 – 625 ÷ 125   **23.** 15625 ÷ (650 – 25)   **24.** (21904 ÷ 148) ÷ 148

25. 696 ÷ 696 – 696 ÷ 696   **26.** 10000 – 800 (75 ÷ 75)

D. Answer *yes* or *no* :

27. If *a* is a whole number other than zero, *a* ÷ *a* = 1   ....

28. If *a* is a whole number other than zero, *a* ÷ 1 = *a*   ....

29. 24375 ÷ 0 is a defined quantity.   ....

30. If *a* is a whole number other than zero, *a* ÷ *a* = *a*   ....

E. Find the value of—

31. p, if $p \div p = p$

32. c if $a \div c = a$ where both a and c are whole numbers.

33. $538 - 125 \div 125$ **34.** $527 + 430 \div 43$

F. 35. 8573 apples were divided equally among 85 students. How many maximum number of apples did each student get. How many apples were left behind ?

36. The product of two number is 504347. If one of the number is 1591, find the other.

37. What smallest number should be added to 10,000 so that the sum may be divisible by 45 ?

38. What smallest number should be subtracted from 10,000 so that the remainder may be divisible by 45 ?

39. Find the greatest number of 5 digits that is divisible by 63.

40. A gardener plans to plant 840 plants in 28 rows so that each row has the same number of plants. How many plants will he plant in each row ?

TESTS OF DIVISIBILITY

In order to find whether a number is exactly divisible by a certain number, we have to carry out actual division. *If we get the remainder 0*, the number **is exactly divisible**. But *if the remainder is not zero*, the number is **not exactly divisible**.

For some common divisors, we have some tests that show whether a number is divisible by the given divisor or not. These common divisors are—

2, 3, 4, 5, 6, 8, 9, 10 and **11.**

Let us try to understand these divisibility tests.

1. DIVISIBILITY BY 10

A number is divisible by 10 only if the digit in its unit place is zero (0) ; as—

20, 30, 50, 100, 500, 1000, 1500 etc.

2. DIVISIBILITY BY 5

A number is divisible by 5 only if the digit in its units place is either 5 or 0 ; as—

10, 15, 20, 25, 165, 4390, 57135 etc.

3. DIVISIBILITY BY 2

A number is divisible by 2, if the digit in its unit's place is either 0 or divisible by 2 ; as—

20, 22, 674, 1856, 190018 etc.

4. DIVISIBILITY BY 4

A number is divisible by 4, if the two digits at its extreme right are zeroes or they form a number that is divisible by 4 ; as—

100, 132, 5112, 22156, 97872 etc.

5. DIVISIBILITY BY 8

A number is divisible by 8 if the three digits at its extreme right are zeroes or they form a number that is divisible by 8 ; as—

1000, 4112, 51424, 57152, 59336 etc.

6. DIVISIBILITY BY 3

A number is divisible by 3, if the sum of all its digits is divisible by 3 ; as—

30, 69, 117, 1425, 92358.

7. DIVISIBILITY BY 9

A number is divisible by 9, if the sum of its digits is divisible by 9 ; as—

72, 90, 162, 9405, 63405 etc.

8. DIVISIBILITY BY 6

A number is divisible by 6 if it is divisible by 2 as well as by 3 ; as—

126, 432, 2832, 23934

9. DIVISIBILITY BY 11

A number is divisible by 11 if the difference between the sums of the digits in its alternate places is either 0 or divisible by 11 ; as—

121, 90728, 863423, 96844 etc.

These divisibility tests are very useful in solving mathematical problems and in making calculations involving four basic operations.

FOUR FACTS ABOUT DIVISIBILITY

FACT 1

If a number is divisible by a certain other number, it is also divisible by all the factors of the divisor ; as—

36 is divisible by 18 and 18 has 1, 2, 3, 6, 9 as its factors.

36 must be divisible by each of these factors, *i.e.* by 2, 3, 6, 9.

FACT 2

If a number is divisible by either of the two given prime numbers, it is divisible by their product as well ; as—

105 is divisible by 5 and 7 both.

We know that 5, 7 are both prime numbers.

So, 105 must be divisible by 5 × 7 = 35 as well.

FACT 3

If a number divides two different whole numbers exactly, it must divide their sum also exactly ; as—

5 divides 15 as well as 20 exactly.

So, it must divide (15 + 20) or 35 exactly as well.

FACT 4

If a number divides two different whole numbers exactly, it must divide their difference also exactly ; as—

5 divides 20 as well as 15 exactly.

So, it must divide (20 – 15) or 5 exactly too.

PRACTICE EXERCISES 7

A. Which of the following numerals are divisible by 2 ?

1. 733	**2.** 2470	**3.** 57986
4. 72645	**5.** 34706	**6.** 436976

B. Which of the following numerals are divisible 3 ?

7. 69435	**8.** 358314	**9.** 10039
10. 882645	**11.** 1790174	**12.** 723406

C. Which of the following numerals are divisible by 4 ?

13. 137200	**14.** 137268	**15.** 428656
16. 946126	**17.** 8790300	**18.** 879964

D. Which of the following numerals are divisible by 8 ?

19. 718000   20. 2424   21. 10032

22. 136000   23. 901456   24. 66823

E. Which of the following numerals are divisible by 6 ?

25. 37056   26. 846126   27. 354660

28. 491628   29. 96435   30. 784932

F. Which of the following numerals are divisible by 9 ?

31. 695844   32. 618093   33. 80503161

34. 50314052   35. 7016985   36. 9020817

G. Which of the following numerals are divisible by 11 ?

37. 8050314052   38. 37565375653

39. 478301967   40. 123456789

H. Which of the following numerals are divisible by 5 and which by 10 ?

41. 3718695   42. 5353350   43. 9020815

44. 7016890   45. 639210   46. 2911440

B. Which of the following are true ?

47. If a number is divisible by 4, it must be divisible by 2.

48. If a number is divisible by 4, it must be divisible by 8.

49. If a number is divisible by 3, it must be divisible by 9.

50. A number divisible by 3 and 2 is divisible by 6 also.

51. The sum of two numbers which are divisible by 3 is also divisible by 3.

52. a and b are both divisible by 7. So, $a - b$ is also divisible by 7.

C. Write—

53. a number which is divisible by 2 but not by 4.

54. a number which is divisible by 3 but not by 9.

55. a number divisible by 4 and 8 but not by 32.

=o=

4 | FACTORS AND MULTIPLES

WHAT IS A FACTOR ?

A **factor** *of a numeral is a numeral that divides it exactly.* For example—

12 is a numeral and the numerals that divide it exactly are **1, 2, 3, 4, 6** and **12**.

These six numerals are factors of 12. It is clear that a numeral may have several factors. But every whole number, except 1, has essentially at least two factors—**itself** and **1**.

COMPOSITE NUMBERS

A number that has more than two factors is called a **composite number**.

4 is a composite number as it has three factors (1, 2 and 4).

The five *smallest composite numbers* are 4, 6, 8, 9 and 10.

PRIME NUMBERS

*A number that has only two factors—***itself*** and ***1***—is a* **prime number**.

7 is a prime number as it has only two factors (1, 7).

The *five smallest prime numbers* are 2, 3, 5, 7 and 11.

Remember that **1 is neither composite nor prime**.

PRIME FACTORS

Prime factors *of a given numeral are those of its factors that are prime numbers.*

These prime factors, when multiplied together, give a product that equals the given numeral.

Each number is a product of only one set of prime factors.

Each prime factor may occur any number of times. For example—

24 is a numeral given to us.

24 is the product of $2 \times 2 \times 2 \times 3$ (in any order).

This prime factorization has 2 (three times) and 3 (only one time).

So, 24 has only two prime factors **2** and **3,** though it has many other factors 1, 4, 6, 8, 12, 24 etc.

COMMON FACTORS

If a numeral is a factor of two or more given numerals, it is their **common factor**.

For example—

15 has its factors **1**, 3, **5** and 15.

20 has its factors **1**, 2, 4, **5**, 10 and 20.

So, **1** and **5** are *common factors* of 15 and 20.

NUMBERS PRIME TO EACH OTHER

Two numbers that have no common factor other than 1 *are called* **prime to each other**. For example—

12 has its factors 1, 2, 3, 4, 6 and 12.

35 has its factors 1, 5, 7 and 35.

$\because$ 12 and 35 have no common factor other than 1.

$\therefore$ 12 and 35 are *prime to each other*.

HIGHEST COMMON FACTOR

Let us take two numerals 30 and 45.

30 has its factors **1**, 2, **3**, **5**, 6, 10 and **15.**

45 has its factors **1**, **3**, **5**, 9 and **15.**

Clearly 30, 45 have 1, 3, 5 and 15 as their common factors.

Out of these four common factors 15 is the highest.

So, **15** is the *highest common factor* of 30 and 45.

MULTIPLE

The numeral, whose factors have been found out, is called the **multiple** *of each of its factors*. A multiple contains each of its factors a number of time exactly, i.e. without remainder. For example—

15 has 1, 3, 5, as its factors.

So, 15 is a multiple of 1. It contains 1 *fifteen times*.

15 is a multiple of 3 also. It contains 3 *five times*.

15 is a multiple of 5 as well. It contains 5 *three times*.

REMEMBER :

1. A *factor* of a whole number is a number that divides it exactly.
2. A number that has only two factors—itself and 1—is a *prime number*.
3. A *prime factor* of a whole number is its factor that is prime.
4. A *common factor* is a numeral that divides two or more numerals exactly.
5. The *highest common factor* of two or more numbers is their largest common factor.
6. A *composite number* is a numeral that is more than 3 and has more than two factors.
7. A prime number has *only two factors—itself* and *1*.
8. A composite number *has more than two factors*.
9. 1 is neither prime nor composite.
10. 2 is the only prime number which is *even*.
11. 2 is the *smallest prime number* while 4 is the *smallest composite number*.
12. A numeral that has been resolved into factors is the multiple of each of its factors.

SIEVE OF ERATOSTHENES

This sieve is a method developed by a Greek mathematician named Eratosthenes. He lived in the third century BC and he developed this sieve for identifying **prime numbers**. This sieve is prepared as under :

1	②	③	4	⑤	6	⑦	8	9	10
⑪	12	⑬	14	15	16	⑰	18	⑲	20
21	22	㉓	24	25	26	27	28	㉙	30
㉛	32	33	34	35	36	㊲	38	39	40
㊵	42	㊸	44	45	46	㊼	48	49	50
51	52	㉝	54	55	56	57	58	㉟	60
㊱	62	36	64	65	66	㊲	68	69	70
㉑	72	㉓	74	75	76	77	78	㉙	80
81	82	㉝	84	85	86	87	88	㉙	90
91	92	93	94	95	96	㉗	98	99	100

1. Write the natural numbers 1 to 100 as shown *above*.
2. Cross out 1 as it is *neither prime nor composite*.
3. Ring 2 as it is the first prime number.
4. Cross out *every alternate number* as it is a multiple of 2.
5. Now ring 3 as it is the prime number next to 2.

6. Cross out every third number as it is a multiple of 3.

7. Now ring 5 as it is the next prime number after 3.

8. Cross out every fifth member as it is a multiple of 5.

9. Go on with the process till every numeral is either ringed or crossed out.

All the *circled numbers* will be **prime numbers**.

All the *crossed out numbers* will be **composite numbers**.

Observe the prime numbers closely. There are pairs of prime numbers that have *only one composite number* between them. Such prime numbers are called **twin primes**. They are—

5, 7 ; 11, 13 ; 17, 19 ; 29, 31 ; 41, 43 ; 59, 61 ; 71, 73.

FACTORIZATION

Let us factorize 36 in different ways :

I

36 = 6 × 6

   = 3 × **2** × **3** × 2

II

36 = 4 × 9

   = 2 × **2** × **3** × 3

III

36 = 3 × 12

   = 3 × **2** × **3** × 2

IV

36 = 2 × 18

   = 2 × **2** × **3** × 3

Each set of factors of 36 has four factors. These factors consist of 2 and 3 only and these numerals are prime. So, such a factorization is called **prime factorization**.

Every composite number has at least *one set of prime factors*. This property of composite numbers is called the **Fundamental Theorem of Arithmetic**.

Example 1 : **Find the prime factors of 468.**

Solution : Dividing 468 by 2, 2, 3 and 3.
We get 13 as the last quotient.
13 is also a prime factor of 468.
So, 468 = **2** × **2** × **3** × **3** × **13** *Ans.*

2	468
2	234
3	117
3	39
	13

FINDING THE HIGHEST COMMON FACTOR

We have already learnt what the *highest common factor* means. It is sometimes called the *greatest common divisor* (G.C.D.) also. Let us see how to find the H.C.F. of various numbers.

Example 2 : **Find the H.C.F. of 120, 144 and 204.**

Solution : Let us find the prime factors of the given numbers :

$120 = 2 \times \mathbf{2} \times \mathbf{2} \times \mathbf{3} \times 5$

$144 = 2 \times 2 \times \mathbf{2} \times \mathbf{2} \times \mathbf{3} \times 3$

$204 = \mathbf{2} \times \mathbf{2} \times \mathbf{3} \times 17$

2	120
2	60
2	30
3	15
	5

2	144
2	72
2	36
2	18
3	9
	3

2	204
2	102
3	51
	17

Comparing the factors closely, we find that 2, 2, 3 are common factors of 120, 144 and 244.

∴ Reqd. H.C.F. = 2 × 2 × 3 = **12** *Ans.*

Example 3 : **Find the H.C.F. of 1197 and 4389.**

Solution : For finding the H.C.F. of large numbers we use the long division method as follows :

1. We divide the larger number by the smaller number.
2. We divide the *first divisor* by the *first remainder*.
3. We carry on this process of dividing each divisor by its remainder till the remainder is 0.
4. The last divisor of the process is the H.C.F. of the given numbers.

```
1197 ) 4389 ( 3
       3591
       ‾‾‾‾
       798 ) 1197 ( 1
              798
              ‾‾‾
              399 ) 798 ( 2
                    798
                    ‾‾‾
                      0
```

∴ Reqd. H.C.F. = **399** *Ans.*

Example 4 : **Find the H.C.F. of 1794, 2346 and 4761.**

Solution : For finding the H.C.F. of three large number, we first find the H.C.F. of any two of them.

The H.C.F. of 4761 and 2346 is 69.

Now we shall find the H.C.F. of this H.C.F. (69) and the third number (1794).

This H.C.F. is also 69.

∴ H.C.F. of 1794, 2346 and 4761 = **69** *Ans.*

```
2346 ) 4761 ( 2
       4692
       ‾‾‾‾
       69 ) 2346 ( 34
            207
            ‾‾‾
            276
            276
            ‾‾‾
              0

69 ) 1794 ( 26
     138
     ‾‾‾
     414
     414
     ‾‾‾
       0
```

Example 5 : **Find the largest number that divides 245 and 1029, leaving 5 as remainder in each case.**

Solution : It is clear that when 245 is divided by the reqd. number, it leaves 5 as remainder.

∴ 245 – 5 = **240** must be divisible by the reqd. number.

Again when 1029 is divided by the reqd. number, it also leaves 5 as remainder.

∴ 1029 – 5 = 1024 must be divisible by it. So, the required.

largest No. is the H.C.F. of 240 and 1024.

Finding the H.C.F. by division, we get 16.

∴ Reqd. largest number = **16** Ans.

```
240)1024(4
    960
    ‾‾‾‾
    64)240(3
       192
       ‾‾‾
       48)64(1
          48
          ‾‾
          16)64(4
             64
             ‾‾
              0
```

Example 6 : **Find the largest number that divides 1478, 2703 and 4052 leaving 8, 15, 20 as remainders respectively.**

Solution : When 1478 is divided by the reqd. largest number, it leaves 8 as remainder.

∴ 1478 – 8 = 1470 must be exactly divisible by it.

Similarly 2703 – 15 or **2688** and 4052 – 20 or **4032** must be divisible by it.

Clearly the reqd. largest number is the H.C.F. of 1470, 2688 and 4032. Finding it by division method, we get this H.C.F. = 42.

∴ Reqd. No. = **42** Ans.

```
2688)4032(1
     2688
     ‾‾‾‾
    1344)2688(2
         2688
         ‾‾‾‾
            0

1344)1470(1
     1344
     ‾‾‾‾
     126)1344(10
         1260
         ‾‾‾‾
          84)126(1
             84
             ‾‾
             42)84(2
                84
                ‾‾
                 0
```

40

Example 7 : **A class-room is 630cm. long and 585cm. wide. Find the largest size of the square tile with which its floor can be paved without breaking any tile. How many tiles will be required for it ?**

Solution : Length of the class-room = 630cm.

Width of the class-room = 585cm.

The side of the reqd. tile will be the H.C.F. of 630 and 585.

Finding it by division, we get this H.C.F. = 45

The side of the tile = 45 cm.

Area of the tile = 45 × 45 sq. cm.

Area of the floor = 630 × 585 cm.

Reqd. Number of tiles = $\dfrac{630 \times 585}{45 \times 45}$ = **182** *Ans.*

```
585) 630 (1
     585
      45) 585 (13
          45
         135
         135
          ×
```

PRACTICE EXERCISES 8

A. Answer :

1. How many factors has a prime number got ? ....

2. How many sets of prime factors does a composite number have ? ....

3. Is 1 a composite or a prime number ? ....

4. What is a number with more than two factors called ? ....

5. Which country did Eratosthenes belong to ? ....

6. Which is the only even prime number ? ....

7. Which prime factor is 27 made up of ? ....

8. 27 is divisible by 3. What is 27 to 3 ? ....

9. 3 is a factor of 45 as well as of 54. What will you call it ? ....

B. Show that—

10. 27 is a factor of 6588.

11. 10000 is product of only two composite numbers.

12. 729 is a product obtained from a number multiplied by itself.

13. 729 is a product of only one prime number.

C. Resolve into prime factors :

14. 144   **15.** 1024   **16.** 15625   **17.** 3016

18. 576   **19.** 786   **20.** 180   **21.** 768

D. Answer yes or no :

22. 3 is a prime number. ....

23. 2 is the only even prime number. ....

24. 1 is neither a composite number nor a prime one. ....

25. 23 is a multiple of 3. ....

26. A factor of a number divides it exactly. ....

27. The H.C.F. is the product of all other factors. ....

28. Two numbers with no common factors are **co-prime**. ....

29. Two prime numbers with only one composite number between them are called *twin primes*. ....

E. Find the H.C.F. using prime factors :

30. 36 and 96   **31.** 61 and 73   **32.** 24 and 32

33. 72 and 117   **34.** 125 and 625   **35.** 102 and 153

36. 144 and 208   **37.** 108 and 252   **38.** 13, 143, 273

39. 144, 180, 192   **40.** 252, 324, 288   **41.** 208, 494, 949

42. 516, 1935, 1548   **43.** 216, 312, 720   **44.** 165, 341, 651

F. Find the H.C.F. by division method :

45. 1380 and 1495   **46.** 1628 and 5336   **47.** 4205 and 4640

48. 7020 and 103868   **49.** 39480 and 39904   **50.** 8217 and 2241

51. 3239, 3075, 1599   **52.** 6868, 1870, 2210   **53.** 4816, 6321, 8127

54. 5330, 10660, 7995   **55.** 494, 741, 988,   **56.** 4210, 7210, 8240

G. 57. Find the largest factor that divides 1631 and 5339 leaving 11 as remainder in each case.

58. Find the largest tape that can be used to measure exactly the following lengths : 2·40m, 1·65m, 2·10m and 2·55m.

59. Find the highest number that will divide 31530 and 14490 leaving 6 as remainder in either case.

60. Find the largest number that divides 13528 and 11296 leaving 23 and 11 as remainders respectively.

61. How will you show that 68401 and 53477 are prime to each other ?

62. A bath-room is 2·24 metres long and 1·89 metres wide. We want to pave its floor with marble tiles. What is the size of the largest square tile that can be used to pave it without breaking any tile ? How many tiles will be required in all ?

63. In finding the H.C.F. of two numbers by division method, the last divisor is 35 while the quotients are 1, 2, 1, 3 respectively. Find both the numbers.

64. In a long division sum, the quotient is made up of two digits. If the dividend is 40051 and the two remainders are 173 and 294, find the divisor and the quotient.

65. Simplify : *(a)* $\dfrac{203}{261}$ *(b)* $\dfrac{217}{279}$ *(c)* $\dfrac{584}{657}$

66. What will be the H.C.F. of :

(a) two prime number   *(b)* two consecutive number

67. Explain the difference between :

(a) a prime number and a composite number

(b) a common factor and a highest common factor

(c) a factor and a multiple

68. Define :

(a) Twin Primes   *(b)* Fundamental Theorem of Arithmetic

═○═

5 LOWEST COMMON MULTIPLE

> *KNOW THESE TERMS :*
> 1. **common multiple**—number that is exactly divisible by two or more numbers
> 2. **lowest common multiple**—smallest number that is exactly divisible by two or more numbers
> 3. **common prime factor**—prime number that is a factor of two or more numbers
> 4. **co-primes**—two or more numbers that have no common factor except 1

MULTIPLE

We learnt the definition of—**multiple**—in the previous lesson. It reads as under :

The multiple of a given number is the number that contains it several times without any remainder.

COMMON MULTIPLE

A **common multiple** *of two or more numbers is a number that contains each of them an exact number of times.* For example—

42 contains 2, 3, 6, 7 and 14 each an exact number of times. In other words, it is exactly divisible by these five numbers. So, 42 is their **common multiple**.

LOWEST COMMON MULTIPLE

From the above example, it follows that 42 is the common multiple of 3 and 7. There are other multiples of 3 and 7 as well.

They are 21, 63, 84, 105 etc.

But the smallest or lowest of these multiples is 21.

So, 21 is the lowest common multiple of 3 and 7.

PROPERTIES OF L.C.M.

1. L.C.M. of some given numbers is never smaller than any of them. It is larger than most of them.

2. L.C.M. of two or more co-primes is equal to their product.

3. If a number a is a factor of another number b then the L.C.M. of a and b is b while their H.C.F. is a. So, it follows that the product of such numbers is equal to the product of their H.C.F. and L.C.M.

4. The H.C.F. of two given numbers is always a factor of their L.C.M.

Example 1 : **Find the L.C.M. of 18, 28, 105 and 108.**

Solution : Let us resolve the given numbers into their prime factors.

$18 = 2 \times 3 \times 3 = 2 \times 3^2$

$28 = 2 \times 2 \times 7 = \mathbf{2^2} \times 7$

$105 = 3 \times 5 \times 7 = 3 \times \mathbf{5} \times \mathbf{7}$

$108 = 2 \times 2 \times 3 \times 3 \times 3 = 2^2 \times \mathbf{3^3}$

$\therefore$ L.C.M. $= 2^2 \times 3^3 \times 5 \times 7$

$= 4 \times 27 \times 5 \times 7$

$= \mathbf{3780}$ *Ans.*

2	18
3	9
	3

2	28
2	14
	7

3	105
5	35
	7

2	108
2	54
3	27
3	9
	3

Another method of resolving the given numbers into prime factors for finding their L.C.M. is as follows :

1. Write all the given numbers as shown.
2. Divide the numbers with the smallest common prime factor of any two or more of the given numbers. We generally start with 2.
3. Write as such the numbers that are not divisible by the dividing prime factor.
4. Follow the process till all the quotients are prime numbers.
5. Multiply all the divisors and the final quotients to get the L.C.M.

2	18 – 28 – 105 – 108
2	9 – 14 – 105 – 54
3	9 – 7 – 105 – 27
3	3 – 7 – 35 – 9
7	1 – 7 – 35 – 3
	1 – 1 – 5 – 3

L.C.M. $= 2 \times 2 \times 3 \times 3 \times 7 \times 5 \times 3$

$= 4 \times 27 \times 7 \times 5 = \mathbf{3780}$ *Ans.*

Example 2 : **Find the lowest number which when increased by 4 is exactly divisible by 18, 28, 105 and 108.**

Solution : We know that the smallest number divisible by 18, 28, 105 and 108 is their L.C.M.

We shall find this L.C.M by division.

L.C.M. $= 2 \times 2 \times 3 \times 3 \times 3 \times 7 \times 5 = 3780$

$\because$ Reqd. number becomes divisible by the given numbers after being increased by 4.

2	18 – 28 – 105 – 108
2	9 – 14 – 105 – 54
3	9 – 7 – 105 – 27
3	3 – 7 – 35 – 9
7	1 – 7 – 35 – 3
	1 – 1 – 5 – 3

$\therefore$ Required No. $= 3780 - 4 = \mathbf{3776}$ *Ans.*

Example 3 : Find the least number which when diminished by 4 becomes divisible by 18, 28, 105 and 108.

Solution : Clearly, the required number is larger than the L.C.M. of the given numbers.

We saw in the previous examples that the L.C.M. of 18, 28, 105 and 108 = 3780

∴ Reqd. Number = 3780 + 4 = **3784** *Ans.*

Example 4 : The H.C.F. of two numbers is 7 and their L.C.M. is 630. If one of the numbers is 126 find the other.

Solution : We know that the product of any two numbers is equal to the product of their L.C.M. and H.C.F.

L.C.M. of the numbers = 630 and their H.C.F. = 7

Product of the numbers = H.C.F. × L.C.M.

= 7 × 630

∵ One of the numbers = 126

∴ Other Number = $\dfrac{7 \times 630}{126}$ = **35** *Ans.*

Example 5 : Anil, Atul and Amit start from the same point and at the same time to run round a race course. Anil completes a round in 252 seconds, Atul in 308 seconds while Amit in 198 seconds. Find when they will be at the starting point together again.

Solution : Clearly, the three runners will be together at the starting point again after a period that equals the L.C.M. of 252, 308 and 198 seconds.

L.C.M. of 252, 308 and 198
= 2 × 2 × 3 × 3 × 7 × 11
= 4 × 9 × 7 × 11 = 2772

∴ The runners will meet after 2772 seconds

or $\dfrac{2772}{60}$ minutes, *i.e.* **46 minutes 12 seconds** *Ans.*

2	252 – 308 – 198
2	126 – 154 – 99
3	63 – 77 – 99
3	21 – 77 – 11
7	7 – 77 – 11
11	1 – 11 – 11
	1 – 1 – 1

46

Example 6 : **Three bells ring after intervals of 18, 24 and 32 seconds respectively. If they start ringing at the same time, after how long will they ring together again ?**

Solution : It is clear that the bells will ring together again after a gap of seconds that equal the L.C.M. of 18, 24 and 32.

Let us find their L.C.M.

2	18 – 24 – 32
2	9 – 12 – 16
2	9 – 6 – 8
3	9 – 3 – 4
	3 – 1 – 4

L.C.M. of 18, 24, 32 = 2 × 2 × 2 × 3 × 3 × 4 = 288

∴ The bells will ring together after 288 seconds or 288 ÷ 60 minutes, *i.e.* **4 minutes 48 seconds** *Ans.*

PRACTICE EXERCISES 9

A. Answer :

1. What is the L.C.M. of two co-primes ? ....

2. Which is the larger—H.C.F. or L.C.M. of two numbers ? ....

3. Can the L.C.M. of two numbers be smaller than each of the two numbers ? ....

4. a is a factor of b. What is the H.C.F. of a and b ? ....

5. a is a factor of b. What is the L.C.M. of a and b ? ....

6. What is the H.C.F. of two numbers to their L.C.M. ? ....

B. Find the L.C.M. of :

   7. 2 and 4   **8.** 2 and 6   **9.** 3 and 6   **10.** 3 and 9

   11. 21 and 28   **12.** 18 and 24   **13.** 6 and 8   **14.** 6 and 9

   15. 10 and 15   **16.** 28 and 35   **17.** 60 and 75   **18.** 42 and 63

C. Find the L.C.M. of :

   19. 2, 4, 6   **20.** 3, 5, 6   **21.** 5, 9, 10   **22.** 12, 18, 20

   23. 60, 70, 108   **24.** 48, 72, 112   **25.** 42, 70, 84   **26.** 35, 40, 45

   27. 28, 36, 42   **28.** 30, 40, 50   **29.** 16, 28, 40   **30.** 36, 45, 60

D. Find the L.C.M. of :

   31. $2^3 × 2$ and $3 × 3^2$ **32.** $2 × 5^2$ and $5 × 2 × 3^2$

   33. $5^2 × 2^2$ and $2^3 × 5$ **34.** 14, 21, 42, 63

   35. 18, 30, 45, 60   **36.** 42, 64, 70, 112

E. Find the L.C.M. as well as the H.C.F. :

37. 2117 and 104   **38.** 221 and 533   **39.** 165 and 195

40. 242 and 330   **41.** 234 and 312   **42.** 154 and 168

F. **43.** What is the least amount of money that can be distributed exactly in 50-paisa coins and 5-rupee coins ?

44. Which is the smallest number that is exactly divisible by 156, 168, 208 and 432 ?

45. Four men can walk 105, 112, 126 and 168 kilometres in a week respectively. Find the smallest distance that each of them can walk in exact number of weeks.

46. Three bells toll at intervals of 9, 12 and 20 minutes respectively They rang together at 8 a.m. When will they toll together again ?

47. Find the smallest number which when divided by 18, 28 and 105 leaves 5 as remainder in each case.

48. L.C.M. of two numbers 667 and 437 is 12673. Find their H.C.F.

49. The H.C.F. of two numbers 221 and 195 is 13. Find their L.C.M.

50. The H.C.F. of two number is 29 and their L.C.M. is 1160. If one of the numbers is 232, find the other.

51. Find the L.C.M. of 435, 580 and 725.

52. The H.C.F. of two numbers is 16. Which can be their L.C.M. — 260 or 256 ?

53. Four walkers start off at the same time. Their steps measure 65, 70, 75 and 80 centimetres respectively. After covering how much distance will their steps fall together again.

54. Which number will be exactly divisible by 20, 21, 28 and 30 when diminished by 17 ?

55. Which number will be exactly divisible by 16, 20, 24 and 28 when increased by 17 ?

56. Find the least number of five digits which when divided by 15, 20, 25, 30 and 35 will leave 7 as the remainder in each case.

57. Find the lowest number which when divided by 25, 40 and 60 leaves 13 as remainder.

58. The H.C.F. of two numbers is 14 and their L.C.M. is 2548. If one of the numbers is 196, find the other.

6 INTEGERS—I

KNOW THESE TERMS :
1. **positive numbers**— natural numbers above zero
2. **negative numbers**— numbers below zero
3. **absolute value**— numerical value of an integer regardless of its sign of + or –
4. **integers without a sign before them** are taken to be positive.

WHAT ARE INTEGERS ?

We studied *natural numbers* and *whole numbers* in detail in the foregoing chapters of this book. We know the following facts :

1. To begin with, *counting numbers* were invented. They came to be called **natural numbers**.

2. When the *natural numbers* could not serve all the purposes of calculations, **0 was invented** in India by *Bhaaskaraachaarya*. Thus a new set of numbers came into being (natural numbers + 0). These numbers came to be known as **whole numbers**.

3. Later on, it was felt that even *whole numbers* were not able to meet all the requirements of calculations. For example :

There were no whole numbers to represent the results of 2 – 3, 3 – 7 and 5 – 9 etc. as subtraction of a larger number from a smaller number was not possible. So, introduction of new numbers became necessary.

Just as 0 was added below the natural numbers to change the natural numbers into whole numbers, **negative numbers** were added below 0.

As a result, a new and larger set of numbers came into being. These numbers came to be called **integers**. Clearly, integers include—

(a) *natural numbers* (1, 2, 3, 4...) etc. which are called **positive integers**.

(b) *0* which is *simply an integer*. **It is neither positive nor negative**.

(c) *negative numbers* or *minus numbers* (–1, –2, –3....) etc. which are called **negative integers**.

For each positive integer, there is an opposite negative integer. For example, for 1, there is –1 and for 2 there is –2. These positive and negative integers are **opposites** of each other and they have a relation as 1 + (–1) = 0 and 2 + (–2) = 0

Negative integers are particularly useful in opposite situations.

For example—

(a) *Profit* and *Loss* are indicated by using *negative integers* along with *positive integers*.

(b) *Heights* above and below the sea-level and *temperatures* more than and less than 0°C are also stated the same way.

INTEGERS ON A LINE

While indicating positive and negative integers on a line, we have got to follow the position of **0** clearly. We know that—

(a) 0 is the lowest whole number. So, *every positive integer is more than 0.*

(b) Therefore, *every positive integer is higher than every negative integer.*

(c) Every negative integer is smaller than 0.

Negative Integers   Positive Integers

Remember that—

1. On a horizontal line, we show *positive integers* to **the right** of 0 and *negative integers* **to the left** of 0.

2. On a vertical line, we show *positive integers* **above the 0** and *negative integers* **below the 0**.

3. –1 is more than –2 which is more than –3..... and so on.

4. +1 is less than +2 which is less than +3.... and so on.

ABSOLUTE VALUE

The **absolute value** of *an integer is its* **numerical value** *regardless of its sign of + or –*

In other words, both –5 and +5 have the same absolute value. Similarly, the absolute value of :

+**7** = 7 and also of –**7** = 7   +**9** = 9 and also of –**9** = 9

The absolute value of an integer is shown by drawing two vertical lines on both sides of the integer ; as—

Absolute value of +3 is expressed by $|+3|$

Absolute value of –3 is expressed by $|-3|$

We have already learnt that—

$|+5| = 5$ and also $|-5| = 5$

50

$|+7| = 7$ and also $|-7| = 7$

$|+12| = 12$ and also $|-12| = 12$ So, we conclude that—

1. Positive integers are natural numbers and they can be written **without the sign + also** ; as +7 can be written as **7** and +9 as **9**.

2. $|a| = a$ **if a is positive or zero**.

3. $|a| = -a$ **if a is negative**.

PRACTICE EXERCISES 10

A. Which is +ve and which is –ve ?

1. Population increase ....
2. Going North ....

3. Climbing up ....
4. Going East ....

5. Population decrease ....
6. 5° above 0°C ....

7. Withdrawing Rs. 25 ....
8. 3° below 0°C ....

9. Going South ....
10. Depositing Rs. 100 ....

11. Gaining weight ....
12. Losing weight ....

B. Which number in each pair will be to the right of the other on a horizontal line ?

13. 2, 5   14. – 1, – 6   15. 1, – 5

16. 0, – 1   17 – 2, 9   18. 3, – 3

C. Which is the higher integer ?

19. 112 or – 180   20. – 12 or 11   21. – 72 or 74

22. 120 or – 175   23. 231 or 457   24. – 504 or 51.

D. Which is the lower integer ?

25. – 99 or 99   26. – 487 or – 320   27. 1 or 6

28. – 2 or 0   29. – 5 or 18   30. – 526 or 556

31. 7 or – 7   32. – 3 or – 5   33. – 701 or – 700

34. – 240 or 240   35. 201 or –201   36. – 20 or – 19

E. Which is correct out of a and b ?

37. (a) 0 is the smallest whole number.   (b) Zero is the smallest integer.

38. (a) Zero is a positive integer.   (b) Zero is neither +ve nor –ve.

39. (a) – 18 is greater than – 7.   (b) – 7 is greater than – 18.

40. (a) Zero is an integer.   (b) Zero is not an integer.

F. Answer *yes* or *no* :

41. The absolute value of an integer depends on its sign.

42. Every positive integer has an opposite negative integer.

43. Absolute value of $(x - 4)$ is $(x - 4)$ if $x > 4$.

44. Absolute value of $(x - 4)$ is $(4 - x)$ if $x < 4$.

45. Zero is a higher integer than any negative integer.

46. If $a > b$, then $-a < -b$.

G. Write the number, which is—

47. 2 more than -7

48. 5 less than -4

49. 1 less than -2

50. 3 more than 2

H. Write in the ascending order :

51. 1, -4, 0, 7, -8, -1

52. -4, -12, 0, 7, -9, 9

I. Fill up each blank :

53. 0, ..., 2, ...4

54. 0, ..., -2, ...

55. -3, ..., ..., ..., ..., ..., 3

56. -9, ..., ..., ..., ..., -4

J. Write the correct term for—

57. The numerical value of an integer. ....

58. The numbers originally used for counting. ....

59. The numbers including natural numbers and 0. ....

60. The numbers including natural numbers, whole numbers and negative numbers. ....

ADDITION OF INTEGERS

Integers include *positive numbers* and *negative numbers*.

Positive integers are added *just like whole numbers*.

But the addition involving all negative integers or mixed integers (positive as well as negative) needs much care. Let us find a rule for this type of addition.

We know that—

(a) Rise in temperature by $4°$ C $= + 4$

Rise in temperature by $5°$ C $= + 5$

Total rise in temperature $= + 4 + 5 = + 9$, *i.e.* $9°$C

(b) Gain of 7 rupees = +7

Loss of 4 rupees = –4

Net gain = +7 + (–4)

= **Rs. 3** *Ans.*

Example 1 : **Add up** *(a)* **4 and 11**   *(b)* **234 and –636**

(c) **–5728 and 429**   *(d)* **–1176 and –636**

Solution :   *(a)* $|4| = +4$ and $|11| = +11$

$\therefore 4 + 11 = +4 + 11 = +15$ or **15** *Ans.*

(b) $|234| = 234$

$|-636| = 636$

As the signs of the addends are different, we shall take the difference of the absolute values

$636 - 234 = 402$

The larger absolute value has a *negative sign*

$\therefore$ Sum of 234 and –636 = **–402** *Ans.*

(c) $|-5728| = 5728$

$|429| = 429$

signs of the addends are different

$\therefore$ We shall take the difference of the absolute values

$5728 - 429 = 5299$

As the larger absolute value is *negative*

$\therefore$ Sum of –5728 and 429 = **–5299** *Ans.*

(d) $|-1176| = 1176$

$|-636| = 636$

both the addends have similar signs

$\therefore$ They will be added

$1176 + 636 = 1812$

As both the addends are *negative*

$\therefore$ Sum of –1176 and –636 = **–1812** *Ans.*

Example 2 : Find the sum of :
373, –245, –373, 145, 3000

Solution : 373 + (–245) + (–373) + 145 + 3000
= (373 + 145 + 3000) + [(–245) + (–373]
= 3518 + (–618)
= 3518 –618= **2900** *Ans.*

PRACTICE EXERCISES 11

A. Answer *yes* **or** *no* :

1. The sum of two negative integers is always –ve. ....

2. The sum of an integer and its opposite is 0. ....

3. The sum of two positive integers is always –ve. ....

4. The consecutive successor of –286 is –285. ....

5. The sum of a +ve and a –ve integer may
be negative or positive. ....

B. Find the sum :

6. –3, –2, 5   **7.** –1, 4, –6, 3   **8.** 2, –7, –5

9. 17, –6, –9   **10.** 3, –4, –4, 6   **11.** –4, –6, –3

12. –2, –3, 7, –4   **13.** –5, 8, 6, –8   **14.** –5, –7, –1, 2, 9

C. Add up :

15. –145, 211, –320   **16.** –948, –230, 10000

17. 1001, –999, –498   **18.** –982, –2304, 3419

19. –18, –2, –245, 312   **20.** –9458, 0, –320, –2548

21. –2547, –2884, –2816, 10001   **22.** –21, –9, 64, –23, –29

23. 99+(–66)+(–33)+7   **24.** –931+(–18)+9+(–81)

25. 566+(–366) +1252+(–962)   **26.** –391+(–81)+9+(–145)

27. 1+(–385)+(–385)+769   **28.** 525+(–373)+(–300)+149

29. 16+(–9)+(–81)+(34)   **30.** (–638)+(–1262)+665+(–181)

31. (–110)+250+(–123)+(–27)   **32.** 1587+(–212)+(–1587)+212

SUBTRACTION OF INTEGERS

Suppose you deposit rupees 8 in a bank and then withdraw Rs. 10. It means that you owe Rs. 2 to the bank. In other words, there are –2 rupees left in your account.

Suppose you withdraw Rs. 4 more. Clearly you owe Rs. 6 to the bank. In other words, Rs. (–2) + (–4) will be left in your account.

$(–2) + (–4) = –2 –4 = –6$

Similarly $–2 –(–4) = –2 +4 = +2$ or 2

Let us solve some examples :

Example : **Subtract :**

(a) **15 from –31**	(b) **–41 from –29**
(c) **–62 from 0**	(d) **–49 from –21**
(e) **–21 from 47**	(f) **250 from –337**

Solution : (a) We are to subtract 15 from –31

$$–31 –(+15) = –31 –15 = \textbf{–46} \; Ans.$$

(b) We are to subtract –41 from –29

$$–29 – (–41) = –29 + 41 = \textbf{12} \; Ans.$$

(c) We are to subtract –62 from 0

$$0 – (–62) = 0 + 62 = \textbf{62} \; Ans.$$

(d) We are to subtract –49 from –21

$$–21 – (–49) = –21 +49 = \textbf{28} \; Ans.$$

(e) We are to subtract –21 from 47

$$47 – (–21) = 47 + 21 = \textbf{68} \; Ans.$$

(f) We are to subtract 250 from –337

$$–337 – (+250) = –337 –250 = \textbf{–587} \; Ans.$$

PRACTICE EXERCISES 12

A. Subtract :

1. –13 from 5	**2.** –6 from 9	**3.** 20 from –2
4. –25 from 15	**5.** –400 from 200	**6.** 901 from –102

7. 625 from –2070   **8.** 7640 from –84   **9.** 8739 from –9041

10. –454 from 332   **11.** 430 from –165   **12.** 351 from –620

13. –1155 from 0   **14.** 0 from –1105   **15.** 2483 from –3240

B. Fill up the blanks :

16. –6 + ... = 0   **17.** 17 + ... = 0   **18.** 14 + (–14) = ...

19. –4 + ... = 14   **20.** –526 + ... = –874   **21.** ..... –215 = 94

22. –112 + ... = 33   **23.** –12 + ... = 86   **24.** –7 + 84 = ...

C. Answer :

25. To subtract –8 from an integer, we add .... to the integer.

26. To subtract 15 from an integer, we add .... to the integer.

27. Subtract –6 from 10 and 10 from –6. Are both the remainders same ?

28. The sum of two integers is 68. If one of them is –46 find the other.

29. The sum of two integers is 496. If one of them is –96, find the other.

30. What is the difference between 12°C and –5°C.

31. Find the distance between two places if one is 4800 metres above the level of the sea and the other 3465 metres below the level of the sea.

32. Subtract the sum of –28 and –29 from the sum of –11 and –27.

33. a and b are two integers such that a is the consecutive predecessor of b. Find the value of $a - b$.

34. * is an operation such that $a * b = a - b + 2$, find the values of 2 * 1 and –3 * –4.

Hint : 2 * 1 = 2 – 1 + 2 = 3

–3 *–4 = –3 – (–4) +2

D. Find the value of :

35. –13 + 23 – 19 + 1   **36.** –40 – (–42) – (–5) + 6

37. –7 + (–8 + 84) +1   **38.** –19 + [(–4) + 14] + 5

39. –11 – [(–14) + (–4) –6]   **40.** 1– 2 + 3 – 4 + 5 – 6 + 7 – 8

INTEGERS—II

We studied *addition* and *subtraction* of integers in the previous lesson. In this lesson, we shall study **multiplication** and **division** of integers.

MULTIPLICATION OF INTEGERS

In regard to the multiplication of integers, commit the following facts to memory.

1. To find the product of two integers, we multiply their absolute values and then put the sign ..... as explained under.

2. *When a* **positive integer** *is multiplied by another positive integer, the* **product is positive**.

3. *When a* **negative integer** *is multiplied by another* **negative integer**, *the* **product positive**.

4. *When a* **positive integer** *is multiplied by a* **negative integer**, *the* **product is negative**.

5. *While multiplying more than two negative integers, remember :*
   (a) If the number of negative integers is **even**, *the* **product is positive**.
   (b) If the number of negative integers is odd, the **product is negative**.

Let us solve examples :

Example : Multiply :
    (a) **2 × 7**   *(b)* **–6 × –6**   *(c)* **3 × –15**
    (d) **–3 × –9 × –1 × –4 × –5 × –2**
    (e) **–6 × –8 × –2 × –7 × –9 × –1 × –5**

Solution : *(a)* 2 × 7 = **+14**   (∵ both integers are +ve)
        (b) (–6) × (–6) = **+36** (∵ both integers are –ve)
        (c) 3 × (–15) = **–45**   (∵ one integer is –ve and one +ve)

(d) $(-3) \times (-9) \times (-1) \times (-4) \times (-5) \times (-2)$

$\quad = + (27 \times 4 \times 10)$
$\quad = + \mathbf{1080} \; Ans.$ $\left.\right] \because$ No of negative terms is even

(e) $(-6) \times (-8) \times (-2) \times (-7) \times (-9) \times (-1) \times (-5)$

$\quad = - (48 \times 14 \times 45)$
$\quad = - \mathbf{30240} \; Ans.$ $\left.\right] \because$ No of negative terms is odd

PRACTICE EXERCISES 13

A. What will the sign of the product be, if —

1. we multiply two positive integers ? ....

2. we multiply two negative integers ? ....

3. we multiply a positive and a negative integers ? ....

4. we multiply 8 negative integers together ? ....

5. we multiply 5 negative integers together ? ....

6. we multiply 11 negative and 2 positive integers ? ....

7. we multiply 8 positive and 1 negative integers ? ....

8. we multiply –40 with –1 ? ....

B. Multiply :

9. $3 \times (-25)$ 10. 125×6 11. $(-13) \times (-15)$

12. $5 \times (-10) \times 7$ 13. $11 \times (5) \times (8)$ 14. $(-15) \times (-18) \times (-16)$

15. $(-2) \times 28 \times (-5)$ 16. $(-8) \times (-42) \times 0$ 17. $16 \times (-185) \times (-4)$

18. $(-42) \times 52 \times (-10)$ 19. $(-3) \times (-4) \times 48$ 20. $(-18) \times (-5) \times 7$

21. $(-6) \times (-5) \times (-2) \times (-3) \times (-5)$

22. $(-5) \times (-8) \times (-11) \times (-15)$

23. $(-10) \times 0 \times 57 \times (-57)$

24. $(-181) \times (-44) + (-181) \times (-56)$

25. $(-8) \times (10 - 5 - 45 + 96)$

C. Which is more ?

26. $(5 + 6) \times 7$ or $5 + 6 \times 7$

27. $(5 - 6) \times 10$ or $5 - 6 \times 10$

28. $[(-1) - (-4)] \times (-6)$ or $(-1) \times -5 \times (-6)$

29. $(-9) \times 6 + (-9) \times 4$ or $8 \times (-12) + 7 \times (-12)$

30. $(-3) \times (-7) \times (-6)$ or $(-8) \times 3 \times (-5)$

D. Answer *yes* **or** *no* :

31. Every integer multiplied by -1 gives its opposite integer.

32. Product of two positive and one negative integers is negative.

33. Product of a positive and a negative integers is positive.

DIVISION OF INTEGERS

We have already learnt that **division** is the operation inverse to the operation called *multiplication*. So, each multiplication fact can be expressed as one or more division facts ; as—

(a) $4 \times 5 = 20$ (Multiplication Fact)

$\left.\begin{array}{l} 20 \div 4 = 5 \\ \text{and } 20 \div 5 = 4 \end{array}\right]$ (Division Facts)

(b) $(-2) \times 3 = -6$ (Multiplication Fact)

$\left.\begin{array}{l} (-6) \div 3 = -2 \\ \text{and } (-6) \div (-2) = 3 \end{array}\right]$ (Division Facts)

We also know :

The number to be divided is called **dividend**.

The number that divides is called **divisor**.

The result of division is called **quotient**.

Now observe the above two examples.

In *(a)*, we observe that—

1. a *positive dividend* divided by a *positive divisor* gives a **positive quotient**. $(20 \div 4 = 5$ and $20 \div 5 = 4)$.

2. a *negative dividend* divided by a *negative divisor* also gives a **positive quotient** $[(-6) \div (-2) = 3$.

3. a *negative dividend* divided by a *positive divisor* gives a **negative quotient** $[(-6) \div 3 = -2]$.

4 A *positive dividend* divided by a *negative divisor* also gives a **negative quotient** $[6 \div (-3) = -2]$.

Example : Divide :

  (a) 72 by 9   (b) 65 by (–5)

  (c) (–81) by (–9)   (d) (–63) by 7

Solution : (a) $|72| = 72$

  $|9| = 9$

  ∵ Both the *dividend* and the *divisor* are **+ve**.

  ∴ Quotient will be +ve.

  So, $72 \div 9 = \mathbf{8}$ *Ans.*

  (b) $|65| = 65$

  $|-5| = 5$

  dividend is **+ve** but the *divisor* is **–ve**

  ∴ Quotient will be –ve

  So, $65 \div (-5) = \mathbf{-13}$ *Ans.*

  (c) $|-81| = 81$

  $|-9| = 9$

  Both the *dividend* and the *divisor* are **–ve**

  ∴ Quotient must be +ve

  So, $(-81) \div -9 = \mathbf{9}$ *Ans.*

  (d) $|-63| = 63$

  $|7| = 7$

  Dividend is **negative** and *divisor* is **+ve**

  ∴ Quotient must be –ve

  So, $-63 \div 7 = \mathbf{-9}$ *Ans.*

PRACTICE EXERCISES 14

A. What sign will the quotient have, if—

  1. a +ve dividend is divided by a +ve divisor ? ....

  2. a + ve dividend is divided by a –ve divisor ? ....

  3. a –ve dividend is divided by a +ve divisor ? ....

  4. a –ve dividend is divided by a –ve divisor ? ....

B. Divide and find the quotient :

5. $18 \div 3$ **6.** $21 \div 7$ **7.** $15 \div 5$

8. $(-15) \div (-5)$ **9.** $45 \div (-9)$ **10.** $(-64) \div (-16)$

11. $0 \div (-10)$ **12.** $(-102) \div 17$ **13.** $(-144) \div (-12)$

14. $(-3125) \div 25$ **15.** $(-729) \div (-9)$ **16.** $1375 \div (-1375)$

17. $(-243) \div (-27)$ **18.** $16825 \div (-1)$ **19.** $1728 \div (-12)$

20. $(-152) \div (-19)$ **21.** $147 \div (-21)$ **22.** $(-161) \div (-23)$

23. $0 \div (-278)$ **24.** $-2061 \div 229$ **25.** $-639 \div -71$

C. Fill up each blank :

26. $-121 \div$ .... $= 121$ **27.** $505 \div$ .... $= 5$

28. .... $\div 670 = 0$ **29.** $-3819 \div$ .... $= 201$

30. .... $\div 256 = -2$ **31.** $-657 \div$ .... $= -1$

32. .... $\div (-12) = -9$ **33.** $720 \div$ .... $= 36$

34. .... $\div (-1) = 18$ **35.** .... $\div 306 = -1$

36. If the dividend and the divisor have like signs, their quotient is ....

37. If the dividend and the divisor have .... signs, their quotient is –ve.

POWER OF INTEGERS

If a number is multiplied by itself once, twice, thrice or any number of times, we can write the product as a **power of the number** in a short way. Observe the following :

How often multiplied	Product	How to Read It
2×2	$4 = 2^2$	Two squared or 2 raised to power 2
$2 \times 2 \times 2$	$8 = 2^3$	Two cubed or 2 raised to power 3
$2 \times 2 \times 2 \times 2$	$16 = 2^4$	2 raised to power 4
$2 \times 2 \times 2 \times 2 \times 2$	$32 = 2^5$	2 raised to power 5
$2 \times 2 \times 2 \times 2 \times 2 \times 2$	$64 = 2^6$	2 raised to power 6

The term—2^4—has two parts. 2 is the **base** and 4 is called the **exponent/index**. In case of negative numbers—

$(-2) \times (-2)$ $= (-2)^2$ $(-3) \times (-3)$ $= (-3)^2$

$(-2) \times (-2) \times (-2)$ $= (-2)^3$ $(-3) \times (-3) \times (-3)$ $= (-3)^3$

$(-2) \times (-2) \times (-2) \times (-2) = (-2)^4$ $(-3) \times (-3) \times (-3) \times (-3) = (-3)^4$

Inversely—

$(-2)^4 = (-2) \times (-2) \times (-2) \times (-2)$

$(-3)^4 = (-3) \times (-3) \times (-3) \times (-3)$

Remember that—

(a) $2^2 = 4$, $3^2 = 9$ and $4^2 = 16$ and $a \times a = a^2$

Numbers 4, 9, 16 and **a²** are called PERFECT SQUARES.

(a) $2^3 = 8$, $3^3 = 27$, $4^3 = 64$ and $a \times a \times a = a^3$

Numbers **8, 27, 64** and **a³** are called PERFECT CUBES.

PRACTICE EXERCISES 15

A. Write the base and the exponent of each term :

1. 2^8 ....

2. $(-3)^5$ ....

3. $(-3)^3$ ....

4. $(-a)^7$ ....

B. Write in power notation :

5. $3 \times 3 \times 3 \times 3 \times 3 \times 3$ ....

6. $7 \times 7 \times 7 \times 7 \times 7 \times 7 \times 7$ ....

7. $(-11) \times (-11) \times (-11) \times (-11) \times (-11)$ ....

8. $5 \times 5 \times 5 \times 5 \times 5 \times 5 \times 5 \times 5$ ....

C. Find the value of :

9. 30^2 10. $(-24)^2$ 11. $(-8)^3$ 12. $(-1)^{50}$

13. $(-2)^6$ 14. $(-3)^5$ 15. $(-1)^{16}$ 16. $(-21)^3$

17. $(-4)^6$ 18. $(-5)^5$ 19. $2^3 \times 3^2$ 20. $3^6 \div 3^2$

D. Do as directed :

21. Write the *squares* of the first nine natural numbers on your note-book.

22. Write the *cubes* of the first nine natural·numbers.

23. Write 16, 25, 49, 81 and 121 in power notation.

24. Find the squares of 13, 15, 17, 19, 21, 23, 27 and 29.

25. Find the cubes of 11, 20, 25, 30 and 40.

26. Find the difference between 4^5 and 5^4.

27. Find the sum of 7^3 and 9^3.

E. Answer *yes* **or** *no* :

28. The square of a negative integer is positive. ....

29. The cube of a negative integer is negative. ....

30. $a^3 \times a^4 = a^7$ ....

USE OF BRACKETS

We have read about the four operations (*addition, subtraction, multiplication* and *division*) in detail. These operations are performed from left to right in a set sequence—*division, multiplication, addition* and *subtraction*. For example :

(a) $25 \div 5 + 4 = 5 + 4 = 9$ (*Division* is performed before *addition*)

(b) $6 - 8 \div 2 = 6 - 4 = 2$ (*Division* is performed before *subtraction*)

But **brackets** if introduced have to be given the first preference ; as—
$9 \div (7 - 4) + 6$ has $7 - 4$ within brackets which is to be solved first of all.
$9 \div (7 - 4) + 6 = 9 \div 3 + 6 = 3 + 6 = 9$

Clearly brackets are used to group terms together. They are marked in pairs. The *left mark* shows its **beginning** while the *right mark* shows its end.
Moreover, brackets are of three chief types as shown below :

1. **Simple Brackets** (*Parentheses*) ....( )
2. **Curly Brackets** (*Braces*)............... { }
3. **Square Brackets** (*Crotchets*)..........[ ]
4. Another symbol called **bar/vinculum** is also sometimes put over two or more terms. **It is solved before the brackets even**.

The squence in which brackets are used is [{ (2+3–2)}]

Another sign—**of**—is also used which has the function of *multiplication*. But **it is solved before the division even.** Let us solve a few examples

Example : Simplify :

(a) $24 + 15 \div 5$ (b) $28 - 5 \times 6 + 2$

(c) $3 - 5 - 6 \div 3$ (d) $36 \div (5 + 7) + 2$

(e) $81 \times [79 - \{7 \times 8 + (13 - \overline{2 - 5})\}]$

Solution : (a) $24 + 15 \div 5 = 24 + 3 =$ **27** Ans.

(b) $28 - 5 \times 6 + 2 = 28 - 30 + 2$
$$= 30 - 30 = \mathbf{0} \text{ Ans.}$$

(c) $3 - 5 - 6 \div 3 = 3 - 5 - 2$
$$= 3 - 7 = \mathbf{-4} \text{ Ans.}$$

(d) $36 \div (5 + 7) + 2 = 36 \div 12 + 2$
$$= 3 + 2 = \mathbf{5} \text{ Ans.}$$

(e) $81 \times [79 - \{7 \times 8 + (13 - \overline{2 - 5})\}]$
$$= 81 \times [79 - \{7 \times 8 + (13 - 2 + 5)\}]$$
$$= 81 \times [79 - \{7 \times 8 + 16\}]$$
$$= 81 \times [79 - \{56 + 16\}]$$
$$= 81 \times [79 - 72] = 81 \times 7 = \mathbf{567} \text{ Ans.}$$

PRACTICE EXERCISES 16

A. Simplify :

1. $(8 + 6) \div 7$ **2.** $12 + 25 \div 5$ **3.** $125 + 32 \div 4$

4. $2 \div 4 + 2$ **5.** $(-58) \times (-1) + (-42) \div 7$ **6.** $35 \div 5 + 7$

7. $4 - (6 \div 3 - 2)$ **8.** $7 - \{6 - 12 \div (5 + 9 \times 2 - 19)\}$

9. $(-15) + 4 \div (7 - 5)$

10. $17 - [3 + \{18 - (19 - 2)\}]$

11. $14 - [12 - \{9 - (7 - \overline{6 - 2})\}]$

12. $65 - [47 - \{7 \times 8 + (9 - \overline{6 + 4})\}]$

B. Make mathematical statements :

13. I bought 9 mangoes from one shop and 5 from another. Mixing them together, I distributed them equally among 7 children.

14. Seven multiplied by 4 and the product divided by 2.

15. Fifty divided by one more than the sum of four and five.

MISCELLANEOUS EXERCISES I

A. Name—
1. The lowest natural number : ....
2. The lowest whole number : ....
3. The largest negative number ....
4. The number with only one factor : ....
5. A number with only two factors : ....
6. a number with two or more factors : ....
7. The smallest two natural numbers ....
8. The largest divisor of two numbers : ....

B. Tick (✓) the correct statements and cross (×) the wrong ones :
9. 1 is neither a prime number nor a composite number. ( )
10. 0 is neither a positive number nor a negative number. ( )
11. Every natural number is a whole number too. ( )
12. Every whole number is a natural number too. ( )
13. The largest number of 6 digits is 100000. ( )
14. The number symbols 0, 1, 2, 3,....... 9 are called digits. ( )
15. 0 has no digit/numeral as its consecutive predecessor. ( )
16. A numeral with two 0's on its right is divisible by 25. ( )
17. A numeral with three 0's on its right is divisible by 125. ( )
18. A number with one zero on its right is divisible by 5 and 10. ( )
19. The function **of** is performed before *division* even. ( )
20. The **vinculum** is solved before the *simple brackets* even. ( )

C. Define—
21. natural numbers
22. whole numbers
23. co-primes
24. twin primes
25. consecutive predecessor
26. consecutive successor
27. addends
28. minuend
29. subtrahend
30. dividend
31. multiplicand
32. divisor
33. integers
34. positive integers
35. negative integers

D. Complete each statement :

36. Divisor × Quotient + Remainder = ...

37. 0 was invented by .... in the country of ....

38. A number is only an .... but a numeral is a symbol/group of symbols.

39. 0 has no .... as its consecutive predecessor.

40. A composite number is more than .... and has more than two factors.

41. The sieve of .... was developed to identify prime numbers.

42. The HCF of two or more number is always a .... of their LCM.

43. The absolute value of an integer is its...................... value irrespective of the sign before it.

44. When two integers with....................... signs are multiplied together, the product is +ve.

45. When two integers with different signs are multiplied together, the product is..............................

46. In the term 4^5, 4 is called the............. and 5 is called the ....

47. Complete each sum :

(a)
```
  6 4 7
+ * 8 *
-------
  9 * 6
```

(b)
```
  5 8 7 2
- * * 9 *
---------
  4 4 * 9
```

(c)
```
  5 8 3 7
- * * 4 *
---------
  4 5 9 4
```

(d)
```
    9 8 3 7
    * 3 * 8
    * 8 6 * 6
  2 9 * 1 1
-----------
* * * 9 7 * 6
```

(e)
```
         **5
715 )1 5 3 7 2 5
     1 4 * 0
     -------
     1 * 7 *
       7 1 5
     -------
       3 5 7 5
       3 5 7 5
       -------
             0
```

E. Simplify :

48. 34 × 483 + 17 − 38 × 483 + 33 × 483

49. Which of the numbers 87903000 and 94612600 is divisible by 125 as well as by 8 ?

50. Find the H.C.F. of 1470, 2688 and 4032 by division method.

51. Find the largest number that divides 249 and 1033 leaving 9 as remainder in either case.

52. Simplify = (a) $\dfrac{259}{333}$　(b) $\dfrac{155}{248}$　(c) $\dfrac{511}{584}$

53. Find the smallest number which when increased by 9 is exactly divisible by 18, 28, 105 and 108.

54. The L.C.M. of two number is 8700 and their H.C.F. is 145. If one of the numbers is 725, find the other.

F. Solve :

55. 7 – [6 – {5+(2 –3 +5)}]

56. –8 × [4 +(–9) +(–5)] +[–4 × [6 +(–5) +(–2)]

G. Write :

57. – 31, –29, 0, 7, 29, 31 in the descending order.

58. 87612475 in the expanded form.

59. 5^5 in its expanded form.　**60.** $(-1)^{12}$ in its expanded form.

H. Write in power notation :

61. 1331　　　**62.** 1024　　　**63.** 15625

I. Simplify :

64. –12 +[(–8) ÷ 2] – [–5 × (–4) –3 –7 –9]

65. 101 – [121 ÷(11 × 11) – (–4) – {1 –7 –4}]

J. Prepare two charts on the next page as directed below :

66. (a) Prepare the Place Value charts in the Indian System

(b) Prepare the Place Value charts in the International System :

MEMORABLE FACTS

1. The smallest natural number is 1.
2. The smallest whole number is 0.
3. Every natural number is a whole number too.
4. Every natural number is a whole number too.
5. No number can be said to be the largest whole number or natural number.
6. If u, a, b, c are said to be the largest whole number of natural number.
   (a) $a + b$ and $a \times b$ are whole numbers
   (b) $a - b$ and $a \div b$ are not essentially whole numbers
   (c) $a + b = b + a$ and $a \times b = b \times a$
   (d) $a + 0 = 0 + a = a$ and $a \times 0 = 0 \times a = 0$
   (e) $a \times 1 = 1 \times a = a$
7. 1 is the only number with only 1 factor (itself)
8. a number with only two factors is called a prime number.
9. The only even prime number is 2.
10. The H.C.F. of the two co-prime number is 1.
11. 1 is neither a prime number nor a composite number.
12. Divisor $\times$ Quotient + Remainder = Dividend.
13. 0 is neither positive nor negative.
14. Integers include all natural number, whole number and negative numbers.
15. The absolute value of a number is its numeral value.
16. Twin primes are two prime numbers that differ by 2 only and have a composite number between them.

COMMERCIAL ARITHMETIC

Commercial Arithmetic means the use of Arithmetic in business. *Accountants* and *book-keepers* use it to maintain financial records, to calculate pricing of articles, to check stocks and to work out profits etc.

Not only this, *farmers, doctors, transporters, air-companies* and *navigators* can't do without Arithmetic as well.

Arithmetic is so important, indeed, that along with *Reading* and *Writing*, it forms the **Three R's—** the backbone of all education.

IN THIS UNIT—

8. Ratio and Proportion
9. Unitary Method
10. Percentage
11. Profit and Loss
12. Simple Interest

8 RATIO AND PROPORTION

KNOW THESE TERMS :
1. **ratio**—number of times one quantity contains another
2. **proportion**—relation of equality between two ratios
3. **terms**—(a) A ratio has only two terms—*first* and *second*
   (b) A proportion has four terms—*first, second, third* and *fourth*
4. **extremes**—*first* and *fourth* terms of a proportion
5. **means**—*second* and *third* terms of a proportion

WHAT IS A RATIO ?

If we take two quantities of the same kind or take two numbers, we can compare them in three different ways. Let us take an example.

Suppose we have two piles of books A, B. *Pile A* contains **8 books** while the *Pile B* has **4 books.** We can compare them as under :

(a) *Pile A* contains 8 – 4 or 4 books **more than** *Pile B.*

(b) *Pile B* is 50% of *Pile A.*

(c) *Pile A* has $\dfrac{8}{4}$, *i.e.* **twice the number** of books in *Pile B.*

The third method is called the **ratio method**. In this method, we express one quantity as a fraction of the other.

Clearly, *ratio* **is the relation which one quantity bears to another quantity of the same kind in terms of magnitude.**

We write a ratio in the following two ways :

(a) $\dfrac{\text{Pile A}}{\text{Pile B}} = \dfrac{8}{4} = \dfrac{2}{1}$

(b) Pile A : Pile B = 8 : 4 = 2 : 1
   We read it as—
   Pile A **is to** *Pile B* **as** *2* **is to** *1.*

☞**Remember that—**
1. *A ratio can be there between two quantities of the same kind only.*
2. *While writing a ratio, we never mention any unit.*
3. *The first term of a ratio is called* **antecedent** *while the second term is called* **consequent***.*

Example 1 : **Express the following as ratios :**

(a) A school has *540 boys* and *450 girls*.

(b) A hall is *10 metres long* and *8 metres wide*.

(c) A dozen has *12 articles* while a score has *20 articles*.

Solution :

(a) No. of *boys* in the school = 540

No. of *girls* in the school = 450

∴ No. of boys : No of girls = 540 : 450 } *By simplification*

= 54 : 45

= **6 : 5** *Ans.*

(b) Length of the room = 10 metres

Width of the room = 8 metres

∴ Length : Breadth = 10 : 8

= **5 : 4** *Ans.*

(c) A dozen = 12 articles

A score = 20 articles

∴ A dozen : A score = 12 : 20

= **3 : 5** *Ans.*

Example 2 : **Ram Swroop earned Rs. 50,000 in 1999 and paid Rs. 5,000 as** *income tax.* **Find the ratio of his** *income tax* **to his** *income.*

Solution :

Yearly income of Ram Swroop = Rs. 50,000

Yearly income tax paid by him = Rs. 5,000

∴ Income tax : Income = 5000 : 50,000

= 5 : 50

= **1 : 10** *Ans.*

Example 3 : **India has 5,00,000 villages out of which 3,75,000 villages have been electrified. Find the ratio of electrified villages to their total number.**

Solution :

Total No. of villages in India = 500000

No. of *electrified* villages = 375000

∴ Electrified villages : Total No. of villages = 375000 : 500000

= 375 : 500

= 15 : 20

= **3 : 4** *Ans.*

Example 4 : Milk costs Rs. 6 a cup while tea costs Rs. 2 a cup. Find the ratio between their prices.

Solution : Price of milk per cup = Rs. 6
Price of tea per cup = Rs. 2
∴ Required Ratio = 6 : 2 = **3 : 1** *Ans.*

Example 5 : **The ratio of gold and copper in a ring is 24 : 1. If the ring weighs 5·5 grams, how much copper has been mixed in its gold.**

Solution : Weight of the ring = 5·5 grams
Gold : copper = 24 : 1
It means that 1 gram of copper is mixed with 24 grams of gold to get 24+1 = 25 grams of metal for the ring.
In other words—

Copper in 25 grams of metal = 1 gram
Copper in 1 gram of metal = (1÷25) grams
Copper in 5·5 grams of metal = (1÷25×5·5) grams

$$= 1 \times \frac{1}{25} \times \frac{55}{10} \text{ grams}$$

$$= \frac{11}{50} \text{ grams} = \frac{1 \cdot 1}{5} \text{ grams}$$

$$= \textbf{0·22 grams } \textit{Ans.}$$

COMPARISON OF RATIOS

In order to compare ratios, we must reduce them to the **same denominator**. Let us solve some examples :

Example 6 : Compare the ratios 2 : 3 and 4 : 7

Solution : $2 : 3 = \dfrac{2}{3}$ and $4 : 7 = \dfrac{4}{7}$

To reduce these ratios to the same denominator,
we shall have to provide them with the denominator $3 \times 7 = 21$

Now $\dfrac{2}{3} = \dfrac{2 \times 7}{3 \times 7} = \dfrac{14}{21}$

and $\dfrac{4}{7} = \dfrac{4 \times 3}{7 \times 3} = \dfrac{12}{21}$

Clearly $\dfrac{14}{21} > \dfrac{12}{21}$ or $\dfrac{2}{3} > \dfrac{4}{7}$ *Ans.*

Example 7 : A quantity a was added to both the terms of a ratio $8 : 5$. As a result, a new ratio $7 : 5$ was obtained. Find the value of a.

Solution : Given ratio $= 8 : 5 = \dfrac{8}{5}$

The quantity added to its terms $= a$

New ratio $= \dfrac{8 + a}{5 + a}$ and it is equal to $\dfrac{7}{5}$

$\therefore \dfrac{8 + a}{5 + a} = \dfrac{7}{5}$

$\therefore 5 (8 + a) = 7 (5 + a)$

or $40 + 5a = 35 + 7a$

or $40 - 35 = 7a - 5a$

or $5 = 2a$ or $a = \dfrac{5}{2} = \mathbf{2 \cdot 5}$ *Ans.*

Example 8 : Divide 720 in the ratio 13 : 11.

Solution : Sum of the terms of the ratio $= 13 + 11 = 24$

The number to be divided $= 720$

$\therefore$ First Part $= \dfrac{720}{24} \times 13 = \mathbf{390}$

and Second Part $= \dfrac{720}{24} \times 11 = \mathbf{330}$ ⎤ *Ans.*

Example 9 : Divide 350 in the ratio 8 : 16 : 11.

Solution : Sum of the terms of the ratio $= 8 + 16 + 11 = 35$

The number to be divided $= 350$

$\therefore$ First part $= \dfrac{350}{35} \times 8 = \mathbf{80}$

Second part $= \dfrac{350}{35} \times 16 = \mathbf{160}$ ⎤ *Ans.*

Third part $= \dfrac{350}{35} \times 11 = \mathbf{110}$

PRACTICE EXERCISES 17

A. Express each of the following as a ratio :

1. Two line-segments AB, CD are 5 cm and 7 cm long respectively.
2. One part of oxygen mixes with 2 parts of hydrogen to form water.
3. Ram and Sham have 9 pens and 12 pens respectively.
4. A class of 30 students has 12 girls and 18 boys.
5. Out of a class of 30 students, only 3 failed the test. Find the ratio of the passed students to the total number of students.

B. Fill up each blank :

6. The ratio of 5 to 9 is ....
7. The ratio of 4 to .... is 4 : 9.
8. The ratio of .... to 6 = 1 : 3.
9. The *first* term of a ratio is called its ....
10. The second term of a ratio is called its ....

C. Express each of these ratios in its simplest form :

11. 120 : 96	**12.** 68 : 204	**13.** 100 : 1000
14. Rs. 2·25 : Rs. 1·75	**15.** 320 m : 640 m	**16.** Rs.7 : Rs 4·90

17. 1024 Apples : 256 apples.

D. 18. A clerk gets Rs. 50000 as his yearly salary. Out of it, he has to pay Rs. 5000 as income tax. He saves Rs. 1000 at the end of the year. Find the ratio of—

(a) his *income tax* to his *salary*.   (b) his *saving* to his *salary*.
(c) his *saving* to his *income tax*.

19. A factory has a staff of 80 persons. Out of them 36 are women while others are men. Find the ratio of—

(a) *women* to *men*   (b) *women* to *the total staff*.
(c) *men* to *the total staff*.

20. Two numbers are in the ratio 7 : 2. If their sum is 54, find the numbers.
21. Divide Rs. 615 in the ratio 7 : 8.

22. Divide Rs. 1525 among A, B and C in the ratio 5 : 9 : 11.

23. Compare each of the following pairs of ratios.

(a) 5 : 6 and 2 : 3 (b) 3 : 4 and 2 : 3 (c) 17 : 25 and 3 : 5

(d) 5 : 8 and 4 : 5 (e) 7 : 8 and 7 : 10 (f) 15 : 16 and 37 : 40

24. A worker makes 540 electric switches in a month. If 1 switch out of every 10 is defective, find the total number of defective switches.

25. The ratio of a man's *income* to his *saving* is 7 : 2. If his monthly saving is Rs. 440, find his monthly expenditure.

26. If a number p is added to both the terms of the ratio 6 : 7, it becomes 9 : 10. Find the value of p.

27. Two numbers are in the ratio 14 : 9. If their sum is 690, find the numbers.

SIMPLE PROPORTION

A **proportion** is formed when two ratios are termed to be equivalent. Clearly, a proportion consists of four quantities. These quantities are said to be in proportion if **ratio of the** *first* **to the** *second* is equal to **ratio of the** *third* **to the** *fourth*.

We write a proportion as under :

14 *is to* 21 *as* 26 *is to* 39   or   14 : 21 :: 26 : 39.

Remember that out of the four terms of a proportion, *the first* and *the fourth* (last) are called **extremes** while the *second* and the *third* are called **means**.

Bear in mind the following points regarding a proportion :

1. The *extremes* (1st and 4th terms) are of the same kind.

2. The *means* (2nd and 3rd) are also of the same kind.

3. **Product of the extremes = Product of the means.**

4. The last term of a proportion is called the **fourth proportional**—if a proportion consists of four different terms, *i.e.* $a : b = c : d$.

5. The last term of a proportion is called the **third proportional** if a proportion consists of three different terms, *i.e.* $a : b = b : c$. In this case, b is called the **mean proportional**.

Example 1 · Are 16, 24, 20, 30 in a proportion ?

Solution   : For 16, 24, 20 and 30 to be in proportion,

16 : 24 must be equal to 20 : 30

Now $16 : 24 = \dfrac{16}{24} = \dfrac{2}{3}$

and $20 : 30 = \dfrac{20}{30} = \dfrac{2}{3}$

$\therefore 16 : 24 = 20 : 30$

Hence **16, 24, 20, 30 are in a proportion.** *Ans.*

Example 2 : **The first, third and fourth terms of a proportion are 6, 10 and 25 respectively. Find its second term.**

Solution : Suppose the second term = a

$\therefore$ 6, a, 10 and 25 are in proportion

$\therefore$ $6 : a :: 10 : 25$

Now, product of the means = product of the extremes

or $a \times 10 = 25 \times 6$

or $10\,a = 150$

$\therefore \qquad a = 150 \div 10 = \mathbf{15}$ *Ans.*

Example 3 : **Given that $100 \times 75 = 150 \times 50$, how will you write the proportion ?**

Solution : $100 \times 75 = 150 \times 50$

If we consider 100×75 as the *product of extremes*, 150×50 will be the *product of means* so—

100 will be *the first term* and 50 will be *the fourth term.*

150 will be *the second term* and 50 *the third term.*

So, the proportion = **100 : 150 :: 50 : 75** *Ans.*

But if we consider 150×50 as the *product of extremes*, 100×75 will be the *product of means.*

150 will be the *first term* and 50 will be the *fourth term.*

100 will be the *second term* and 75 will be the *third term.*

So, the proportion will be **150 : 100 :: 75 : 50 Ans**

Example 4 : **Are the numbers 25, 45 and 81 in continued proportion?**

Solution : We see that the given terms are 25, 45, 81. Clearly, 45 occurs twice.

For these terms to be in **continued proportion,** 45 must be the second and third term.

i.e. 25 : 45 :: 45 × 81

Now 25 × 81 = 2025   and 45 × 45 = 2025

∴ So **25, 45 and 81 are in continued proportion.** *Ans*

Example 5 : **Set up all the possible proportions using the four numbers 45, 30, 24 and 16.**

Solution : We shall have to try these four numbers in various combinations.

(a) 45 × 30 = 1350   (b) 45 × 24 = 1080
(c) 45 × 16 = **720**   (d) 30 × 24 = **720**
(e) 30 × 16 = 480   (f) 24 × 16 = 384

Out of these combinations, we see that—

45 × 16 = **720** and also 30 × 24 = **720**

∴ **45 × 16 = 30 × 24**

We can write this equation in four ways. So, there can be four different proportions.

Equations	*Proportions*
(a) 45 × 16 = 30 × 24	(a) **45 : 30 :: 24 : 16**
(b) 45 × 16 = 24 × 30	(b) **45 : 24 :: 30 : 16**
(c) 16 × 45 = 30 × 24	(c) **16 : 30 :: 24 : 45**
(d) 16 × 45 = 24 × 30	(d) **16 : 24 :: 30 : 45**

Example 6 : **The ratio of the length of a play-field to its width is 5 : 2. If the length of the field is 40 metres, find its width.**

Solution : Length : Breadth = 5 : 2

∴ Breadth × 5 = 2 × Length

or Breadth = (2 × 40) ÷ 5 = **16 metres** *Ans*

Example 7 : **What sum of money bears the same ratio to Rs. 2·25 as 24 metres bear to 5 metres ?**

Solution : Suppose the required sum = Rs. x

according to the proportion—

$$\text{Rs. } x : \frac{\text{Rs. } 225}{100} = 24 \text{ metres} : 5 \text{ metres}$$

or $x \times 5$ should be equal to $\frac{225}{100} \times 24$

or $x = \frac{225}{100} \times 24 \times \frac{1}{5}$

$$= \frac{9}{4} \times 24 \times \frac{1}{5} = \frac{54}{5}$$

∴ Required sum = Rs. $\frac{54}{5}$ = **Rs. 10·80** *Ans.*

Example 8 : **Find the fourth proportional to Rs. 8, Rs. 27 and 384 metres.**

Solution : Suppose the fourth proportional is x metres

Writing the given quantities as a proportion, we have—

Rs. 8 : Rs. 27 :: 384 metres : x metres

or $\dfrac{\text{Rs. } 8}{\text{Rs. } 27} = \dfrac{384 \text{ metres}}{x \text{ metres}}$

or $\dfrac{8}{27} = \dfrac{364}{x}$, *i.e.* $8x = 27 \times 364$

or $x = (27 \times 384) \div 8 = 27 \times 48 = 1296$

Hence the fourth proportional = 1296 metres *Ans*

Example 9 : **Find the mean proportional between 16 and 25.**

Solution : A mean proportional is there if three quantities are in continued proportion.

Let the mean proportional between 16 and 25 = x

∴ The continued proportion = 16 : x :: x : 25

$\because$ Product of the means = product of the extremes

$\therefore$ $\quad x \times x = 25 \times 16$ or $x^2 = 400$

$\therefore$ $\quad \sqrt{x^2} = \sqrt{400}$ or $x = 20$

Hence the reqd. mean proportional = 20 Ans.

PRACTICE EXERCISES 18

A. Which of the following proportions are true ?

1. 30 : 40 :: 45 : 60   **2.** 20 : 18 :: 5 : 6

3. 36 : 81 :: 28 : 63   **4.** 40 : 200 :: 5 : 25

5. 99 kilograms : 45 kilograms :: Rs. 44 : Rs. 20

B. Which of following are in proportion ? Write *yes* or *no*

6. 40, 30, 60, 45   **7.** 100, 50, 75, 150

8. 45, 63, 25, 35   **9.** 36, 24, 24, 16

C. Find the fourth proportional to :

10. 24, 51, 104   **11.** 5, 4, 210

12. 15, 20, 24   **13.** 2, 10, 3

14. 49, 56, 56   **15.** 45, 63, 25

D. Find the third proportional to :

16. 0·5, 1·5   **17.** x, y   **18.** 5·6, 0·84

19. $\dfrac{2}{3}$, $\dfrac{4}{5}$ **20.** $5\dfrac{1}{4}$, 7   **21.** 25, 35

E. Find the mean proportional to :

22. 49, 64   **23.** 49, 121   **24.** 25, 144

25. 4, 64   **26.** 121, 4   **27.** 7, 63

28. 9, 4   **29.** a^3b, ab^3 **30.** 3, 27

F. Answer :

31. When are four numbers in a *proportion* ? Give an example.

32. When are three numbers in a *continued proportion* ? Give an example.

33. What are the *extremes* of a proportion ? Give an example.

34. What are the *means* of a proportion ? Give an example.

35. What is the relation between the *means* and *extremes* of a proportion. Explain giving an example.

36. What is meant by the *mean proportional* of a proportion ? Explain giving an example.

37. Is it correct to say that the square of a mean proportional equals the product of its extremes ?

G. 38. The ratio of the number of girls in a school to the number of its boys is 5 : 4. If the girls number 210, find the number of boys.

39. The ratio of the sale of tickets on a cinema hall on a Sunday was 2 : 9 to the total sale for rest of the six days of the week. the total sale of tickets during the week was Rs. 44000. Find the amount of sale on Sunday.

40. The monthly expenditure of a family is in ratio to its monthly income as 6 : 7. If its total monthly income is Rs. 14000, find the monthly saving of the family.

41. The ratio of books on Mathematics to those on Science is 15 : 17 in a library. If the books on Science are 1054, find the total number of books in the library. Also, find the number of books on Mathematics

42. The monthly consumption of tea-leaves has a ratio 3 : 16 to the consumption of sugar in a family. If the family uses 0·5 kg. tea-leaves every month, how much sugar does it use monthly.

43. A pole is 6 metres in height and it casts a shadow 8 metres long. How long a shadow will a 20 metre tall tree cast ?

   Hint : height of the pole : Its shadow :: height of the tree : Its shadow.

44. Terms *a, b, c* are continued proportion. Find *b* if *a* and *c* are 16 and 4 respectively.

45. Find the value of *x* if 81, 36, *x* and 16 are in proportion.

46. A map is drawn to a scale. 1cm = 100 km, find—
   (a) actual distance between two place shown 1·8 cm. apart.
   (b) how far apart will Mumbai and Kanya Kumari be shown on a map it they are 1330 kilometres apart actually ?

9 UNITARY METHOD

> KNOW THESE TERMS :
> 1. **unitary method**—process in which cost of one article is calculated for further calculations\
> 2. **direct variation**—decrease/increase in cost according to decrease or increase in number of articles
> 3. **inverse variation**—decrease or increase in the number of workers in contrast to the decrease or increase in number of time-units etc.

WHAT IS UNITARY METHOD ?

The word—**unitary**—has been formed from the word **unit** which means *one*. So, *unitary method* is an arithmetical process in which the *value* **or** *time etc. is first calculated for one unit of a quantity* and then for a *higher number of that quantity*. Let us take two examples :

1. **A worker earns Rs. 162·50 in 5 days. What will he earn in 28 days at the same rate ?**

   In 5 days, the worker earns Rs. 162·50

   In **1 day**, he will earn Rs. 162·50 ÷ 5 or **Rs. 32·50**

   and in 28 days, he will earn Rs. 32·50 × 28 = **Rs. 910·00**

2. **6 masons build a house in 12 days. How long will 12 masons take to build it ?**

   6 men take 12 days to build the house

   1 man will take a longer time, *i.e.* 12 × 6 = **72 days**

   and 12 men will take less time, *i.e.* 72 ÷ 12 days = **6 days**.

DIRECT VARIATION

In example 1—

1. If the days decrease in number, the earning also decreases.
2. If the days again increase in number, the earning also increases.

In other words, the earning varies **directly** as the days vary in number. Such a variation is called **direct variation**.

INVERSE VARIATION

In example 2—

1. If the workers *decrease*, the time required for the work *increases*.
2. If the workers *increase* again, the time required for the work *decreases*.

In other words, the *time* varies **inversely** as the workers *decrease* or *increase* in number. Such a variation is called **inverse variation**.

Let us now solve some examples :

Example 1 : **A train covers 165 kilometres in 2·5 hours. How long will it take to cover 660 kilometres.**

Solution :   Time taken by the train to cover 165 km. = 2·5 hours

Time taken by the train to cover **1 km**. = 2·5 ÷ 165 hours

$$= \frac{25}{10} \times \frac{1}{165} \text{ hours} = \frac{1}{66} \text{ hours}$$

and time taken by the train to cover 660 km.

$$= \frac{1}{66} \times 660 \text{ hours} = \mathbf{10 \text{ hrs.}} \textit{ Ans.}$$

Example 2 : **35 men can do a piece of work in 6 days. In how many days can 15 men do it ?**

Solution :   Time taken by 35 men to do the work = 6 days

Time taken by **1 man** to do the work will be **more,** *i.e.*

It will be = **6 × 35 days.**

Time taken by 15 men to do it will be **less,** *i.e.*

It will be (6 × 35) ÷ 15 days = **14 days** *Ans.*

☞ Be careful while performing the middle step where unitary method is actually applied.
1. Ask yourself whether in the step on unitary process, the result will be *smaller* or *larger*.
2. If it is to be smaller division is applied.
3. If it is to be larger, multiplication is applied.

Example 3 : **How long will it take me to earn Rs. 68 if I earn Rs 51 in 3 weeks ?**

Solution :   Time taken to earn Rs. 51 = 3 weeks

Time taken to earn **Re. 1** will be **less,** *i.e.*

It will be 3 ÷ 51 weeks.

and time taken to earn Rs. 68 will be **more**, *i.e.*

It will be (3 ÷ 51) × 68 weeks

$$= \frac{3 \times 68}{51} = \mathbf{4 \text{ weeks}} \textit{ Ans.}$$

Example 4 : **125 men can do a piece of work in 120 days. How many men can do it in 100 days ?**

Solution : To do the work in 120 days, we need 125 men

To do it in **1 day,** we shall need **more** men, *i.e.*

$$= 120 \times 125 \text{ men.}$$

And to do it in 100 days we shall need less men, *i.e.*

$$(120 \times 125) \div 100 \text{ men}$$

$$= \frac{120 \times 125}{100} \text{ men} = \textbf{150 men } \textit{Ans.}$$

Example 5 : **How far will a bus travel in 17 minutes at a speed of 30 kilometres an hour.**

Solution : In 60 minutes, the bus covers 30 km.

In **1 minute**, it will cover **less distance**, *i.e.* $30 \div 60$ km.

In 17 minutes, it will cover more distance, *i.e.*

$$(30 \div 60) \times 17 \text{ km.}$$

$$= 30 \times \frac{1}{60} \times 17 \text{ km.} = \frac{17}{2} \text{ km.} = \textbf{8·5 km.} \textit{Ans.}$$

PRACTICE EXERCISES 19

A. Solve orally and answer :

1. 8 apples cost Rs. 16, find the cost of 1 apple.   ....

2. One toy costs Rs. 5, what will 8 such toys cost ?   ....

3. 4 men do a work in 3 days. In what time will 1 man do it ? ....

4. Ribbon sells Re. 1 a metre. How much will 40 cm. of it cost ? ....

5. 7 pencils cost Rs. 14. How much will 5 pencils cost ?   ....

6. 4 kg. sugar costs Rs. 60. How much will 24 kg. sugar cost ?   ....

7. 1 dozen pens cost Rs. 12. How much will 20 pens cost ?   ....

8. 5 persons use 10 kg. sugar in 15 days. In how many days will 1 man use it ? ....

B. Solve :

9. The price of 14 articles is Rs. 210. Find the price of 21 articles.

10. The railway freight for 25 tonnes of weight is Rs. 350. What will it be for 14 tonnes ?

11. The cost of 23 books is Rs. 584·20. How many books can be bought for Rs. 431·80 ?

12. A bus travels 246 kilometres in 6 hours. Find—

    (a) in how much time will it cover 328 kilometres ?

    (b) how far will it travel in 10 hours ?

13. 16 packets of bread each weighing 400 grams cost Rs. 160. What will be the cost of 20 packets of bread each weighing 500 grams ?

14. 135 kilograms of flour last 15 days for a family of 9 persons. How long will this flour last for 15 persons ?

15. A car covers 36 kilometres in 40 minutes. How much time will it take to cover 162 kilometres ?

16. A map-scale shows 3 cm for 24 kilometres. How far apart are two towns if the map-scale shows them 7·5 cm. apart ?

17. The distance between two towns is 119 kilometres. Find the speed of the car that can cover this distance in 2 hours 20 minutes ?

18. A man gives one-tenth of his property to his wife and one-twelfth to his daughter. Rs. 4900 are still left with him. Find the total value of his property.

19. A child spends Rs. 87·50 in 35 days as his pocket money. How much money will he spend in a year at this rate ?

20. A watch loses 2 hours 13 minutes in 7 days. How much does it lose in 36 hours ?

21. $\frac{3}{8}$ of an amount is Rs. 930. find the whole amount.

22. A plot of 15 metres square is sold for Rs. 4725. Find the price per sq. metre.

23. After covering $\frac{17}{20}$ of his journey, a traveller has still 6 km. to go. How much distance has he covered ?

10 PERCENTAGE

WHAT IS PERCENTAGE ?

The word—**percentrage**—has come from the phrase **per cent** which means *on/after every hundred*. It is the abbreviation of the Latin phrase *per centum*.

In order to understand the meaning of *per cent*, look at the square given in front. It has been divided into 100 small squares. 20 of these 100 squares have been shaded while the remaining 80 squares have been left white.

Now, *20 shaded squares* out of the total 100 squares form the **20 per cent** of the large square

Similarly *80 white squares* out of the total 100 squares form the **80 per cent** of the large square.

In order to express a quantity as a percentage, we write it as **numerator** and write 100 as its **denominator** ; as—

$$3 \text{ per cent} = \frac{3}{100}, \quad 11 \text{ per cent} = \frac{11}{100}, \quad 21 \text{ per cent} = \frac{21}{100}$$

In mathematical language, we write them as **3%, 11%, 21%** and read them as **3 per cent, 11 per cent, 21 per cent**.

A *percentage* **is a ratio which has 100 as its second term** (*consequent*).

APPLICATION OF PERCENTAGE

Percentage is used in many areas of daily life. Read these examples :
1. Mohan has got **97%** marks in English.

2. Books are sold at a discount of **10%**.

3. **70%** of the people in India live in villages.

4. I borrowed money at an interest of **5 per cent** per annum.

5. Every shopkeeper earns **some per cent** on the things that he sells.

6. There is an increase of **some percent** in the population of a country every year.

A. EXPRESSING A FRACTION AS A PER CENTAGE AND VICE VERSA

Example 1 : **Express $\frac{2}{7}$ as a percentage.**

Solution : To express $\frac{2}{7}$ as a percentage, we shall find $\frac{2}{7}$ **of 100**

∵ **of** means *multiplication*, therefore $\frac{2}{7}$ of $100 = \frac{2}{7} \times 100$

∴ $\frac{2}{7} = \frac{2}{7} \times 100$ per cent $= \frac{200}{7}\% = \mathbf{28\frac{4}{7}}\%$ *Ans.*

Example 2 : **Express 0·24 as a percentage.**

Solution : $0.24 = \frac{24}{100} = \frac{6}{25}$ and we are to find $\frac{6}{25}$ **of 100**

$\frac{6}{25} = \frac{6}{25} \times 100$ p.c. $= \mathbf{24\%}$ *Ans.*

Example 3 : **Express $12\frac{1}{2}\%$ as a fraction, as a decimal fraction and also as a ratio.**

Solution : To express $12\frac{1}{2}\%$ as a fraction, we shall divide it by 100

$12\frac{1}{2}\% = 12\frac{1}{2} \times \frac{1}{100} = \frac{25}{2} \times \frac{1}{100} = \frac{25 \times 1}{100 \times 2} = \mathbf{\frac{1}{8}}$

$\frac{1}{8}$ is a fraction which can be written as **·125** in *decimal form* and as **1 : 8** as a *ratio*

Hence $12\frac{1}{2}\% = \mathbf{\frac{1}{8}}$ or **·125** or **1 : 8** *Ans.*

Example 4 : **Find 7 % of Rs. 225 and** $4\frac{1}{2}$ **% of Rs. 950.**

Solution : (a) $7\% = \dfrac{7}{100}$

$\therefore$ 7 % of Rs. 225 = Rs. $\dfrac{7}{100} \times 225$

$= \text{Rs.} \dfrac{1575}{100} = $ **Rs. 15·75** Ans.

(b) $4\dfrac{1}{2}\% = \dfrac{9}{2} \times \dfrac{1}{100} = \dfrac{9}{200}$

$\therefore 4\dfrac{1}{2}$ % of Rs. 950 = Rs. $\dfrac{9}{200} \times 950$

$= \text{Rs.} \dfrac{8550}{200} = \text{Rs.} \dfrac{4275}{100} = $ **Rs. 42·75** Ans.

Example 5 : **What per cent of Rs. 125 is Rs. 10 ?**

Solution :   Rs. 10 is $\dfrac{10}{125}$ of Rs. 125

and *fraction* $\dfrac{10}{125} = \dfrac{10}{125} \times 100 \% = $ **8 %** Ans.

Example 6 : **Express Rs. 6·60 as a percentage of Rs. 52·80.**

Solution :   Rs. 6·60 = 660 paise and Rs. 52·80 = 5280 paise

660 paise $= \dfrac{\textbf{660}}{\textbf{5280}}$ of 5280 paise

and fraction $\dfrac{660}{5280} = \dfrac{660}{5280} \times 100 \% = \dfrac{100}{8}\%$

$= \dfrac{25}{2}\% = \mathbf{12\dfrac{1}{2}}$ % Ans.

Example 7 : $\mathbf{33\dfrac{1}{3}}$ **% of which number is 21 ?**

Solution : $33\dfrac{1}{3}$ % of the Required Number = 21

or $\dfrac{100}{3}$ % of the Required Number = 21

or $\dfrac{100}{3} \times \dfrac{1}{100} \times$ Required Number $= 21$

$\therefore$ Required Number $= 21 \times \dfrac{3}{100} \times \dfrac{100}{1} = \textbf{63}$ *Ans.*

Second Method :

Suppose the Required No $= 100$

$33\dfrac{1}{3}$ % of $100 = 33\dfrac{1}{3} = \dfrac{100}{3}$

Using unitary method—

If the given number is $\dfrac{100}{3}$ the Reqd. No. $= 100$

" " " " " 1, " " " $= 100 \times \dfrac{3}{100}$

" " " " " 21, " " " $= \dfrac{100 \times 3 \times 21}{100}$

$= \textbf{63}$ *Ans.*

Example 8 : **A shopkeeper announced a discount of 25 % on the prices of all his wares. Find the reduced price of a bicycle which previously cost Rs. 2240.**

Solution : Previous price of the bicycle = Rs. 2240

Announced discount = 25 %

$\therefore$ Total discount on Rs. 2240 = Rs.$\dfrac{25}{100} \times 2240$ = Rs. 560

Hence the Reqd. Reduced Price = Rs. (2240 − 560)

$= \textbf{Rs. 1680}$ *Ans.*

Example 9 : **The population of a city was 450,000 in a certain year. Within a year, it rose to be 495,000. Find the increase per cent.**

Solution : New population of the city = 495000

Original population of the city = 450000

$\therefore$ Increase = 45000

This increase is on 450000

$\therefore$ Increase % $= \dfrac{45000}{450000} \times 100 = \textbf{10\%}$ *Ans.*

Example 10: **A team won 10 out of the 16 matches played in all. Another team won 12 matches out of 20 matches. Which team played better ?**

Solution :   The first team won 10 matches out of 16 matches

∴ It won $(\frac{10}{16} \times 100)$ % or **62·5 % matches**

The second team won 12 out of 20 matches

∴ It won $(\frac{12}{20} \times 100)$ % or **60 % matches**

Hence the **first team played better.** *Ans.*

PRACTICE EXERCISES 20

A. Express each of these fractions in per cent form :

1. $\frac{7}{16}$ 2. $\frac{5}{8}$ 3. $\frac{11}{21}$ 4. $\frac{5}{7}$ 5. $\frac{5}{17}$

6. $\frac{3}{5}$ 7. $\frac{7}{20}$ 8. $\frac{1}{6}$ 9. $\frac{2}{3}$ 10. $\frac{1}{2}$

B. Express each percentage into a fraction, a decimal fraction and a ratio :

11. 32 %   12. 80 %   13. 6·25 %   14. $33\frac{1}{3}$ %   15. $6\frac{1}{3}$ %

16. 2·5 %   17. $7\frac{1}{2}$ %   18. 1·5 %   19. $1\frac{7}{8}$ %   20. 1·3 %

C. Express each of these ratios as a percentage :

21. 4 : 5   22. 2 : 3   23. 5 : 6   24. 3 : 5   25. 1 : 5
26. 3 : 8   27. 1 : 4   28. 1 : 6   29. 1 : 2   30. 2 : 5

D. Express each percentage as a decimal fraction :

31. $3\frac{1}{3}$ %   32. $12\frac{1}{2}$ %   33. $33\frac{1}{3}$ %   34. 7·5 %   35. 25 %

36. 75 %   37. 7 %   38. $13\frac{1}{2}$ %   39. $13\frac{3}{4}$ %   40. 26 %

E. Express each of these decimals in per cent form :

41. 0·4   42. 0·02.   43. 0·0275   44. 0·063   45. 0·56
46. 0·08   47. 0·125   48. 0·03   49. 0·7   50. 0·09

F. Find the value of :

51. 9 % of Rs. 700   **52.** 5 % of Rs. 35   **53.** 7 % of Rs. 225

54. $3\frac{1}{8}$ % of Rs. 1174   **55.** 8 % of Rs. 2200   **56.** $4\frac{1}{8}$ % of Rs. 950

G. What per cent is—

57. Rs. 17·25 of Rs. 60   **58.** 35 P of Rs. 105·70   **59.** 528 gms of 22·4 kg.

60. 21 metres of 1·5 km.   **61.** 4 kg. of 5 quintals   **62.** 4 metres of 36 metres

63. Rs. 20 of Rs. 450   **64.** 42 kg. of 126 kg.   **65.** 6 minutes of 2 hours

H. Which is greater ?

66. 0·05 or 6 %   **67.** 0·75 or 60 %   **68.** 0·9 or 9 %

69. 2·5 or 25 %   **70.** 1·6 or 16 %   **71.** 0·09 or 90 %

72. $\frac{1}{4}$ or 20 %   **73.** $\frac{1}{8}$ or 6·25 %   **74.** $1\frac{5}{8}$ or 150 %

I. What percentage of each picture is coloured ?

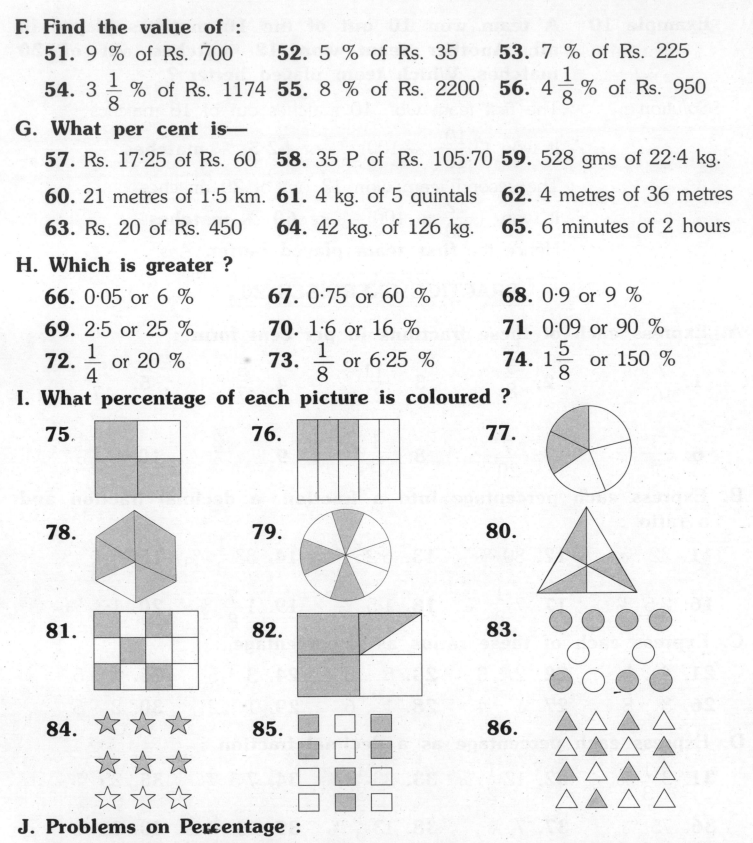

75.　　　**76.**　　　**77.**

78.　　　**79.**　　　**80.**

81.　　　**82.**　　　**83.**

84.　　　**85.**　　　**86.**

J. Problems on Percentage :

87. A basket contains 350 apples. If 12 % of them go bad, how many apples are saleable ?

88. A house-holder spends 95 % of his earning. Thus he is able to save Rs. 230 every month. Find his monthly earning.

89. A factory has both men and women workers. 18 % of its workers are women while total number of men workers is 328. How many workers are there in the factory in all ?

90. A worker got an increment of 15 % in his salary. He now earns Rs. 3243 a month. What was his monthly salary before the increment.

91. 52 % of the total students of a school are girls. The number of boys in the school is 312. Find the total number of students in the school.

92. The population of a city was 1800000 in 1981. It became 2100000 in 1985. Calculate the increase per cent.

93. A dealer marks his articles at 20 % less for a mass sale. Find the reduced price of a TV-set whose previous price was Rs. 8750.

94. In an election, candidate A got 42 % of the total votes polled that were 400000. How many votes did his opponent obtain in the elections ?

95. 40 % marks are necessary to be obtained to pass a test. Raman got 68 marks out of 200 marks. By how many marks did he fail ?

96. An army marched to a battle-front. Due to sudden outbreak of cholera, $12\frac{1}{2}$ % of the total number of soldiers died and 15 % of the soldiers fell fighting. The number of still soldiers was 1082280. How strong was the army in the beginning ?

97. There are two roads from town A to town B. One of them is $7\frac{1}{2}$ % of itself longer than the other. If the longer road is 430 metres long, find the length of the shorter road.

98. A trader wants to have his wares insured. The rate of premium is $7\frac{1}{2}$ %. The value of the wares is Rs. 37000. For what sum should the wares be insured so that in case of loss the value of the wares and also the premium may be recovered.

99. Bhavanesh was given 30 sums to solve by his tutor. He could solve only 80 % of them correctly. How many sums could he not solve correctly ?

100. Three friends Ram, Krishna and Prashant undertook a job for Rs. 300. Ram did 30 % of the job while Krishna did $26\frac{1}{2}$ % of it. The rest of the job was done by Prashant. What will each of them get ?

11 PROFIT AND LOSS

Every town has a market where people buy articles of daily use. The shopkeepers who sell these articles buy them from wholesale markets at cheaper rates. Then they sell these articles to people in retail at higher rates and earn profits. An example will clarify this point.

A shopkeeper buys a carton of 144 crayon-boxes for Rs. 216 from a wholesale market. He sells the crayon-boxes in retail at Rs. 2·50 each box.

Clearly the shopkeeper buys each crayon box for Rs. 216 ÷ 144 or Rs. 1·50. But he sells it for Rs. 2·50. Thus he earns a profit of Re. 1 on each crayon-box.

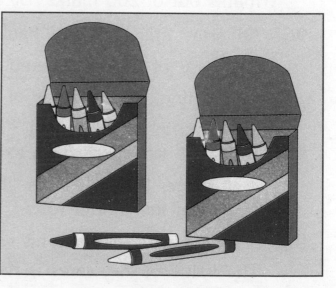

Cost of 1 crayon-box = Rs. 1·50
Sale of 1 crayon-box = Rs. 2·50
Sale of all the boxes brings
Rs. 144 × 2·50 = Rs. 360.
So, there is a profit of
Rs. (360–216) = Rs. 144.

We see that goods are bought at a *certain price* and then sold at a *higher price* generally. In such a case, there is a **profit** or **gain.** Sometimes the goods have to be sold at a price lower than the price at which it was bought. In such a case, there is a **loss**.

By calculating gain or loss separately on each *purchase and sale*, we cannot compare various transactions. But if gain or loss is calculated on every 100, (**in per cent form**), it is easy to compare various transactions.

A. FINDING GAIN OR LOSS %

Gain or loss % means gain or loss on 100

We calculate gain/loss % by *unitary method*. Here are some examples :

Example 1 : **Find the actual gain and the gain per cent if the CP of an article is Rs. 640 and SP is Rs. 800.**

Solution : CP = Rs. 640 and SP = Rs. 800

SP> CP ; so, there is a **gain**.

Actual gain = SP—CP = Rs. (800 – 640) = **Rs. 160**

This gain is on Rs. 640 while gain % is on Rs. 100

If the CP is Rs. 640, gain = Rs. 160

If the CP is Rs. 1, gain = Rs. 160 ÷ 640

If the CP is Rs. 100, gain = Rs. $\dfrac{160}{640} \times 100$ = Rs. 25

Hence **Actual gain = Rs. 160** and **gain % = 25 %** *Ans.*

Example 2 : **Find the actual loss and loss % if a bicycle is bought for Rs. 1560 and sold for Rs. 1508.**

Solution : CP = Rs. 1560 and SP = Rs. 1504.

SP< CP ; so, there is a **loss.**

Actual loss = CP — SP = Rs.(1560 –1508) = **Rs. 52**

This loss is on Rs. 1560 while loss % is on Rs. 100

If the CP is Rs. 1560, loss = Rs. 52

If the CP is Rs. 1, loss = Rs. 52 ÷ 1560

If the CP is Rs. 100, loss = Rs. $\dfrac{52}{1560} \times 100$ = Rs. $\dfrac{10}{3}$

∴ **actual loss = Rs. 52** and **loss %** = $\dfrac{10}{3}$ % = $3\dfrac{1}{3}$ % *Ans.*

Example 3 : Sandeep bought a stereo for Rs. 5548. As some defect developed in it, he had to pay Rs. 152 to a mechanic for its repairs. Sandeep sold it for Rs. 5510. What was his loss per cent ?

Solution : CP of the stereo $\quad$ = Rs. 5548

Expenses on the repairs = Rs. 152

∴ Actual CP of the stereo $\quad$ = Rs. 5548 + Rs. 152 = Rs. 5700

SP of the stereo $\quad$ = Rs. 5510

SP< CP ; So, is there is loss

Actual loss $\quad$ = Rs. 5700 Rs. – 5510 = Rs. 190

$$\text{Loss \%} = \frac{\text{Loss} \times 100}{\text{CP}} = \text{Rs.} \ \frac{190 \times 100}{5700} = \text{Rs.} \ \frac{10}{3} = 3\frac{1}{3}\% \ Ans.$$

If you observe carefully calculations of gain and loss % using unitary method in examples 2 and 3 the following formula can easily be evolved for finding gain or loss per cent.

$$\textbf{gain/loss \%} = \frac{\textbf{Actual gain/loss} \times \textbf{100}}{\textbf{CP}}$$

B. FINDING SELLING PRICE

Example 4 : An article was bought for Rs. 130 and sold at a profit of 10 %. Find its selling price.

Solution : $\quad$ CP of the article = Rs. 130 ; Profit = 10 %

It means that an article costing Rs. 100 was sold for Rs. 110

By unitary method—

If the CP is Rs. 100, SP = Rs. 110

If the CP is Re. 1, SP = Rs. $\dfrac{110}{100}$

If the CP is Rs. 130, SP = Rs. $\dfrac{110}{100} \times 130$ = **Rs. 143** *Ans.*

Example 5 : I bought an article for Rs. 11·20 and sold it at a loss of 10 %. Find its selling price.

Solution : $\quad$ CP of the article = Rs. 11·20 ; Loss = 10 %

It means that an article costing Rs. 100 was sold for Rs. 90

By unitary method—

If the CP is Rs. 100, SP = Rs. 90

If the CP is Re. 1, SP = Rs. $\dfrac{90}{100}$

If the CP is Rs. 11·20, SP = Rs. $\dfrac{90}{100} \times \dfrac{56}{5}$ = **Rs. 10·08** *Ans.*

If you observe carefully the calculation of SP, you will see that the following formula can be evolved easily for finding selling price (SP)

$$\text{S.P} = \frac{100 + \text{gain \%}}{100} \times \text{CP} \quad \text{or} \quad \frac{100 - \text{loss \%}}{100} \times \text{CP}$$

C. FINDING COST PRICE

Example 6 : An almirah was sold for Rs. 2900 earning a gain of 16 %. Find the cost price of the almirah.

Solution : Suppose the CP of the almirah = Rs. 100

Gain = 16 %

∴ SP of the almirah = Rs. 100 + Rs. 16 = Rs. 116

Real SP of the almirah = Rs. 2900

By unitary method—

If the SP of the almirah is Rs. 116, CP = Rs. 100

" " " " " " " Rs 1, CP = Rs. $\frac{100}{116}$

Rs. 2900, CP = Rs. $\frac{100}{116} \times 2900$

= **Rs. 2500 Ans.**

If you observe carefully the calculation of CP, you will see that the following formula can be evolved easily for finding cost price. (CP)

$$\text{C.P.} = \frac{100}{100 + \text{gain \%}} \times \text{SP} \quad \text{or} \quad \frac{100}{100 - \text{loss \%}} \times \text{SP}$$

D. MISCELLANEOUS

Example 7 : A merchant buys wheat at Rs. 752 per quintal. At what rate should be sell it so as to gain 25 % ?

Solution : CP of the wheat = Rs. 752

Desired gain = 25 %

Desired S.P. = Rs. $\frac{125}{100} \times 752$ = **Rs. 940 Ans.**

Example 8 : A shopkeeper buys 300 eggs at Rs. 9·60 per dozen. He sells them at Rs. 85 per hundred. Find his gain or loss %.

Solution :

Buying Rate of the eggs = 9·60 per dozen

∴ CP of 300 eggs = Rs. $\frac{960}{100} \times \frac{1}{12} \times 300$ = Rs. 240

Selling Rate of the eggs = Rs. 85 per hundred

∴ SP of 300 eggs = Rs. $\frac{85}{100} \times 300$ = Rs. 255

Clearly, there is a gain as SP > CP

Actual gain : Rs. (255 – 240) = **Rs. 15**

gain % = $\frac{15}{240} \times 100 = \frac{25}{4} = 6\frac{1}{4}$ % Ans.

Example 9 : A man buys a plot for Rs. 36000. He sells two-fifths of it at a gain of 25 % and one-third of it at a loss of 20 %. At what gain % should he sell the remaining part of the plot so as to gain 10 % on the whole.

Solution :

CP of the plot = Rs. 36000
Required gain = 10 %

Required SP = Rs. $\frac{110}{100} \times 36000$ = **Rs. 39600**

CP of the two-fifths plot = Rs. 36000 $\times \frac{2}{5}$ = Rs. 14400

SP of the two-fifth plot at a gain of 25 % = Rs. $\frac{125}{100} \times 14400$

= **Rs. 18000**

CP of the one-third plot = Rs. 36000 ÷ 3 = Rs. 12000

SP of the one-third plot at a loss of 20 %

= Rs. $\frac{80}{100} \times 12000$ = **Rs. 9600**

CP of the remaining plot = Rs. (36000 – 12000 – 14400) = **Rs. 9600**

Reqd. SP of the remaining plot = Rs. (39600 – **9600 – 18000**) = Rs. 12000

gain on the remaining plot = Rs. (12000 – 9600) = Rs. 2400

∴ Reqd. gain % = Rs. $\frac{2400}{9600} \times 100$ = **25 %** Ans.

A. Find gain and gain %, if—

1. CP = Rs. 560 and SP = Rs. 630 **2.** CP = Rs. 400 and SP = Rs. 500

3. CP = Rs. 840 and SP = Rs. 910 **4.** CP = Rs. 6000 and SP = Rs. 6500

5. CP = Rs. 200 and SP = Rs. 250 **6.** CP = Rs. 2500 and SP = Rs. 2600

B. Find loss and loss % if—

7. CP = Rs. 400 and SP = Rs. 336   **8.** CP = Rs. 6000 and SP = Rs. 5700

9. CP = Rs. 25 and SP = Rs. 21   **10.** CP = Rs. 540 and SP = Rs. 495

11. CP = Rs. 54 and SP = Rs. 48   **12.** CP = Rs. 340 and SP = Rs. 306

C. Find the selling price if—

13. CP = Rs. 64 and gain per cent = $56\frac{1}{4}$ %

14. CP = Rs. 2500 and gain per cent = 16 %

15. CP = Rs. 250 and gain per cent = 20 %

16. CP = Rs. 300 and gain per cent = $5\frac{5}{6}$ %

17. CP = Rs. 800 and loss per cent = $20\frac{1}{2}$ %

18. CP = Rs. 1400 and gain per cent = 30 %

19. CP = Rs. 3400 and loss per cent = 2 %

20. CP = Rs. 490 and loss per cent = 5 %

D. Find the cost price if—

21. SP = Rs. 585 and loss per cent = 10 %

22. SP = Rs. 120 and gain per cent = 25 %

23. SP = Rs. 4590 and gain per cent = 8 %

24. SP = Rs. 42·90 and loss per cent = $13\frac{1}{3}$ %

25. SP = Rs. 537·50 and loss per cent = $16\frac{2}{3}$ %

26. SP = Rs. 52·50 and gain per cent = 25 %

27. SP = Rs. 306 and loss per cent = 15 %

28. SP = Rs. 1026 and loss per cent = 5 %

E.29. Write the formula for finding *gain or loss per cent*, if CP and SP are given :

$$\text{Gain \%} = \frac{\cdots\cdots \times \cdots\cdots}{\cdots\cdots}$$

$$\text{Loss \%} = \frac{\cdots\cdots \times \cdots\cdots}{CP}$$

30. Complete the formula for finding SP if CP and **gain/loss %** are given :

$$SP = \frac{\cdots\cdots \times (\ 100 + \cdots\cdots)}{100} \quad \text{or} \quad SP = \frac{\cdots\cdots \times (\ 100 - \cdots\cdots)}{100}$$

31. Complete the formulas for finding CP if SP and **gain/loss %** are given :

$$CP = \frac{\cdots\cdots \times \cdots\cdots}{(100 + \cdots\cdots)} \quad \text{or} \quad CP = \frac{\cdots\cdots \times \cdots\cdots}{(100 - \cdots\cdots)}$$

F. Problems on Profit/Loss

32. A buffalo was bought for Rs. 18000 and was sold for Rs. 19800. Find the gain per cent.

33. A number of articles were bought at Rs. 35 per score and sold at Rs. 24 per dozen. Find the gain or loss per cent.

34. An article was bought for Rs. 130 and sold at a profit of 10 per cent. Find its selling price.

35. By selling a mirror for Rs. 55·20, there is a loss of 8 per cent. What is its cost price ?

36. A toy-gun was sold for Rs. 54 at a loss of 28 per cent. What would have been the gain per cent if it had been sold for Rs. 90 ?

37. A shopkeeper announced a discount of 10 per cent in the prices of all his articles. At what price should he mark the item, which he wants to sell for Rs. 6 ?

38. If an article is sold at a profit of 13 % instead of at a profit of 6 %, it brings in Rs. 14 more. Find its cost price.

39. A watch costs Rs. 320 at its production house. It was sold to a dealer at a gain of 25 % and the dealer sold it further to the retailer at a gain of 12 %. What will a retailer pay for it ?

40. A fruit-seller sells oranges at Rs 24 per dozen and loses 20 % of his cost price. What per cent will he gain or lose if he sells them at Rs. 240 per hundred.

41. A cloth-seller will gain 20 % more if he sells a shirt-piece for Rs. 45·50 instead of Rs. 39·00. Find the cost price of the shirt-piece.

42. A sells an article to B gaining 4 % and B sells it to C gaining 5 %. If C buys it for Rs. 273, what did the article cost to A ?

43. The making cost of a bicycle is Rs. 1600. The maker sells it to dealers gaining 25 %. The dealers sell it to retailers at Rs. 2500. What is the dealers' gain ?

44. An egg-seller buys eggs at 7 for Rs. 10·50 and sells them at a gain of 40 %. How many eggs will a customer get for Rs. 10·50 ?

45. A milkman buys milk at Rs. 16 a litre and sells it at Rs. 19·20 a litre. If he makes a profit of 60 %, how much water does he mix per litre of milk ?

46. A person sells an article at a gain of 5 %. Had he bought it at 5 % less and sold it for Re. 1 less, he would have gained 10 per cent. Find the cost price of the article.

47. A person buys an old house for Rs. 30,000 and spends 10 % of the cost price on its repairs. Then he sells it at a gain of $9\frac{1}{11}$ %. Find the selling price of the house.

48. A grocer buys rice at Rs. 160 a quintal. At what rate should he sell it so as to gain 25 % ?

49. A fruiterer buys 12 dozen oranges at Rs. 16 a dozen and another 12 dozen oranges at Rs. 15 a dozen. He sells them at Rs. 15·75 per dozen. Find his gain or loss per cent.

50. An egg-seller buys 600 eggs at 75 paise an egg. Out of the lot, 50 eggs were found to be bad. At what rate should he sell the remaining eggs in order to gain 10 % ?

51. A man sells 10 oranges at the same price as he had bought 11 oranges. Find his gain per cent.

52. A shopkeeper buys toffees at 6 for a rupee. How many a rupee must he sell to gain 20 %.

53. The cost price of 12 books is equal to the selling price of 9 books. Find the gain or loss per cent.

12 SIMPLE INTEREST

We have to borrow money from friends, relatives or banks etc. to meet our needs. Two parties are involved in this process.

1. The **lender** who lends money. It may be a person or an agency.

2. The **borrower** who borrows money from the *lender*.

Also, remember the following points :

1. The lender charges some additional money when the borrower returns the money. This additional money is called INTEREST.

2. The money that a lender lends is called the PRINCIPAL. The total money that a borrower returns is called AMOUNT.

3. The money is borrowed for a **specific period**. At the end of this period, the loan has to be returned along with its interest.

4. Interest is calculated at a **certain rate per cent** on the principal for each year or month till the loan is paid back.

It is clear from the above discussion that—

Amount = Principal + Interest

An agreement is made between the lender and the borrower in which the *principal* (borrowed money), *time* (period for which the money is borrowed) and the *rate of interest* are given.

The interest is calculated on the principal throughout the loan-period. So, this interest is called **simple interest**.

We use the terms **P** for the *principal*, **T** for the *time*, **R** for the *rate of interest*, **I** or **S.I.** for *simple interest* and **A** for the *amount*.

Let us now solve some examples to understand how simple interest is calculated.

Remember that we **multiply** the **principal** by the **rate per cent** and the **time** and then **divide** the product **by 100** to find the simple interest. This rule can be written as—

$$S.\ I. = \frac{P \times R \times T}{100}$$

Example 1 : **A sum of Rs. 500 is borrowed for a period of 3 years at the rate of 12 per cent per annum. Find the simple interest.**

Solution :   P = Rs. 500 ; T = 3 years ; R = 12 % per year

clearly—

Int. on Rs. 100 for 1 year = Rs. 12

Int. on Re. 1 for 1 year   = Rs. 12 ÷ 100

Int. on Re 1 for 3 years   = Rs. (12 ÷ 100) × 3

Int. on Rs. 500 for 3 years = Rs. (12 ÷ 100) × 3 × 500

$$= Rs.\ \frac{12 \times 3 \times 500}{100} = \textbf{Rs. 180}\ \textit{Ans.}$$

Second Method :

We know that S.I. $= \dfrac{P \times R \times T}{100}$

$$\therefore Reqd.\ Int. = \frac{500 \times 12 \times 3}{100} = \textbf{Rs. 180}\ \textit{Ans.}$$

Example 2 : **Find the simple interest on Rs. 315 for 73 days at 5 % per year.**

Solution :   P = Rs. 315 ; R = 5 % ; T = 73 days $= \dfrac{73}{365}$ or $\dfrac{1}{5}$ yr

$$\therefore S.I. = \frac{P \times R \times T}{100} = Rs.\ \frac{315 \times 5 \times 1}{100 \times 5}$$

$$= Rs.\ \frac{315}{100} = \textbf{Rs. 3·15}\ \textit{Ans.}$$

Example 3 : **Find the amount of Rs. 547 for 146 days at $2\frac{1}{2}$ % per annum.**

Solution :   P = Rs. 547 ; R = $2\dfrac{1}{2}$ % = $\dfrac{5}{2}$ % ; T = $\dfrac{146}{365}$ or $\dfrac{2}{5}$ yr

$$\therefore \text{S.I.} = \frac{P \times R \times T}{100} = \text{Rs.} \frac{547 \times 5 \times 2}{100 \times 2 \times 5} = \text{Rs.} \frac{547}{100}$$

$$= \text{Rs. } 5 \cdot 47$$

Amount $\qquad = \text{Rs. } (547 + 5 \cdot 47) = \textbf{Rs. } \textbf{552} \cdot \textbf{47}$ *Ans.*

B. TO FIND THE PRINCIPAL

Example 4 : **Find the sum of money that will produce Rs. 17 as simple interest in 8 months at the rate of $2\frac{1}{2}\%$ per year.**

Solution : Int. $= \text{Rs. } 17$; $R = 2\frac{1}{2}\% = \frac{5}{2}\%$; $T = 8$ months

$$= \frac{8}{12} \text{ yr } = \frac{2}{3} \text{ yr.}$$

Now, $\text{S.I.} = \dfrac{P \times R \times T}{100}$ or $\dfrac{P \times 5 \times 2}{100 \times 2 \times 3} = \text{Rs. } 17$

or $\dfrac{P}{60} = \text{Rs. } 17$ or $P = \text{Rs. } 17 \times 60 = \text{Rs. } 1020$.

Hence Principal $= \textbf{Rs. } \textbf{1020}$ *Ans*

Example 5 : **Find the principal that will amount to Rs. 1417 in 5 years at 6 % rate of simple interest per year.**

Solution : Suppose $P = \text{Rs. } 100$

$R = 6\%$ and $T = 5$ years

$\therefore \text{S.I. on Rs. } 100 = \text{Rs. } \dfrac{100 \times 6 \times 5}{100} = \text{Rs. } 30$

$\therefore$ Amount of Rs. 100 $= \text{Rs. } (100 + 30) = \text{Rs. } 130$

By unitary method

If the amount is Rs. 130, P = Rs. 100

If the amount is Re 1, P = Rs. 100 ÷ 130

If the amount is Rs. 1417, P = Rs. 100 ÷ 130 × 1417

$$= \text{Rs. } \frac{100 \times 1417}{130} = \textbf{Rs. } \textbf{1090} \textit{ Ans.}$$

C. TO FIND TIME

Example 6 : **In how many years will Rs. 2500 produce Rs. 375 as simple interest at 5 % per annum ?**

Solution :   P = Rs. 2500 ; R = 5 % ; S.I. = Rs. 375

Now, $\dfrac{P \times T \times R}{100} = $ S.I or $\dfrac{2500 \times T \times 5}{100} = 375$

or 125 T = 375 or T = 3

Hence the Reqd. time = **3 years** *Ans.*

Example 7 :   **In what time will Rs. 1500 amount to Rs. 1680 at 3 % per annum ?**

Solution :   P = Rs. 1500 ; A = Rs. 1680 ; R = 3 %

Int. = Rs. (1680–1500) = Rs. 180

Now, $\dfrac{P \times T \times R}{100} = $ S.I or $\dfrac{1500 \times T \times 3}{100} = 180$

or 45 T = 180 or T = 4

Hence the required time = **4 years Ans.**

TO FIND RATE PER CENT

Example 8 :   **At what rate per cent will Rs. 375 yield an interest of Rs. 90 in 4 years ?**

Solution :   P = Rs. 375 ; T = 4 years ; S.I. = Rs. 90

Now, $\dfrac{P \times R \times T}{100} = $ S.I or $\dfrac{375 \times R \times 4}{100} = 90$

or 15 R = 90 or R = 6

Hence rate per cent = **6 %** *Ans.*

Example 9 :   **At what rate per cent will Rs. 2500 amount to Rs. 3125 in 5 years ?**

Solution :   A = Rs. 3125 ; P = Rs. 2500 ; T = 5 years

S.I. = Rs. (3125 – 2500) = Rs. 625

Now, $\dfrac{P \times R \times T}{100} = $ S.I, or $\dfrac{2500 \times R \times 5}{100} = 625$

or 125 R = 625 or R = 5 ; So, **Rate = 5 %** *Ans.*

PRACTICE EXERCISES 22

A. Find the *simple interest*, if—

1. P = Rs 350   ;   R = 3 %   ;   T = 4 years
2. P = Rs 731·50 ;   R = 4 %   ;   T = 2·5 years
3. P = Rs 1525   ;   R = 5 %   ;   T = 4 years
4. P = Rs 4000   ;   R = 6 %   ;   T = 3 years
5. P = Rs 7200   ;   R = 8 %   ;   T = 3·5 years

B. Find the *amount*, if—

6. P = Rs 7200   ;   R = 8 %   ;   T = 4 years
7. P = Rs 1835   ;   R = 1·25 %   ;   T = 292 days
8. P = Rs 1605   ;   R = 5·5 %   ;   T = 146 days
9. P = Rs 219   ;   R = 7·5 %   ;   T = Jan. 1 to May 26
10. P = Rs 7000   ;   R = 4 %   ;   T = 292 days

C. Find the *principal*, if—

11. Int. = Rs 203   ;   R = 3·5 %   ;   T = 7·25 years
12. S.I. = Rs 422·50 ;   R = 2·5 %   ;   T = 3·25 years
13. S.I = Rs 217·50   ;   R = 14·5 %   ;   T = 0·5 years
14. S.I = Rs 9·3   ;   R = 7·5 %   ;   T = 62 days
15. A = Rs 3712   ;   R = 4 %   ;   T = 4 years

D. Find the *time*, if—

16. A = Rs 2860   ;   S.I. = Rs. 360 ;   R = 4 %
17. A = Rs 1375   ;   P = Rs. 1250 ; R = 4 %
18. S.I. = Rs 588   ;   P = Rs. 1960 ; R = 3·75 %
19. S.I. = Rs 972   ;   P = Rs. 5400 ; R = 2·25 %
20. A = Rs 256·50   ;   P = Rs. 225   ; R = 3·5 %

E. Find the *rate %* if—

21. P = Rs 422·50 ;   S.I. = Rs. 84·50 ;   T = 4 years
22. P = Rs 375   ;   S.I. = Rs. 90   ;   T = 4 years
23. A = Rs 2550   ;   P = Rs. 2125   ;   T = 5 years
24. P = Rs 250   ;   A = Rs. 287·50   ;   T = 5 years
25. P = Rs 1500   ;   S.I. = Rs. 180   ;   T = 4 years

PROBLEMS ON SIMPLE INTEREST

26. A sum of Rs. 1200 was borrowed for 1 year at 12 % per annum. How much money will have to be returned ?

27. Find the simple interest on Rs. 6250 for four years at 15 % per annum. Find the amount also.

28. A traders borrows Rs. 3400 from a bank for 2.5 years. What will he pay back if the rate of interest is 13 % per annum ?

29. A lady deposited Rs. 8000 in a bank on March 28, 1997 and closed her account on August 21, the same year. If the bank gives interest at the rate of 9 % per annum, what amount shall she get ?

30. A shopkeeper borrowed Rs. 7000 from a money-lender at 13 % per annum on March 23, 1999. How much money did he pay to the money-lender to clear off his debt on June 4, the same year.

31. Monu deposited Rs. 7200 in a company that pays interest at the rate of 15 % per annum. What will he get from the company after 4 years and 6 months.

32. A rich man donated Rs. 2000 to a trust. The interest on this amount is to be used for awarding 4 yearly scholarships of equal value. If the interest earned by the donation is calculated at 10 % per annum, find the amount for each scholarship.

33. A widow deposited Rs. 6280 in a bank that pays interest at the rate of 2.25 per cent per annum. What will the widow get back from the bank after 2 years ?

34. What sum must be placed with a bank for 8 months so that it may earn an interest of Rs. 17 if the rate of interest is 2.5 per cent per annum ?

35. Mohan lends Rs. 564 to Sohan for 5 years. Sohan pays Rs. 705 to to clear Mohan's account. Find the rate per cent.

36. A man invests Rs. 1000 as deposit at 3 per cent on a certain date. On 15th June, the man withdraws the interest of his money to buy a gift for his son. If the gift costs Rs. 12, when was the deposit made ?

37. Which sum will amount to Rs. 2548 in $4\frac{1}{2}$ years at a yearly interest-rate of 5 % ?

38. A widow lent out Rs. 3600 to a person so that she must get Rs. 100 as interest every 5 months. What was the rate per cent settled in the deal ?

MISCELLANEOUS EXERCISES II

1. In a state 13600 villages were electrified in the *First Five-Year Plan* and 15300 villages in the *Second Five-Year Plan*. How many per cent more villages were electrified in the Second Five-Year Plan ?

2. An army lost two-sevenths of its *jawans* in a battle and 6 % of the remaining soldiers due to sickness. If 95,880 soldiers are left behind, what was the original strength of the army ?

3. If eggs are sold at Rs. 24 per dozen, there is a loss of 20 %. Find the cost price of eggs per score.

4. A builder buys a house for Rs. 20,000. But he had to sell it to an agent at a loss of 16 %. The agent was able to sell the house at a gain of 25 %. What did the buyer pay for it ?

5. A producer sells an item at a gain at 20 % to the wholesaler who further sells it to a retailer earning a profit of 20 %. The retailer has to sell it at a loss of 5 % to the customer. What will the customer pay for it if its original cost is Rs. 25 ?

6. A trader marks his prices 12 % above his cost. But he allows a discount of Rs. 10 on a bill of Rs. 280. What is his real profit % ?

7. On what sum will the S.I. for $3\frac{1}{2}$ years at 3 % be Rs. 24·15 ?

8. At what rate will a sum of money lent at S.I. treble itself in 25 years ?

9. In how many days will the S.I. on Rs. 730 be Rs. 3·50 at 5 %.

10. What sum should be invested on simple interest at 5 % to get an income of Rs. 350 a week ?

11. A trader borrowed Rs. 12000 from a bank at 7 % and lent it to another trader at 10 % for 3 years. What will be his total gain ?

12. Manish Graphics opened its account with a bank on 23rd August, 1997 with a deposit of Rs. 5000. The bank paid interest at the rate of 6 % for the deposit. What will his amount be on 4th November, 1997 ?

13. A sum of money lent at simple interest at 15 % per annum for 4 years amounts to Rs. 10,000. What sum was lent out ?

14. A sum of Rs. 3500 was borrowed for a fixed period at 13 % yearly. At the end of the period, it amounted to Rs. 4637·50. For what period was the sum borrowed ?

15. A rectangular garden has an area of 125 square kilometres. Its length is five times its breadth. Find its length and breadth.

16. A square park has an area of 48400 sq. metres. Find the cost of fixing a fence round it at Rs. 2·50 per metre.

17. Two ships cover the same voyage in 2 days 1 hour and $3\frac{1}{2}$ days respectively. Find the ratio between their average speeds per hour.

18. What sum of money bears the same ratio to Rs. 2·25 as 2·4 metric tons to 5 quintals ?

19. Find the third term in the proportion 1·68 : 2·52 = x : 4·29

20. If the ratio of a yard to a metre is 200 : 219, find the value of 2920 yards in metres.

21. If 7·5 kg. of a certain tea cost Rs. 56·25. Find the cost of 2·4 kg. the same tea.

22. A pumping-set of 54 horse-power raises 1530 litres of water per minute. Of how much horse-power a pumping-set will raise 2805 liters of water per minute.

23. 4 men can earn Rs. 9 in 12 hours. How much will 8 men earn in 10 hours ?

24. A regiment of 7500 soldiers attacked by sickness is reduced to 6330 soldiers. What is the loss per cent ?

25. A sells an article to B at a gain of 4%. B sells it to C at a profit of 5%. If C pays Rs. 273 for it find its original cost to A.

26. A builder sells a house worth Rs. 20,000 at a loss of 16 per cent to an agent. The agent sells it further at a gain of 25 pe cent. What does the purchaser pay ?

27. Arun deposits Rs. 6280 in a bank that pays interest at the rate of $2\frac{1}{4}$ % per annum. What sum will he have in the bank at the end of 6 months ?

28. A man puts Rs. 610 in a bank that pays interest at the rate of 5% per annum. He takes his interest when it becomes Rs. 20. After how much time does he take the interest if the year is leap ?

MEMORABLE FACTS

1. In a continued proportion—

   (a) **Product of the extremes = Product of the means**

   (b) a **percentage** *is a ratio with 100 as its second term (consequent)*

2. (a) The price at which an article is bought is its **cost price** (**CP**)

   (b) The price at which an article is sold is its **selling price** (**SP**)

   (c) If SP is higher than CP, there is a **gain** or **profit**.

   (d) If SP is lower than CP, there is a **loss**.

   (e) **gain** = (SP–CP) (f) **Loss** = (CP–SP)

3. (a) **gain**% = $\dfrac{\text{Actual gain} \times 100}{\text{CP}}$ (b) **Loss**% = $\dfrac{\text{actual loss} \times 100}{\text{CP}}$

   (c) **CP** = $\dfrac{\text{SP} \times 100}{100 + \text{gain}\%}$ or $\dfrac{\text{SP} \times 100}{100 - \text{loss}\%}$

   (d) **SP** = $\dfrac{\text{CP} \times (100 + \text{gain}\%)}{100}$ or $\dfrac{\text{CP} \times (100 - \text{loss}\%)}{100}$

4. (a) The person who lends money to another person is the **lender**.

   (b) The person who borrows money from another person is the **borrower**.

   (c) The money borrowed/lent is called the **principal** (**P**)

   (d) The extra money paid by the borrower for the use of the borrowed principal is called the **interest**.

   (e) Interest is calculated at a **rate**% (**R**) fixed when the money is borrowed.

   (f) The period for which money is borrowed is called the **time (T)**.

   (g) The total money including the *principal* and the *interest* is called **amount (A)**.

5. (a) **Interest (S.I.)** = $\dfrac{\text{Principal} \times \text{rate} \times \text{time}}{100}$ = $\dfrac{P \times R \times T}{100}$

   (b) **Principal** = $\dfrac{\text{interest} \times 100}{\text{rate} \times \text{time}}$ = $\dfrac{\text{S.I.} \times 100}{R \times T}$

   (c) **Time** = $\dfrac{\text{Interest} \times 100}{\text{Principal} \times \text{rate}}$ = $\dfrac{\text{S.I.} \times 100}{P \times R}$

   (d) **Rate**% = $\dfrac{\text{Interest} \times 100}{\text{Principal} \times \text{time}}$ = $\dfrac{\text{S.I.} \times 100}{P \times T}$

Algebra is a branch of mathematics that deals with properties of numbers using *letters* and some other *general symbols.*

★ ★ ★ ★ ★ ★

The word—**Algebra**—comes from the Arabic word—**al jabr**— which means *reunion of broken parts, i.e.* **reduction**. But it is widely believed that algebra had its birth in India.

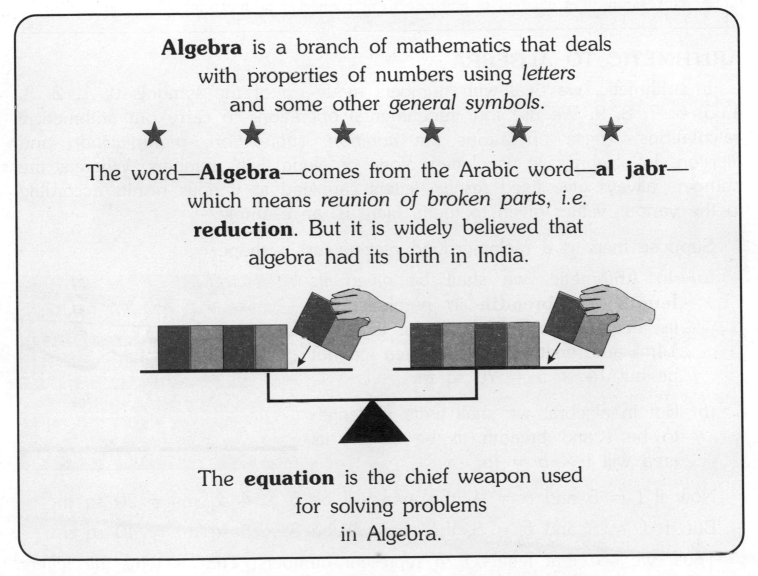

The **equation** is the chief weapon used for solving problems in Algebra.

IN THIS UNIT—
13. Introduction to Algebra
14. Addition and Subtraction
15. Linear Equations

> *KNOW THESE TERMS :*
> 1. **algebra**—it stands for Generalised Arithmetic in which numbers are represented by *letters* generally called *literal numbers*
> 2. **term**—an algebraic term is the product of one or more letters and numbers
> 3. **expression**—it is a group of algebraic terms connected by the symbols + and − only

ARITHMETIC TO ALGEBRA

In arithmetic, we deal with numbers made up of the symbols 0, 1, 2, 3, 4, 5, 6, 7, 8, 9. We use four fundamental operations to carry out arithmetical calculations. These operations are *addition, subtraction, multiplication* and *division*. In algebra, *we* use letters alone or along with numbers. Whereas the numbers always give fixed results, letters can lead to various results according to the various values given to them. Here is an example.

Suppose there is a racing-ground *rectangular* in shape.

(a) In Arithmetic, we shall be given its **length** and **breadth** in numbers. So, its area will be definite. If the length is 14m and width 5m, the area cannot be but 14 × 5 = 70 sq m.

(b) But in algebra, we shall write its length to be *l* and breadth to be *b*. So, its area will *l* × *b* = *lb*.

Now if l = 5 and *b* = 4, the area will be 5 × 4 sq m. = 20 sq m.

But if *I* = 8 and *b* = 5, the area will be 8 × 5 sq m. = 40 sq m.

Thus, we see that letters *l, b* represent numbers. That is why the letters used for numbers are called **literal numbers**.

Remember that literal numbers obey all the rules of Arithmetic including the four fundamental rules.

BASIC OPERATIONS WITH LITERAL NUMBERS

As mentioned above, the literal numbers obey all the four basic operations and their properties—*addtion, subtraction, multiplication* and *division*.

ADDITION

Two literal numbers are written just like numerals when they are to be added ; as—

We add a and b as $a + b$ and also $a + b = b + a$

Similarly $a + 5 = 5 + a$ and $a + (b + c) = (a + b) + c$

SUBTRACTION

We write the difference of two literal numbers as—

$x - 3$; $y - x$; $b - c$; $4 - a$

MULTIPLICATION

(a) $x + x + x + x = 4 \times x = 4x$

(b) The product of a and b = ab

(c) $a \times 0 = 0 \times a = 0$; $x \times 1 = 1 \times x = x$

(d) $a \times b \times c = abc$

DIVISION

$a \div b = \dfrac{a}{b}$ just as $7 \div 4 = \dfrac{7}{4}$

Similarly

$x \div 5 = \dfrac{x}{5}$ and $20 \div 5x = \dfrac{20}{5x}$

POWERS OF A LITERAL NUMBER

If a literal number is multiplied by itself a number of times, the repeated multiplication is indicated by a small number written at its top right ; as—

$a \times a = a^2$ and $a \times a \times a = a^3$

In a^2, a is called the **base** while 2 is called the **power** or **exponent**.

COMMON TERMS USED IN ALGEBRA

1. TERM

    An algebraic term is a quantity that is part of an *expression* ; as—
    x, 4a, 8b, 3c etc.

2. EXPRESSION

    An algebraic expression consists of two or more terms combined together by operation-signs of *addition* and *subtraction*.

3. MONOMIAL

    A monomial is an expression that consists of **one term** only ; as—
    x, 5a, abc.

111

4. BINOMIAL

A binomial is an algebraic expression consisting of **two terms** connected by + or – symbols ; as—

$a + b$ or $4x + 3y$.

5. POLYNOMIAL

A polynomial is an expression (in algebra) consisting of **more than two terms** ; as—

$3x + 4y + 6$.

6. VARIABLE

A variable is a symbol in algebra—usually a letter. It can be replaced by one or more numerical values ; as—

a, b, x, y, z.

7. CO-EFFICIENT

It is a numeral or literal number written before a variable as its multiplier ; as—

5 in $5x$ or **1** in xy.

☞ Remember that if an Algebraic term has no number as its co-efficient, its co-efficient is **1** ; as in xy, we can also say that 1 is its co-efficient

8. CONSTANT

A constant is a numeral or variable that governs only *one number* as its fixed value.

9. FACTOR

Two or more expressions when multiplied together are factors of their product ; as—

$3 \times 4 \times x = 12x$. So, each of 3, 4 and x is a factor of $12x$.

10. EXPONENT

An exponent is a numeral written/printed at the top right end of a number or variable to show how many times the number/variable is to be multiplied by itself ; as : $a^3 = a \times a \times a$; $x^2 = x \times x$.

11. EQUATION

It is a mathematical statement which holds that two expressions are equal to each other ; as : $3 + x = 5$

12. ROOTS OF AN EQUATION

These are numbers that when substituted for the variable used in an equation, prove the equation to be true.

13. AGGREGATION SIGNS

These signs include **three types of brackets** ( ), { }, [ ] and the **bar** that are used to enclose expressions ; as—

$(a+b) \times (a+b) = (a+b)^2$

14. ABSOLUTE VALUE

The absolute value of a number is its unchangeable numerical value whether it is *positive* or *negative*.

Let us now solve some examples :

Example 1 : **Write the following in the language of algebra.**

(a) **5 less than the number *a***

(b) **4 times the sum of *x* and *y***

(c) **3 more than the quotient of *a* ÷ *b***

(d) **product of *b* and *c* added to the quotient of *b* ÷ *c***

(e) **9 less than the sum of *x* and *y***

Solution :

(a) 5 less than the number $a = \boldsymbol{a - 5}$

(b) 4 times the sum of x and $y = \boldsymbol{4 (x + y)}$

(c) 3 more than the quotient of $a \div b = \boldsymbol{3 + \dfrac{a}{b}}$

(d) product of b and c + quotient of $b \div c = \boldsymbol{bc + \dfrac{b}{c}}$

(e) 9 less than the sum of x and $y = \boldsymbol{(x + y) - 9}$

} *Ans.*

Example 2 : **Express the following statement in its algebraic form :**
5 times a number *x* is 3 more than the sum of *x* and *y*.

Solution : The given statement = $\boldsymbol{5x - 3 = x + y}$

or $\boldsymbol{5x = x + y + 3}$ *Ans.*

Example 3 : **Write the following in its exponential form :**
$\boldsymbol{5 \times a \times a \times a \times b \times b \times c \times c \times c \times c}$

Solution : $5 \times a \times a \times a \times b \times b \times c \times c \times c \times c$

$= 5 \times (a \times a \times a) \times (b \times b) \times (c \times c \times c \times c)$

$= 5a^3 \times b^2 \times c^4 = \boldsymbol{5a^3b^2c^4}$ *Ans.*

Example 4 : Write $7a^2b^4c^3$ in its fully expanded form.

Solution :
$$7a^2b^4c^3 = 7 \times a^2 \times b^4 \times c^3$$
$$= 7 (a \times a) \times (b \times b \times b \times b) \times (c \times c \times c)$$
$$= 7 a \times a \times b \times b \times b \times b \times c \times c \times c$$

Example 5 : **The area of the four walls of a room is given by the relation 2 (length + breadth) × height. The length of the room is thrice its height and the breadth is twice its height. Find the area of its four walls if its height is *x*.**

Solution :
The height of the room $= x$

∴ breadth $= 2x$ and length $= 3x$

Now area of the four walls $= 2$ (length + breadth) × height
$$= 2 (3x + 2x) \times x = 2 \times 5x \times x = \mathbf{10x^2} \textit{ Ans.}$$

PRACTICE EXERCISES 23

A. Define—
1. a term　　2. an equation　　3. a variable　　4. a monomial
5. an expression　　6. an exponent　　7. a co-efficient　　8. a factor

B. Fill up each blank :

9. Literal numbers obey all the rules of .... operations.

10. There is .... difference between xy and $x \times y$ ....

11. x is greater than y by ....

12. Multiplication is another word for repeated ....

13. In a^3, a is called the .... while 3 is called the ....

14. In the product xy, both x and y are .... of xy.

15. x^7 is equal to x multiplied by .... seven times.

C. Write each of the following in algebraic language :

16. Sum of 9 and a

17. Difference between b and c if $b>c$.

18. Twice the number x is 4 less than the sum of the numbers y and z

19. Number 8 diminished by literal number a.

114

20. A literal number m multiplied by 8 and then decreased by 7.

21. One third of the sum of a and b.

22. Quotient of $y \div z$ added to the product of y and z.

23. Seven times a literal number x is y less than another literal number z.

D. Do as directed :

24. Write in exponential form : $a \times a \times a \times a$....ten times $\div x \times x \times x \times x \times x \times x$....12 times.

25. Write in expanded form : (a) $a^3 b^8$ (b) $x^4 y^6$ (c) $l^4 m^3$

26. Mohan is a brilliant student. He scores 90 marks in English, $x + 8$ marks in mathematics and 83 marks in science. Find his total score.

E. Which of the following are monomials, binomials and polynomials :

27. $x + y - z$ ....

28. $-6a$ ....

29. $2x^2 - 3$ ....

30. $2x - 5y + 4$ ....

31. $(-b)^5$ ....

32. $3a - b$ ....

33. $a^2 - b^2 + c^2$ ....

34. $a \times a \times a$ ....

F. Separate the terms of each expression :

35. $2a - 3b - 4c$ ....

36. $-5bc - 7ab + 2ab$ ....

37. $bz - 4ac + 2ab$ ....

38. $3x - 4y$ ....

G. Combine the terms of each set in an expression :

39. $3z, 2ab, 3xy$

40. $7lm, 3mn, 8$

41. $4z, -3y, -2x$

42. $5x^2, 2x, 8$

43. $4p^2, -3pq, 8$

H. Write the co-efficient of each term :

44. xy **45.** $2yz$ **46.** $-1ab$ **47.** $6x^2 y$ **48.** $9x^2 y^2$ **49.** axy

14 ADDITION AND SUBTRACTION

Before studying the *addition* and *subtraction* of algebraic expressions, we must understand what **like terms** and **unlike terms** mean.

LIKE AND UNLIKE TERMS

Like terms *in algebra are the terms that are expressed using the same letters with same powers.*

Unlike terms *are the terms that are expressed using different letters or different powers of the same letter..*

Like terms just differ only in their co-efficients which may be purely numerical or literal. They differ in powers as well ; as—

In the expression—

$4yz + 6zx - 3yz - 5xy - 3zx + 2xy$

(a) $-5xy$ and $2xy$ are like terms.
(b) $4yz$ and $-3yz$ are like terms.
(c) $6zx$, $-3zx$ are like terms.

But

(a) $-5xy$ and $4yz$ are unlike terms.
(b) $2xy$ and $6zx$ are unlike terms.
(c) $4yz$ and $6zx$ are unlike terms.
(d) a, a^2, a^3, are also unlike terms.

Like Terms	Unlike Terms
$5x^2$	$5x^2$
$2x^2$	$2xy$
$-7x^2$	$-7yz$
$4x^2$	$4zx$

ADDITION OF ALGEBRAIC EXPRESSIONS

While adding algebraic expressions, we write the expressions in columns such that their like terms come under one another. Then we add them up like numbers to get the sum of the given expressions. Let us solve some examples.

Example 1 : Add up :

$5x^2 + 7y - 5z^3 ; 6y + 2x^2 ; -7x^2 + 8y$ and $4x^2 - 9y - 6z^3$.

Solution :   Writing the expressions in proper columns

$$5x^2 + 7y - 5z^3$$
$$+2x^2 + 6y$$
$$-7x^2 + 8y$$
$$\underline{4x^2 - 9y - 6z^3}$$

By adding   **$4x^2 - 12y - 11z^3$** Ans.

Example 2 : Find the sum of : $4x^2 - 5xy + 3y^2$; $-6x^2 - 4xy + 2y^2$ and $-3x^2 - 2xy - 4y^2$

Solution :   Writing the expressions in proper columns

$$4x^2 - 5xy + 3y^2$$
$$-6x^2 - 4xy + 2y^2$$
$$\underline{-3x^2 - 2xy - 4y^2}$$

By adding $-$ **$5x^2 - 11xy + y^2$** Ans.

SUBTRACTION OF EXPRESSIONS

Subtraction in algebra means *negative addition*. Subtracting $3a$ from $5a$ is the same as adding $-3a$ to $5a$ or to subtract c from b is the same as to add $-c$ to b. So, the rule for algebraic subtraction is as under :

(a) Write the expressions in proper columns of similar terms.

(b) Change the sign before each term of the *expression to be subtracted* from + to $-$ and from $-$ to +.

(c) Then add up both the expressions.

Example 3 : Subtract $4a - 6b - c$ from $6a - 3b + 3c$.

Solution :   Writing the expressions in proper columns.

$$6a - 3b + 3c$$
$$4a - 6b - c$$
$$\underline{-\quad +\quad +\quad} \text{ (changing signs)}$$

By adding   **$2a + 3b + 4c$** Ans.

Second Method :

$$(6a - 3b + 3c) - (4a - 6b - c)$$
$$= 6a - 3b + 3c - 4a + 6b + c$$
$$= (6a - 4a) + (-3b + 6b) + (3c + c)$$
$$= \textbf{2a + 3b + 4c} \textit{ Ans.}$$

Example 4 : What must be added to $3x^3 - 2x^2 + 5x + 1$ so that the sum may be $x^3 - 2x^2 + 4x - 1$?

Solution :

The Reqd. Sum $= x^3 - 2x^2 + 4x - 1$

The given exp. $= 3x^3 - 2x^2 + 5x + 1$

Reqd. addend $= (x^3 - 2x^2 + 4x - 1) - (3x^3 - 2x^2 + 5x + 1)$

$= x^3 - 2x^2 + 4x - 1 - 3x^3 + 2x^2 - 5x - 1$

$= \mathbf{-2x^3 - x - 2}$ Ans.

Example 5 : If $P = 3x^2 - 7x - 8$, $Q = x^2 + 8x - 3$ and $R = -5x^2 - 3x + 2$ find the value of $P - Q + R$.

Solution :

$P = 3x^2 - 7x - 8$

$Q = x^2 + 8x - 3$

$\underline{\qquad - \qquad - \qquad + \qquad}$ (changing signs)

$P - Q = 2x^2 - 15x - 5$

$\underline{R = -5x^2 - 3x + 2 \qquad}$ Adding

$P - Q + R = \mathbf{-3x^2 - 18x - 3}$ Ans.

PRACTICE EXERCISES 24

A. Add up

1. $2a, 7a$ **2.** $3p, 5p$ **3.** $5b, 8b$ **4.** $2a, 3b$

5. $7x, 9y$ **6.** $5xy, 4xy, y$ **7.** $4p, 4q$ **8.** $2x^2, 5x$

9. $3x^2, -5x^2$ **10.** $2ab, - ab$ **11.** $4x^3, -5x^3$ **12.** $15x, -9x$

B. Find the sum of :

13. $3x^2 - x + 7$ and $- 2x^2 + 5x - 8$

14. $5x^2 - 4x + 2$ and $- 3x^2 - 7x + 4$

15. $2x - 3y + 4z$ and $5x + 2y - 5z$

16. $x - 2y + z$; $5y - 2x + 2z$; $- 4x - 3y$

17. $4x^3 + 5x^2 - 3x + 8$ and $-2x^3 + 3x^2 - x - 5$

18. $2x^3 - 3x^2 + x + 5$ and $4x^3 + 5x^2 - 3x + 8$

19. $x^2 + 4xy - 2y^2$ and $3x^2 - 7xy + 5y^2$

20. $3x^2 + 4y - 5z^3$; $7x^2 - 8y - 6z^3$ and $4x^2 - 9y - 7z^3$

21. $p^2 + 2pq + q^2$, $p^2 - 2pq + q^2$ and $-p^2 - q^2$

118

C. Add up :

22. $4pq + 2qr - 7$
$\quad\;\; 6pq + 9qr - 4$
$\underline{-\; 8pq - 7qr + 4}$

23. $-10ab - 6bc + 5zx$
$\quad\;\;\; 3ab + 9bc - zx$
$\quad\;\;\; 2ab - 2bc - 3zx$
$\underline{}$

D. Subtract :

24. $5x$ from $8x$

25. $12a$ from $15a$

26. $-5y$ from $8y$

27. $2a$ from $5b$

28. $4p$ from $6q$

29. $11x$ from $5y$

30. $5x^2$ from $8x^2$

31. $7p^3$ from $4p^3$

32. $-8ab$ from $9ab$

33. $15xy$ from $11xy$

34. $-8x^2$ from $12x^2$

35. $-6ab$ from $-7ab$

E. Find the difference between :

36. $-3a - 7b - c$ and $3a - 8b - 6c$

37. $19x - y + z$ and $8x - 3y - 4z$

38. $2x^3 - 3x^2 + x + 5$ and $4x^3 + 5x^2 - 3x + 8$

39. $2a - 3b + 4c - 6d$ and $4a - 6b - c + 7d$

40. $x^2 - 3xy + 7y^2 - 2$ and $-4x^2 - 6xy - y^2 + 5$

F.41. Subtract $2x^4 - 5x^3 + 2x^2 - 6x - 8$ from the sum of $6x^4 - 3x^3 + 7x^2 - 5x + 1$ and $-3x^4 + 5x^3 - 9x^2 + 7x - 2$.

42. Subtract $4x^2 - 9x + 7$ from the sum of $3x^2 - 5x + 2$ and $5x^2 - 8x + 6$.

43. What must be added to $2x - 3y + z$ to make it $x + 2y - 3z$?

44. How much larger is $2x - 4y - z$ than $x - 2y + 3z$?

45. How much smaller is $x^3 - x^2 + 4x - 1$ than $3x^2 - 5x + 6$?

46. What must be subtracted from x to make it $x - y$?

47. What must be added to $x^4 - x^2y^2 - y^4$ to get $2x^4 - 3x^2y^2 + 4y^4$?

48. What will be the remainder if the expression $2x^3 + 7x^2 + 4x + 9$ is subtracted from 0 ?

49. If $A = 3x^2 - 4x + 1$; $B = 5x^2 + 3x - 8$ and $C = 4x^2 - 7x + 3$, find the value of $(A - B + C)$.

50. If $A = -7x^2 - 5xy + 9y^2$, $B = 4x^2 - xy - 5y^2$ and $C = -4y^2 + 3x^2 + 6xy$ prove that $A + B + C = 0$.

SIMPLIFICATION

In sums on simplification, *three types of brackets* mentioned on pages 63 and 64 and the *bar* are also involved. Remember that when brackets occur one inside the other, we solve/remove simple brackets first of all. Then we remove curly brackets and lastly the square brackets.

Example 7 : Simplify :

(a) $a - (b - c)$ 　　　　(b) $3x - \{x - 2y (5x - 3y)\}$

(c) $x - [2y - \{3x - (2y - 3z)\}]$

Solution :

(a) $a - (b - c) = \mathbf{a - b + c}$ Ans.

(b) $3x - \{x - 2y - (5x - 3y)\}$
$= 3x - \{x - 2y - 5x + 3y$
$= 3x - x + 2y + 5x - 3y = \mathbf{7x - y}$ Ans.

(c) $\quad x - [2y - \{3x - (2y - 3z)\}]$
$= x - [2y - \{3x - 2y + 3z\}]$
$= x - [2y - 3x + 2y - 3z]$
$= x - 2y + 3x - 2y + 3z$
$= \mathbf{4x - 4y + 3z}$ Ans.

PRACTICE EXERCISES 25

A. Simplify :

1. $x - (y - 2z)$　**2.** $4 - (2b - a + 2c)$　**3.** $3x - (2y - 5x + 3z)$

4. $(x^2 - 8xy - 5) - (3xy - 4x^2 + 8)$

5. $(a^2 - b^2 + 2ab + 1) - (a^2 - b^2 + 4ab - 5)$

6. $(5x^2 - y + z + 7) - (-x^2 - 3z)$

7. $(6a + -4b) + (-4b + 2a) + (4b - 7)$

8. $x^4 + (x^4 - 2x^3 + x - 1) - (-x^2 - 1) - (x^4 + 3x - 1)$

9. $x - [y - \{z - (y - z)\}]$

10. $2x - [3x - \{4x - (3y - \overline{2x + 3y})\}]$

11. $- x - 5y - [2x - y - \{3x - 2y - \overline{x + 2y}\}]$

B. If a = 3, b = 2, c = 5 find the value of :

12. $2a - 3c + 4b$	13. $3a + 5b - 4c$	14. $4a^2 + 2b^3 - 3c^2$
15. $a^2 - 3b^3 + abc$	16. $2a^3b^2 - 5b^2c - c^3$	17. $a^3 - b^3 - c^3$
18. $3a^3 + 2b^2 + 4c$	19. $5a^4 - 3b^3 + 2c^2$	20. $a^3 - 2b^3 + c - 8$

15 LINEAR EQUATIONS

KNOW THESE TERMS :
1. **imbalance**—state in which something loses its balance
2. **equality**—state of being equal in value, weight etc.
3. **equation**—statement that explains an equality
4. **mathematically**—in the language of mathematics

WHAT IS AN EQUATION ?

The word—**equation**—has its relation with the word—*equal*. It is a mathematical statement which states that **two expressions are equal to each other in every respect.**

We can compare an equation with a balance that has two pans. One of them is for *standard weights* and the other for *articles to be weighed*. When both the pans have equal weights, the balance has its beam quite straight—parallel to the ground.

If the weights in the pans are not equal, the beam of the balance will not be straight but in a slanting position. This is a condition in which the pans are in an imbalance.

In algebra, we have to put expressions in a state of equality very often. The *statement of such an equality is called an* **equation** ; as—

(a) 16 + 5 = 21   (b) 4 + x = 9   (c) b ÷ 6 = 2

(d) 9 + y = 12   (e) $a^2 = a + 6$ (f) $a^3 = 27$

We can state these equations as under :

(a) 16 added to 5 is 21   (b) x increased by 4 is 9

(c) b divided by 6 is 2   (d) 9 added to y is 12

(e) a squared is 6 added to it   (f) a cubed is equal to 27

An *equation* **is a statement in the language of mathematics that holds two expressions equal to each other.**

WHAT IS A LINEAR EQUATION ?

The word—**linear**—means *of a line, i.e. of one dimension.* **So, a linear equation is an equation that has its variables (literal numbers) in their first degree only** ; as—

$$x + 7 = 9 \text{ or } a + 11 = 15$$

A linear equation may have one or more variables used in it. In this lesson, we shall study how to solve linear equations with one variable only.

Remember that an equation has two sides. One of them is to the left of the sign of *equal to* (=) while the other is to the right of this sign.

The expression to the left of the sign of = is called the **Left Hand Side** *(LHS)* and the expression to its right is called the **Right Hand Side** *(RHS)*.

ROOT OF AN EQUATION

It is the value that can be put in place of the variable used in the equation to satisfy the equation.

Example 1 : Solve the equation $x + 7 = 20$.

Solution : Clearly the value of x is a number which when added to 7 gives 20. So, it is $20 - 7 = 13$

Hence **13 is the root of the given equation**.

We can verify whether this value of x is correct or not.

Verification : Putting 13 in place of x in the equation $x + 7 = 20$

or $13 + 7 = 20$, *i.e.* $20 = 20$ which is a fact.

So, **13** is the correct value of x.

Remember that as in the case of a balance whose beam is straight—

(a) **an equation holds good if the same quantity is added to both of its sides.**

(b) **an equation holds good if the same quantity is subtracted from both of its sides.**

(c) **an equation holds good if both its sides are multiplied by the same quantity.**

(d) **an equation holds good if both its sides are divided by the same quantity.**

Example 2 : Solve the equation $y + 7 = 11$.

Solution :
$$y + 7 = 11$$
$$\text{or } y + 7 - 7 = 11 - 7$$
$$\text{or } y = 11 - 7 \quad \text{or} \quad y = 4 \text{ Ans.}$$

Example 3 : Solve the equation $\frac{x}{4} = 3$

Solution : $\frac{x}{4} = 3$

Multiplying both sides by 4

$$\frac{x}{4} \times 4 = 3 \times 4 \text{ or } x = 12 \text{ Ans.}$$

TRANSPOSITION

If we observe closely the method used to solve examples 2 and 3, we can form a rule which is called the **Rule of Transposition.** According to it—

If **a term is transferred from one side of an equation to the other side, the sign before it changes as under** :

(a) **+ changes** into –   (b) **– changes** into +

(c) **× changes** into ÷   (d) **÷ changes** into ×

Example 4 : Solve the equation $13x - 14 = 9x + 10$.

Solution :
$$13x - 14 = 9x + 10$$
$$\text{or } 13x - 9x = 10 + 14 \text{ (By transposition)}$$
$$\text{or } 4x = 24$$
$$\text{or } x = 6 \text{ Ans.}$$

Example 5 : Solve the equation :
$$5\ (3x + 4) - 8\ (6x - 7) = 9x - 8$$

Solution :
$$5\ (3x + 4) - 8\ (6x - 7) = 9x - 8$$
$$\text{or } 15x + 20 - 48x + 56 = 9x - 8 \text{ (Removing brackets)}$$
$$\text{or } -33x + 76 = 9x - 8$$

Transposing the terms—
$$-33x - 9x = -8 - 76$$
$$\text{or } -42x = -84$$

Dividing both sides by – 42
$$x = 2 \text{ Ans.}$$

A. Define—

1. an equation
2. a linear equation
3. LHS of an equation
4. RHS of an equation
5. root of an equation
6. transposition

B. Write each of the following statements as an equation :

7. A number decreased by 7 equals 14.
8. One-third of a number is 8.
9. Five times a number equals 55.
10. Twice a number diminshed by 11 is equal to 11.
11. If a number is doubled and 15 subtracted from the result, the remainder is 17.
12. The sum of four consecutive number is 26.

C. Separate the LHS and the RHS :

13. $\dfrac{2x}{5} = 6$

14. $7x + 8 = 43$

15. $36 - y = 24$

16. $3x - 6 = 15$

17. $3x + 20 = 62$

18. $19x - 13 = 11x + 35$

D. Solve the following equations :

19. $x + 9 = -5$

20. $3a + 4 = 16$

21. $6x + 7 = 37$

22. $x - \dfrac{1}{2} = 2\dfrac{1}{2}$

23. $3(x + 6) = 21$

24. $\dfrac{y}{3} + 5 = 8$

25. $\dfrac{x}{2} + 7 = 15$

26. $\dfrac{y}{12} = 4$

27. $1{\cdot}5x = 7{\cdot}5$

E. Solve each equation :

28. $2(x - 5) - 3(x - 3) = 4(x - 4)$
29. $11(a - 1) - 3(2a - 8) = 2(3a + 15)$
30. $5y - 3(y - 2) = 3y - 2(y - 1)$
31. $4x - 7 - 3(4x + 5) - 5x + 9 = 0$
32. $3(x - 1) - 2(2x + 3) = 5(x + 3)$
33. $x - 7 = 5 + \dfrac{x}{2}$
34. $3(a + 3) - 2(a - 1) = 5(a - 5)$
35. $\dfrac{a}{8} - \dfrac{1}{2} = \dfrac{a}{6} - 2$

APPLICATION OF EQUATIONS

We have already learnt how to write statements in the form of equations. So, most problems can be solved with the help of equations. At first, the problem is given in the form of an equation and then it is solved. Let us solve some examples :

Example 1 : **If 9 is added to a number, the sum is 37. Find the number :**

Solution : Suppose the reqd. number $= x$

According to the statement of the problem

$9 + x = 37$

or $x = 37 - 9 = 28$ *(By transposition)*

Hence **the required no. = 28** Ans.

Example 2 : **One of the two numbers is thrice the other. If their sum is 124, find the numbers.**

Solution : Suppose one of the numbers $= x$

According to the statement of the problem

The other number $= 3x$

and $x + 3x = 124$

or $\qquad 4x = 124$

or $\qquad x = 124 \div 4 = 31$

Hence **one number = 31**

and **other number = 31×3 = 93** $\Big]$ Ans.

Example 3 : **13 added to twice a number is equal to 5 added to thrice the same number. Find the number.**

Solution : Suppose the reqd. number $= x$

According to the statement of the problem

$13 + 2x = 5 + 3x$

or $\qquad 2x - 3x = 5 - 13$ *(By transposition)*

or $\qquad -x = -8$

or $\qquad x = 8$

Hence **the reqd. number = 8** Ans.

Example 4 : **A 96-centimetre long wire is given the shape of a rectangle such that its length is 12 centimetres more than its breadth. Find the dimensions of the rectangle.**

Solution :

Suppose the breadth of the rectangle = x cm.

According to the statement of the problem

Length of the rectangle = $x + 12$ cm

Length of the wire = 96 cm

This length is equal to 2 (*length + breadth*)

or 2 (length + breadth) = 96

or $\quad 2(x + 12 + x) = 96$

or $\quad 2x + 24 + 2x = 96$

or $\quad\quad 24 + 4x = 96$

or $\quad\quad\quad 4x = 96 - 24 = 72$ *(By transposition)*

or $\quad\quad\quad\quad x = 72 \div 4 = 18$

Hence **breadth** of the rectangle = **18 cm.**

and **length** of the rectangle = 18 + 12 = **30 cm.** *Ans.*

PRACTICE EXERCISES 27

Solve the following problems using equations :

1. A number is 15 more than the other and the sum of both the numbers is 75. Find the numbers.

2. Peter's father is four times as old as Peter. After 18 years, he will be twice as old as Peter. Find the present ages of Peter and his father.

3. The length of a plot is 8 meters more than its breadth. If its perimeter is 80 metres, find its length and breadth.

4. Find two numbers whose sum is 64 while their difference is 8.

5. A rectangular park is twice as long as it is wide. If its perimeter be 228 metres, find its length and breadth.

6. After 32 years, a man will be 5 times as old as he was 8 years ago. How old is he now ?

7. The sum of two consecutive odd numbers is 72. Find the numbers.

8. The sum of three consecutive even numbers is 42. Find the numbers.

9. A man is 80 years old now. Five years ago he was thrice the age of his son. How old is his son now ?

10. A purse has only 25-paisa coins. If 5 more coins are added to the coins, the amount becomes Rs. 20. Find the number of coins in the purse.

11. The length of a rectangle is one-and-a-half times its breadth. If its perimeter is 40 metres, find its dimensions.

MISCELLANEOUS EXERCISES III

A. Define—
  1. a term
  2. an expression
  3. a co-efficient
  4. a factor
  5. an exponent
  6. an equation
  7. transposition
  8. like terms

B. Write the name of —
  9. four basic operations

....

  10. four aggregations signs

....

  11. two sides of an equation

....

C. Write the following in the language of algebra :

12. a less than the number x ....

13. 5 more than the quotient of $a \div b$ ....

14. Product of x and y – quotient of $x \div y$ ....

D. 15. The volume of a block is given by the relation *length × width × height*. The length of block is thrice its height while its width is twice its height. Find the dimensions of the block if its volume is 162 cubic cm.

16. Find the sum of $-6a^2 - 4ab + 2b^2$; $4a^2 - 5ab + 3b^2$ and $-3a^2 - 2ab - 4b^2$

17. Find the difference between $19a - b + c$ and $8a - 3b - 4c$ if the first expression is greater than the second.

18. If $P = -7x^2 - 5xy + 9y^2$; $Q = 3x^2 - 4xy + 1$ and $R = -4x^2 - 6xy + 3y^2$, find the value of $P + Q - R$.

19. **Simplify** : $2x - [3x - \{4x - (3y - \overline{2x + 3y})\}]$

20. If $a = 1$, $b = 2$ and $c = 3$, find $3a^3 + 2b^2 + 4c$

21. What is a linear equation. Give four examples.

22. Complete each sentence :

(a) An equation holds good if the .... quantity is added to both of its sides.

(b) An equation holds good if the same quantity is .... from both of its sides.

(c) An equation holds good if both its .... are multiplied by the same quantity.

(d) An equation holds good if both its sides are divided by the ....

23. Solve the equation : $5(3a + 4) - 8(6a - 7) = 9a - 8$

24. One of the two numbers is thrice the other. If their difference is 62, find the numbers.

25. After 32 years from now, a man will be five times as old as he was 8 years back. How old is the man now ?

26. The sum of two consecutive odd numbers is 88. Find the numbers.

27. The sum of three consecutive even numbers is 72, find the numbers.

28. The sum of the ages of two brothers is 45 years. If the elder brother's age is 1·5 times the age of the younger one, find their ages.

29. Two numbers differ by 18. If the smaller number is increased by 4 and the larger number is increased by 6, the larger number becomes five times the smaller one. Find the numbers.

30. The lengths of two poles differ by 20 cm. Had the longer pole been even longer by 10 cm more, its length would have been 4 times the length of the shorter pole. Find their lengths.

MEMORABLE FACTS

1. *Addition, subtraction, multiplication* and *division* are called **basic operations**.
2. *Three types of brackets* and the *vinculum* are called **aggregation signs**.
3. The **numerical value** of a numeral irrespective of the sign before it is called its **absolute value**.
4. Algebraic terms using the *same letters with same powers* are called **like terms**.
5. Algebraic terms using *different letters* or *different powers of the same letter* are called **unlike terms**.
6. An **equation** is a *mathematical statement* that holds two expressions equal to each other.
7. The **root** of an equation is the *value* of the variable used in it that proves the equation to be true.

Geometry **is a branch of mathematics that studies the shapes, sizes and positions of plane** (*flat*) **as well as solid** (*three-dimensional*) **figures.**

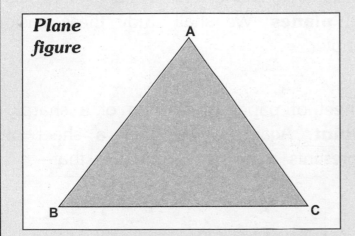

Plane figure

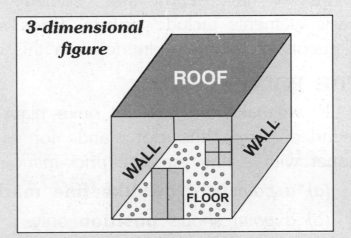

3-dimensional figure

Geometry = *geo* + *metry* = *earth* (*land*) + *measurement*. Geometry had its birth with measurement of land in Egypt. It helps us understand our surroundings in a much better way as all material things are of various shapes. It is practically applied in various fields—*engineering, architecture, metallurgy* and *photography*.

IN THIS UNIT—

16. Basic Geometrical Concepts
17. Line Segments
18. Rays and Angles
19. Parallel Lines
20. Kinds of Angles
21. Triangles
22. Circles
23. Practical Geometry—I
24. Practical Geometry—II

16 BASIC GEOMETRICAL CONCEPTS

As we have learnt that geometry deals with *plane* and *solid figures*, its basic elements include **points**, **lines** and **planes**. We shall study these basic elements of geometry in detail in this chapter.

THE POINT

If we make a *small dot* on a plain sheet of paper by the tip of a sharply mended pencil, the dot stands for a **point.** Again, if we prick a sheet of paper with a fine pin, the *prick-mark* represents a **point**. Remember that—

(a) a point is a **dot-like fine mark**.

(b) a point shows **position** only.

(c) a point has **no length, breadth** or **height.**

(d) in geometry, a point is named using a **capital letter**.

(e) two lines can **meet/intersect** at a point.

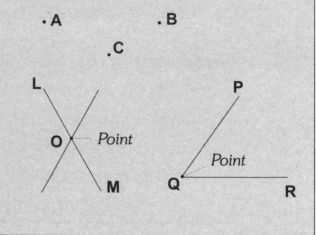

THE LINE

If you hold a thread from its two ends using both of your hands and pull it outside, it will become taut and straight and it will show a **line**.

Take a piece of paper and fold it from the middle. Then press it hard along the fold dragging your thumb on it. When you unfold the paper, you will see a crease formed along the fold. It will be straight and thin. It also stands for a **line**. Remember that the *edge of a table-top* and the *entire corner-length where two walls meet* are other examples of *a line*.

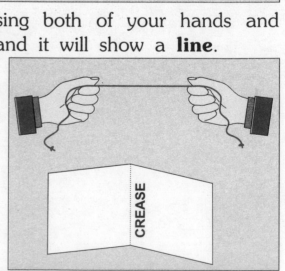

130

Remember the following points regarding a line :

(a) A line has **no end-points**. It can extend to any length in both its directions.

(b) A line **cannot be drawn on paper.** Only a part of it can be drawn. Arrowheads are marked on both-ends of the line. These arrows indicate that a line has no end-points.

(c) A line is **named using a small letter** as shown in front.

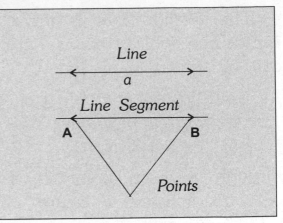

(d) If any two points are taken on a line, they have a **segment** of the line between them.

(e) A **line-segment** is always named using two capital letters.

(f) A line is **made up of points** placed in close proximity.

THE PLANE

Different solids have different types of surfaces—*flat, curved* or *irregular.*

A flat surface is a **plane surface**.

If a flat surface extends indefinitely in all directions, it is called a **plane**.

The surface of a floor, a ceiling, the top of a table and the base of a cone or a cylinder are all examples of *a plane*.

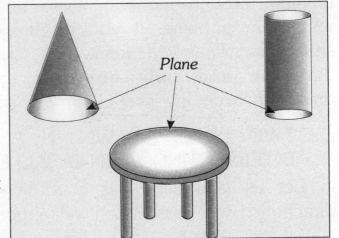

Remember these points about a plane :

1. A plane is a flat surface.

2. A plane has no ends or edges.

3. In geometry, the word—**plane**—always stands for an endless plane, not for any part of it.

4. A plane is named simply by taking three points in it. These three points must not be in the same straight line. So, it is represented by a rectangle or parallelogram as shown below.

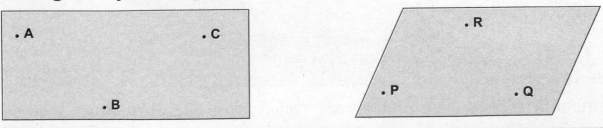

MORE ABOUT THE PLANE

The relation that is there between points and lines in a plane is called **incidence** which means *happening*. Let us study the properties of lines that can be drawn in a plane.

A. UNLIMITED NUMBER OF LINES THROUGH A POINT

How many lines can be drawn through a given point in a plane ? If you try it using a sharp pencil and a ruler, you will see that an **unlimited number of lines** can be drawn through the given point as shown in the figure given in front.

B. ONLY ONE LINE THROUGH TWO GIVEN POINTS

Again, how many lines can be drawn passing through the two given points A and B in a plane. If you try it using a sharp pencil and a ruler, you will find that **one and only one line** can be drawn through the two given points.

C. TWO LINES DRAWN IN A PLANE ARE EITHER PARALLEL OR INTERSECTING (NON-PARALLEL)

Let us take two lines *l, m* in a plane. If we extend them in both the directions, two possibilities will appear :

(a) Either the lines **meet/intersect** each other, as in figure *(a)*.

(b) or they never meet, *i.e.* they **are parallel,** as in figure *(b)*.

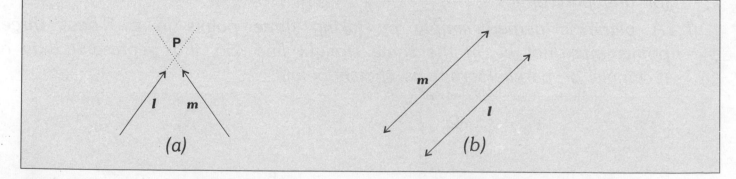

Remember that intersecting lines are called **non-parallel lines** also.

D. COLLINEAR POINTS

Three or more points are said to be *collinear* **if they all lie on the same line. Points A, B, C, D are collinear.**

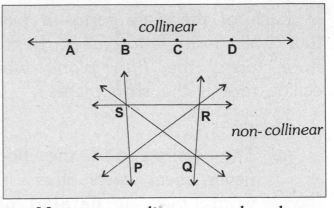

But if these 3 or more points are not on the same line, they are called *non-collinear*.

Points P, Q, R, S are non-collinear points. How many lines can be drawn passing through the various pairs of these four points ? These lines are PQ, QR, RS, SP, SQ, RP. Clearly, there can be only **six lines**.

E. CONCURRENT LINES

Two or more lines passing through the same point in a given plane are called **concurrent lines**.

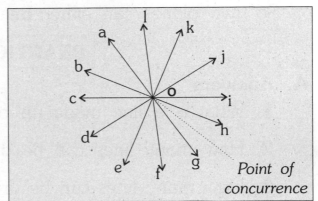

The point through which all such lines pass is called the **point of concurrence**.

STILL MORE ABOUT PLANES

A. **Only one plane can be drawn to contain three non-collinear given points.**

Take three points P, Q, R and join them by straight lines. PQR is part of a plane. Can you draw another plane passing through P, Q, R ? No, not at all. So, it is clear that **one and only one plane** can be drawn to contain the three given non-collinear points.

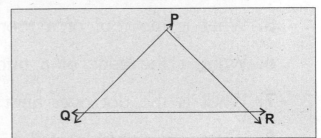

B. **Only one plane can be drawn through two intersecting lines.**

Draw any two lines that intersect at a point O. Try to draw planes that contain these intersecting lines. You will see that **one and only one plane** can be drawn containing the two given intersecting (non-parallel) lines.

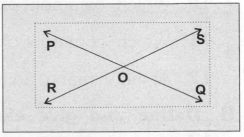

C. **Two planes can either meet in a line or are parallel.**

Observe the picture given on page 134. It shows a room. The room has **four walls, a floor** and a **ceiling roof.**

Each of the walls forms a plane. So, four walls form *four planes*. Besides, the floor forms the *fifth plane* while the ceiling roof is the *sixth plane*.

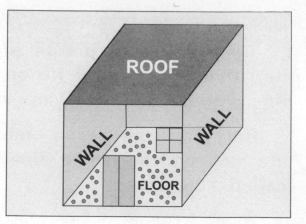

Clearly—

(a) The ceiling and the floor can never meet each other. In other words, they are **parallel planes**.

(b) The walls meet each other along lines called the *corner-lines*. Each two adjacent walls meet along a corner. So, the walls are intersecting planes :

So, two planes can either **be parallel** or **they can meet in a line**.

PRACTICE EXERCISES 28

A. Answers :

1. What is a line made up of ? *dots in close proximity.*

2. How many lines can be drawn through a point ? *∞*

3. How many lines can be drawn through two given points ? *one*

4. What is a wire stretched between two poles like ? *line segment*

5. What is the roof of a room like ? *plane of the*

6. What is the edge of a brick like ? *line Line seg*

7. What is the dot over an *i* like ? *point*

8. What are points located on the same line called ? *collinear*

9. What are points not located on the same line called ? *non-collinear*

10. Which common object has a curved surface ? *ball*

11. Which common object has a flat surface ? *table-top*

12. At how many points can two lines intersect ? *1*

B. Define and give examples :

13. a point   14. a line   15. a line-segment

16. a plane   17. parallel lines   18. non-parallel lines

19. parallel planes   20. intersecting planes   21. concurrent lines

C. 22. A, B and C are three points in a plane. Join them in pairs and find how many lines there can be if—

(a) A, B, C are collinear   (b) A, B, C are non-collinear

23. If there are five non-collinear points P, Q, R, S, T given in a plane and they are joined in pairs, how many lines can be drawn in all ?

PQ, PR, PS, PT, QROS, QJRS RTST

24. Give five examples of common objects that have parallel edges.

phone, house, card book paper

25. Observe the figure given below on the left. How many lines does it have in all ? How many of them are concurrent at O ?   6,3

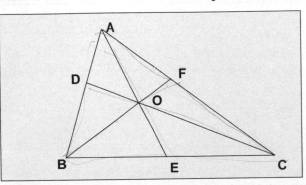   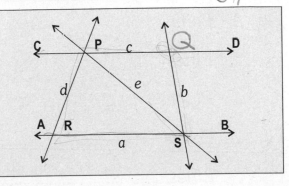

26. Look at the figure given above on the right and name :

(a) four pairs of intersecting lines   ...E,d,c,e,b,a,d;

(b) four non-collinear points   ...P,R,S,Q,

(c) four collinear points   ...ARSB

(d) three concurrent lines at P   ...e,d,e,

(e) three lines intersecting at S   ...a,e,b

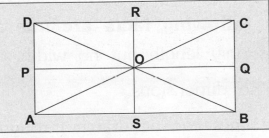

27. In the figure given above, name—

(a) concurrent lines at A, O, Q   ....

(b) eight sets of collinear points   ....

(c) which lines pass through the points D and R   ....

135

28. Given below are two figures. Write in each figure the names of all the—

(a) points   (b) lines   (c) planes

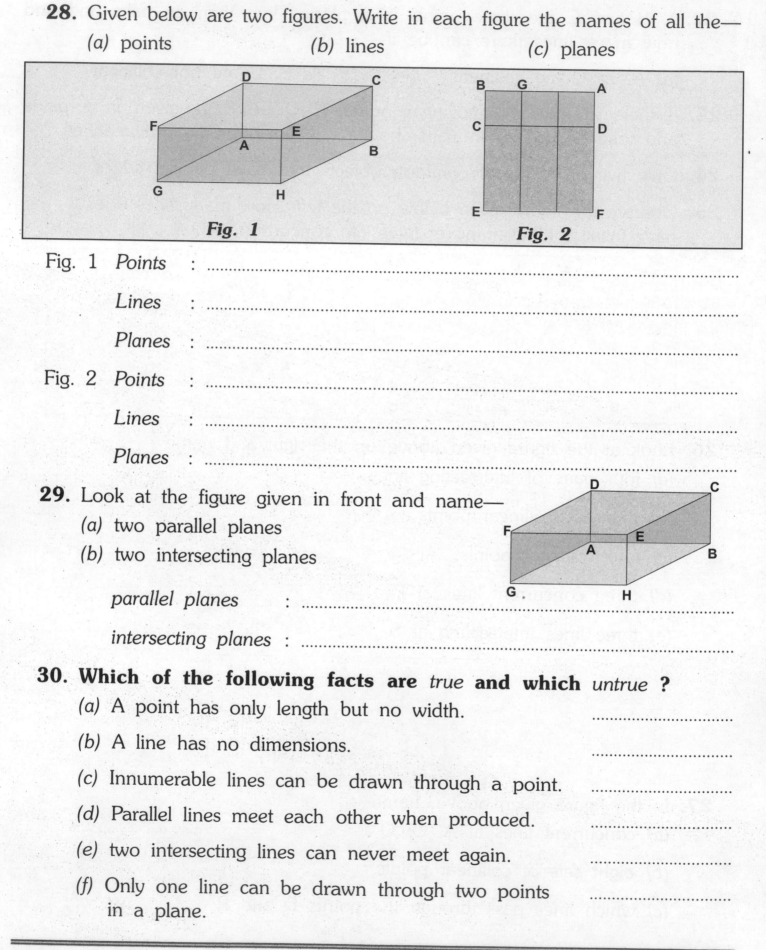

Fig. 1   Fig. 2

Fig. 1 *Points* : ....

      Lines : ....

      Planes : ....

Fig. 2 *Points* : ....

      Lines : ....

      Planes : ....

29. Look at the figure given in front and name—

(a) two parallel planes
(b) two intersecting planes

parallel planes : ....

intersecting planes : ....

30. Which of the following facts are *true* and which *untrue* ?

(a) A point has only length but no width.   ....

(b) A line has no dimensions.   ....

(c) Innumerable lines can be drawn through a point.   ....

(d) Parallel lines meet each other when produced.   ....

(e) two intersecting lines can never meet again.   ....

(f) Only one line can be drawn through two points
    in a plane.   ....

17 LINE-SEGMENTS

WHAT IS A LINE-SEGMENT ?

We studied in the pervious chapter that **lines are of indefinite length** and so they cannot be drawn on paper in their full. We can draw or show only a part of a line on paper. And such parts are called *line-segments*.

The word—**segment**—means *a part cut out of a whole or a larger part.*

The segment of a line is shown by plotting two fixed points on it. The part of the line between these two points is called a **line-segment**. In the figure given in front—

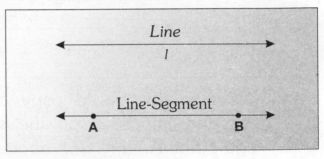

(a) *l is a line that has no end-points.*

(b) *AB is a line-segment. It has its end-points A and B.*

(c) *We can name the line-segment AB as BA also.*

(d) *A line-segment has length only. It has no breadth or height/thickness.*

(e) *We can identify a line-segment if we know its end-points.*

COMPARING LINE-SEGMENTS

Comparing two or more line-segments means to find out which of them is the **shorter/shortest** and which is the **longer/longest**. This comparison is possible by several methods.

A. BY OBSERVATION

This method can be used when the difference in lengths of segments is considerable so that our eyes may be able to locate it at the very first glance. But we cannot know the exact difference

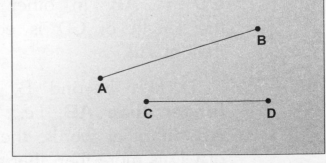

between the lengths of two line-segments by the observation method.

B. BY TRACING

For this method we use a tracing paper and a pencil. Let us see how it is done.

1. Suppose we are given two line-segments AB and CD for comparison. We take a tracing-paper and place it on the line-segment CD. Then we trace it using a ruler and a sharp pencil (Fig *a below*).

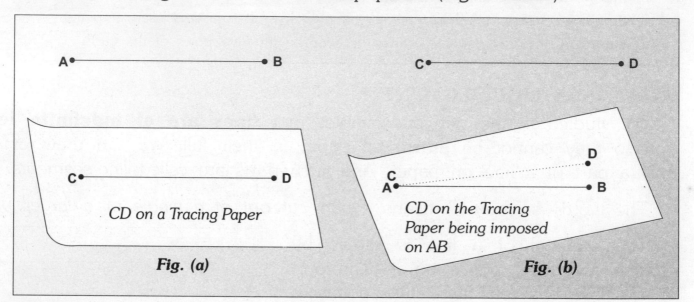

CD on a Tracing Paper

Fig. (a)

CD on the Tracing Paper being imposed on AB

Fig. (b)

2. We take this traced copy of the line-segment CD to the line-segment AB and impose it on the segment AB placing the end-point C on the end-point A. (*Fig. (b) above*). Now there are three possibilities :

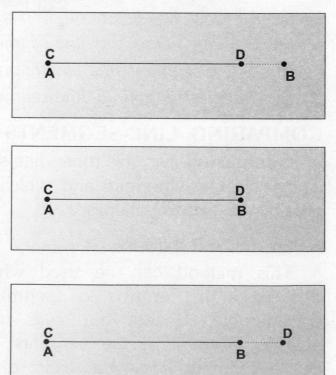

(a) If the end-point D falls short of the end-point B, CD is **shorter than AB**, *i.e.* **CD <AB**. In other words, the length of CD is smaller than that of AB.

(b) If the end-point D falls just on B, CD is **equal to AB**, *i.e.* **CD = AB**. In other words, the length of CD is equal to that of AB.

(c) If D falls beyond B, CD is **longer than AB,** *i.e.,* **CD > AB**. In other words, the length of CD is more than that of AB.

B. USING DIVIDERS

There is an instrument called **dividers** in your geometry-box. Its picture has been given in front. It has two arms hinged together. The arms have pointed ends. Their mutual distance can be adjusted as desired by opening them outwards or closing them inwards. In order to compare two segments AB and CD, take the following steps.

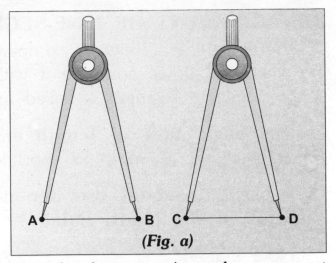

(Fig. a)

1. Place the end-point of one arm of the dividers on A and open out the arms carefully and gently such that the end-point of the other arm falls exactly on B. *(Fig. a)*

2. Lift the dividers carefully so that its opening is not disturbed in any way.

3. Place the end-point of one of the arms of the dividers on C and the other end-point on the segment CD. Now three possibilities arise.

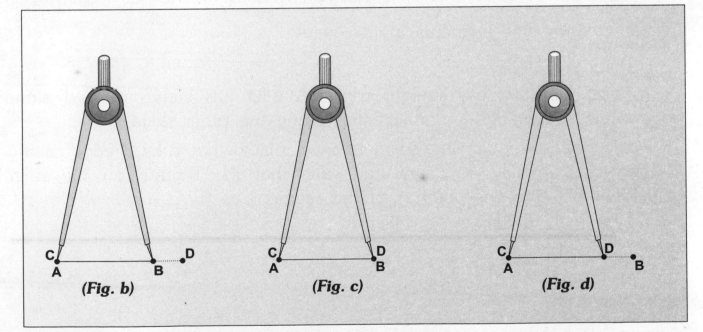

(Fig. b)　　　　*(Fig. c)*　　　　*(Fig. d)*

(a) If the end-point of the second arm of the dividers falls short of D, **AB is shorter than CD**, *i.e.* **AB < CD.** *(Fig. b)*

(b) If the end-point of the second arm falls just on D, **AB is equal to CD**, *i.e.* **AB = CD**. *(Fig. c)*

(c) If the end-point of the second arm falls beyond D, **AB is longer than CD**, *i.e.* **AB > CD**. *(Fig. d)*

MEASUREMENT OF LINE-SEGMENTS

We have learnt how to compare line-segments. Clearly, a line-segment can be measured if we compare it with a segment that has a *standard measured length*. Such a segment is called a **unit segment**.

The **basic unit of length** in the international system of units is **metre** which we write as **m** in its short form.

A *metre* is about one ten-millionth part of the distance from the equator to the North Pole.

Note that—

1 m = 100 centimetres   and   **1 cm.** = 10 millimetres
1 m = 1000 millimetres

Also remember that—

1 inch = 2·54 cm.   **1 foot** = 30·48 cm.
1 yard = ·9144 m   **1 mile** = 1·608 kilometres
1 metre = 1·094 yards   **1 metre** = 39·37 inches

We measure line-segments in two ways :

A. USING A RULER

Take a ruler that has straight edges. A ruler has inches marked along one edge while centimetres and millimetres along the other edge.

While measuring a line-segment, we place the ruler's edge along the segment (say AB) to be measured such that the 0-mark on the ruler just coincides with the end-point A of the segment.

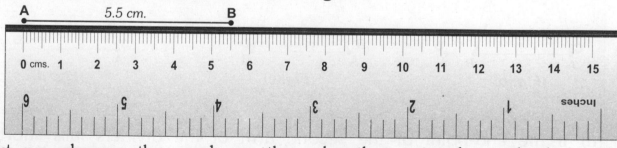

Next we observe the mark on the ruler that coincides with the end-point B. The divisions between the marks A and B on the ruler give the length of the line-segment AB.

In the figure given above, there are 5 full divisions on the ruler between the end-point A and B. Besides there are 5 small divisions also. So, the length of the line-segment AB = **5·5 cm**.

B. USING DIVIDERS

It has often been seen that the ends of rulers are broken. Moreover, there is no uniformity in the divisions on rulers. So, there can be an error in the measurement. To avoid all this, line-segments are measured using dividers as well. For it, we have to proceed as follows :

1. Open the dividers to an optimum width.

2. Place one end-point of the dividers on A.

3. Adjust the dividers such that the other end-point of the dividers falls on B.

4. Lift the dividers carefully so that its opening is not disturbed at all.

5. Place the end-point of one of the arms of the dividers on the zero-mark on the ruler as shown in front.

6. Place the end-point of the other arm of the dividers on the ruler and read the division of the ruler that coincides with it.

   This reading will give the length of the given line.

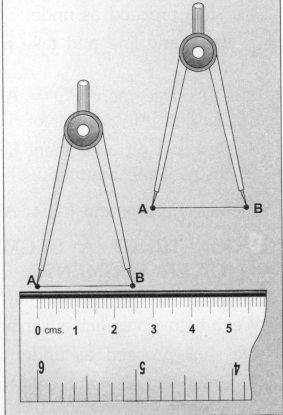

CUTTING A SEGMENT OUT OF A GIVEN LINE-SEGMENT

Suppose a line-segment AB is given. Also, given is a line *l*. We have to cut a line-segment equal in length to the given segment AB out of the line *l*. For it, take the following steps :

1. Take any point P on the given line *l*.

2. Take your dividers and open their arms to an optimum length.

3. Measure the length of the given segment AB using the dividers.

4. Now place one end of the dividers on the point P.

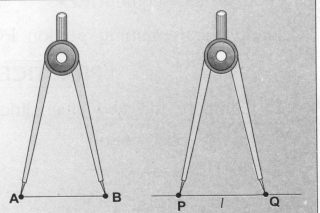

5. Place the other end of the dividers on the line and mark the point where it falls as Q. The portion of the line *l* named PQ is equal to the given line-segment AB.

TO CONSTRUCT A SEGMENT EQUAL TO THE SUM OF TWO GIVEN SEGMENTS.

Suppose we are given two segments AB and CD and we are to construct a segment equal to AB + CD.

We shall proceed as under :

1. Draw any line and take a point P on it.

2. Cut off segment PQ = AB out of the line using a pair of dividers.

3. Next, cut off a segment QR = CD in the same manner.

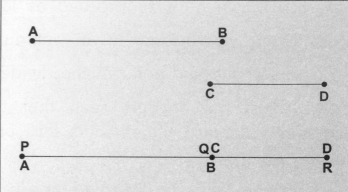

Clearly, the segment PR = AB + CD

TO CONSTRUCT A SEGMENT EQUAL TO THE DIFFERENCE OF TWO GIVEN SEGMENTS.

Suppose we are given two segments AB and CD. Such that AB > CD. We are to construct a segment equal to AB − CD.

We shall proceed as under :

1. Draw any line and take a point P on it.

2. Cut off a segment PR = AB out of the line.

3. Next cut off segment RQ = CD out of the segment RP.

Clearly, the remaining portion PQ of the segment PR = AB − CD.

PRACTICE EXERCISES 29

A. 1. Compare the two given line-segments AB and CD

   (a) By observation

   (b) Using dividers

   (c) By tracing

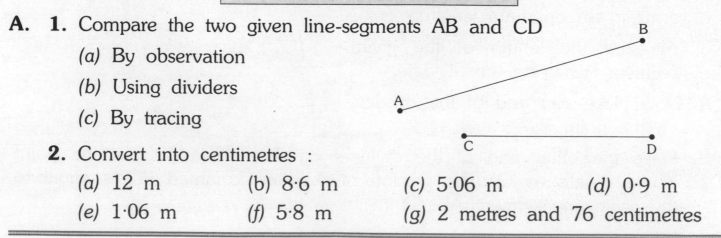

2. Convert into centimetres :

   (a) 12 m   (b) 8·6 m   (c) 5·06 m   (d) 0·9 m

   (e) 1·06 m   (f) 5·8 m   (g) 2 metres and 76 centimetres

3. Convert into millimetres :

(a) 17 cm.   (b) 5·3 cm.   (c) 8·63 metres   (d) 12·7 cm.

(e) 4·6 cm.   (f) 6·7 cm.   (g) 1 m 35 cm   (h) 3·4 cm.

4. Construct line-segments equal to the following lengths :

(a) 7·2 cm.   (b) 4·6 cm.   (c) 5·2 cm.   (d) 3·4 cm.

5. The end-point A of a given line-segment coincides with 1 cm.-mark on a ruler. Its end-point B coincides with the 4·6 cm.-mark on the ruler. What is the length of the segment AB ?

6. Measure the lengths of the following line-segments using dividers and a ruler.

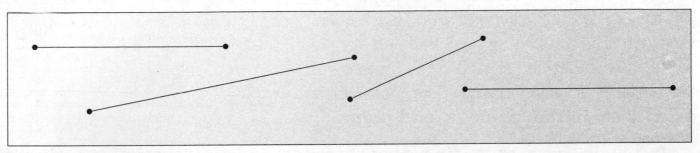

7. Draw two line-segments 3·8 cm. and 2·8 cm. long respectively. Draw another segment equal in length to their sum. Check its length with a ruler.

8. Given in front is a figure. Observe it and answer :

(a) How many line-segments are there in all in it ?

(b) Which three line-segments are concurrent at O ?

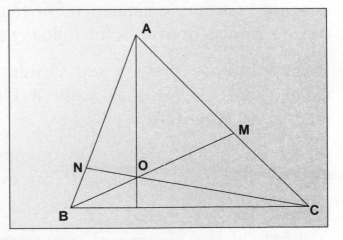

9. Draw a line-segment 10 cm. in length. Out of it, cut off a segment AB 3·6 cm. in length. Measure the remaining segment.

10. Draw two segments AB and CD 4·3 cm. and 2·7 cm. long respectively. Draw a segment equal in length to their sum.

18 RAYS AND ANGLES

WHAT IS A RAY ?

We know that a line is of unlimited length. But when we take any point (say O) on it, it gets divided into two parts. One of these parts is to the left of O while the other is to its right. Either of these parts is called a **ray**. The point O is called their **initial point** or **end-point**.

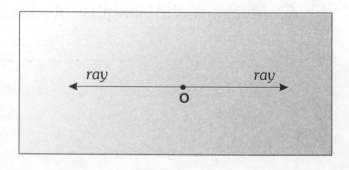

A *ray* **is part of a line that extends indefinitely in one direction from a given point on the line.**

Observe the figure given in front. A number of rays shoot from the point O.

A ray has only one end-point. But it can be extended indefinitely in one direction. Clearly, unlimited number of rays can be drawn from a point *(initial point)*.

Suppose we draw a ray OA from the initial point O. We shall write it OA and read it as **Ray OA**.

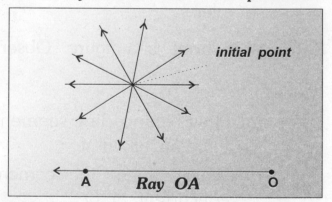

To be more precise, OA means that the ray starts from O and passes through the point A. Nay, it can extend indefinitely in the direction OA.

WHAT IS AN ANGLE ?

Look at the pictures of some common objects given on page 145. Each of them has two arms joined together by a hinge with their other ends open.

If we observe these objects closely, we can consider each of them to be made of two rays shooting from a **common initial point.** And this is the idea at the base of each and every **angle** in geometry.

The angle is a most important element in almost every physical phenomenon. You will read about this fact in your higher classes.

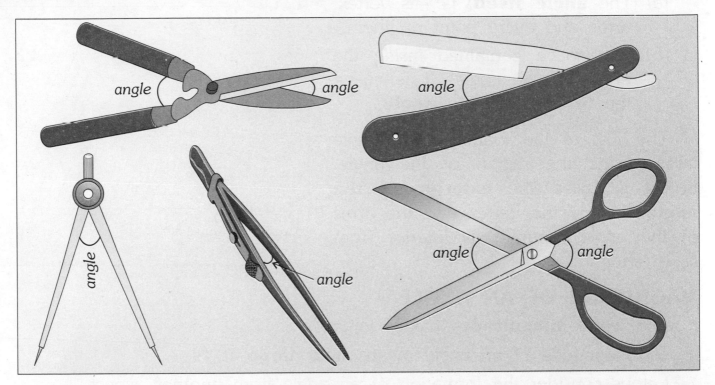

An *angle* **is a figure formed by two rays that shoot from the same initial point in different directions.**

The common initial point is called the **vertex** or **angular point** of the *angle*.

The rays forming the angle are called the **arms** of the *angle*.

In the figure given in front—

(a) O is the *vertex* of the angle

(b) OA and OB are the *arms* of the angle.

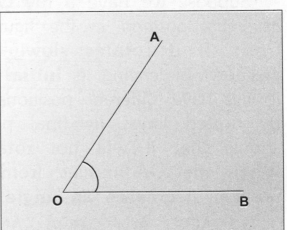

(c) Angle AOB is the *angle* made by the two arms. It may be written as ∠O or we may name it as ∠1 etc.

(d) While naming an angle, its vertex-point must be in the centre as ∠AOB or ∠BOA.

INTERIOR AND EXTERIOR OF AN ANGLE

The end-points of the rays/segments forming an angle are not collinear. Clearly, every angle lies in a plane. And in its plane it has its own region which is called its **angular region**.

The angular region of an angle has two parts :

(a) The **angle itself**, *i.e.* its vertex, arms and every point on them.

(b) The space contained *inside* the arms of the angle. It is called the **interior of the angle**.

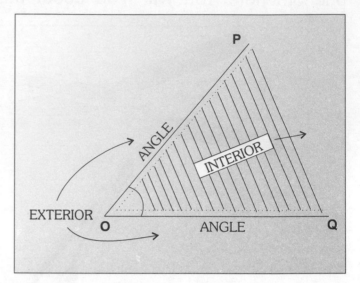

The rest of the plane of the angle falls outside the region of the angle. So, it is called the **exterior of the angle**. Clearly the vertex and the arms of the angle separate its *interior* from its *exterior*.

MAGNITUDE OF AN ANGLE

The word—**magnitude**—means *largeness*.

So, magnitude of an angle means **how large it is**.

Let us consider the formation of an angle from another aspect.

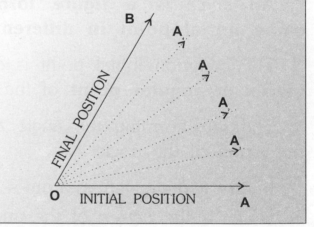

Suppose we have a ray OA. Observe its *initial position* in the figure given in front. If it rotates slowly from this position not leaving its **initial point** (O), it will have different positions as shown by dotted lines. Its final position OB shows that it will not rotate further. When ray OA moves from its initial position, it **creates an angle**, thus—

(a) AOA_1, AOA_2, AOA_3, AOA_4 and AOB are all angles.

(b) $\angle AOA_2 > \angle AOA_1$ and $\angle AOA_3 > \angle AOA_2$ while $\angle AOA_4 > \angle AOA_3$

(c) Clearly, the size or magnitude of rotation of the ray OA shows the size or **magnitude of the angle**.

Magnitude **of an angle depends on the amount of rotation of one of its arms from its initial point.**

COMPARING ANGLES

Comparison between different angles is an essential need. We have got to know sometimes whether an angle is equal to another angle or it is larger or

146

smaller than it. Angles can be compared just as we compare line-segments. There are three similar methods of comparing angles.

A. BY OBSERVATION

If two angles differ considerably in terms of magnitude, we can easily know which of them is the larger or smaller. But this comparison cannot lead to exact facts about the comparison of the angles.

B. BY SUPER-IMPOSITION

The second method of comparing angles is *super-imposition*. We first trace one of the angles on a tracing paper and then super-impose the traced image on the other angle.

Suppose we want to compare two angles ABC and PQR by super-imposition method. The following steps will be taken.

1. Take a tracing paper and trace ∠PQR using a sharp pencil and a ruler.
2. Place the traced ∠PQR on ∠ABC such that vertex Q falls on vertex B.
3. Adjust the tracing paper such that arm QR of ∠PQR coincides with arm BC of ∠ABC.
4. In regard to the arm QP, three possibilities arise :

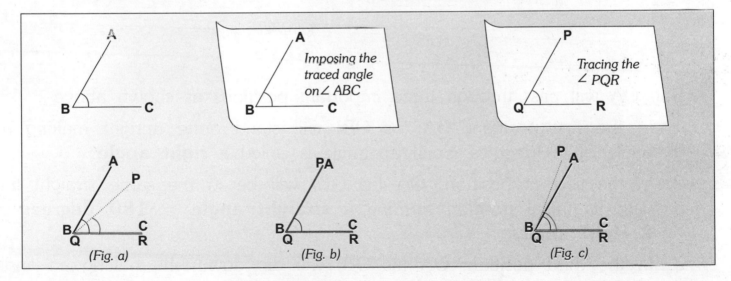

(Fig. a)   (Fig. b)   (Fig. c)

(a) If QP falls in the interior of ∠AOB, ∠**PQR is shorter than** ∠**ABC**, *i.e.* ∠**PQR** < ∠**ABC**.

(b) If QP falls just on arm AB, **both the angles are equal,** *i.e.* ∠**PQR** = ∠**ABC**.

(c) If QP falls in the exterior of ABC, **PQR is larger than** ∠**ABC,** *i.e.* ∠**PQR** >∠**ABC**.

C. BY MEASUREMENT

The third way of comparing two angles is by measuring them in degrees. **Degree** is the *standard unit* for measuring angles.

What is a **degree** ?

We read about the rotation of ray OA in this very chapter. If OA keeps rotating anti-clockwise, it will come to its initial position after taking a full round. Thus, it will rotate through 360 degrees.

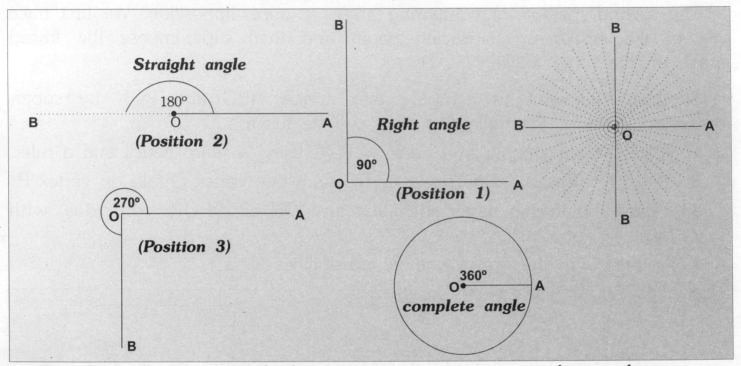

Ray OA will pass through three important positions as shown above :

1. In the first position, OA (as OB) will stand quite upright making an angle of 90 degrees. Such an angle is called a **right angle**.

2. In the second position, OA (as OB) will be in the same straight line with its initial position forming a **straight angle = 180 degrees = 2 right angles**.

3. In the third position, OA (as OB) will dip downright making an angle of **270 degrees**. Such an angle is equal to **three right angles**.

4. Next, OA will return to its initial position traversing an angle of **360 degrees** which is called a **complete angle** or **circle**.

Clearly a degree is 360th part of a complete angle. The sign of degree is °. So, we write the measurement of angles in degrees as follows :

90°   180°   270° etc.

We can measure the angles to be compared using a *protractor*. A protractor is a geometrical instrument similar in shape to a half-circle.

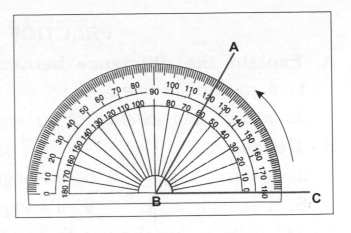

When we have known the measures of both the angles, we can know which of them is the larger and which the smaller.

HOW TO MEASURE AN ANGLE

Suppose we have to measure a given angle PQR. We shall use the protractor to measure it in the following manner :

1. Place the protractor such that its centre falls exactly on the vertex Q of the angle.

2. Also see that 0-mark of the instrument is exactly on the arm QR of the given angle.

3. Now see which mark on the protractor falls on the arm QP.

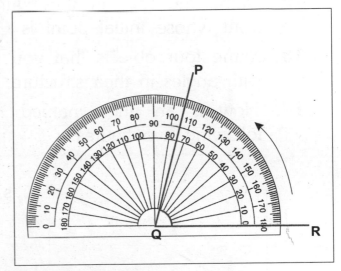

The reading of this mark 75° will give the measure of the given angle.

CONSTRUCTING ANGLES WITH A PROTRACTOR

Suppose we want to construct an angle of 45° using a protractor. We shall proceed as under :

1. Draw any ray BA.

2. Place the protractor on it such that its centre falls on B.

3. Make sure that the 0-mark of the protractor falls on ray BA.

4. Starting from the 0°, discover the 45°-mark on the protractor.

5. Using a sharp pencil, plot a point C just against the 45°-mark.

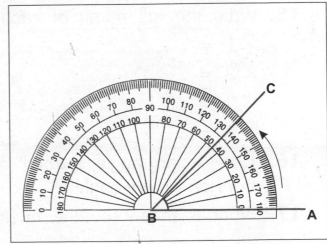

6. Remove the protractor and join BC. ∠**ABC will be the required angle = 45°.**

PRACTICE EXERCISES 30

A. Explain the difference between—

1. a *ray* and a *line*
2. a *ray* and a *line-segment*
3. *interior* and *exterior* of an angle
4. *end-point* and *vertex*

B. Define—

5. a ray
6. an angle
7. a right angle
8. a straight angle
9. a complete angle
10. initial point

C. 11. With its initial point P draw a ray that passes through another given point Q.

12. Name the rays in the figure given in front whose initial point is O.

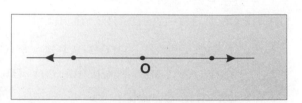

13. Name four objects that you see around with angles in their structure.

14. How is an angle named ? Mark and name all the angles in the following two figures :

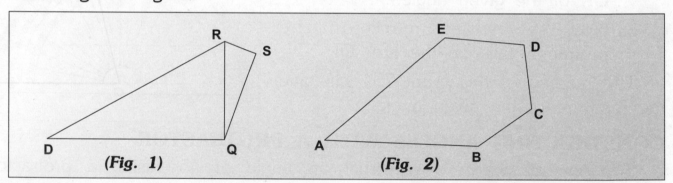

(Fig. 1)   (Fig. 2)

15. Write the full name of each angle in the figure given below :

∠1 = ...

∠2 = ...

∠3 = ...

∠4 = ...

16. How is an angle formed ? What do you mean by the *interior* and *exterior* of an angle ?

17. What is meant by the *magnitude* of an angle ? What does it depend on ?

18. How can we compare two angles ?

19. How will you measure a given angle using a protractor ?

20. How will you construct an angle of 60° using a protractor ?

19 PARALLEL LINES

KNOW THESE TERMS :
1. **parallel lines**—lines that always remain at the same distance from each other
2. **transversal**—a line that cuts two other lines at two different points
3. **vertically opposite angles**—angles formed at a common vertex on opposite sides
4. **interior angles**—angles formed on the same inner sides of the lines cut by a transversal

We already know an important fact about lines in a plane. It is that—

(a) two distinct lines in a plane can either meet/intersect each other or

(b) they can never meet.

Clearly, the second type of lines are called **parallel lines**. Look at the lines *l* and *m* given in front.

However long may we produce these lines on either side, they will never meet or intersect. So, they are **parallel lines**. We can write them as—

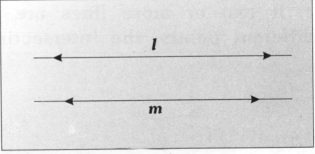

(a) *l//m*   (b) *l* is parallel to *m*

Remember that the distance between two parallel lines is always the same.

Some more examples of parallel lines are as under—

(a) opposite edges of a ruler   (b) rails of a railway-line

(c) opposite edges of a table top   (d) opposite edges of the page of a book

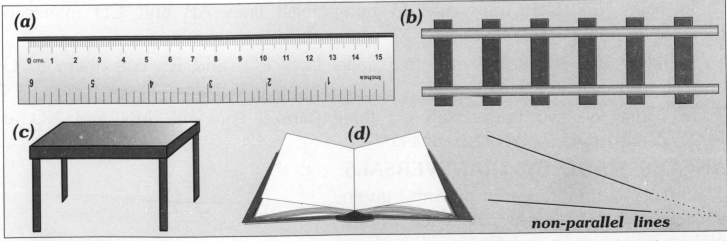

(a)

(b)

(c)

(d)

non-parallel lines

Remember that if two lines meet when produced on one side, they are **non-parallel lines**.

So, there are two distinct properties of parallel lines :

1. **Parallel line are always equally apart everywhere.**
2. **Parallel lines do not meet even when they are produced on either side**.

PARALLEL RAYS

Two rays are parallel if their corresponding lines are parallel.

(Parallel Rays)   **(Parallel Line-segments)**

PARALLEL LINE-SEGMENTS

Two line-segments are parallel if their corresponding lines are parallel.

TRANSVERSALS

If two or more lines are intersected/cut by another line at two different points, the intersecting line is called their *transversal.*

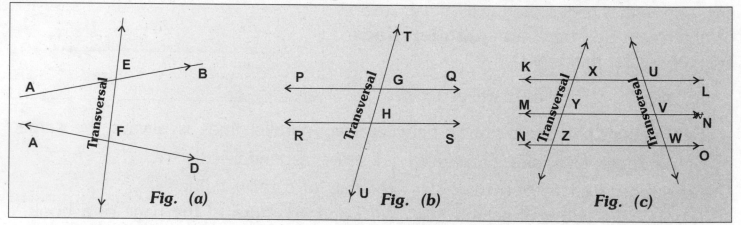

Fig. (a)   Fig. (b)   Fig. (c)

In figure *(a)*, is a transversal to non-parallel lines AB and CD intersects them at E and F respectively.

In figure *(b)*, is a transversal to parallel lines PQ and RS cuts them at G and H respectively.

In figure *(c)*, two transversals cut three parallel lines LK, MN and NO at X, Y, Z and at U, V, W respectively.

ANGLES MADE BY TRANSVERSALS

Observe the three diagrams given above. Each transversal cuts each of the given lines at a point making four angles. The figure given on the right clarifies this point.

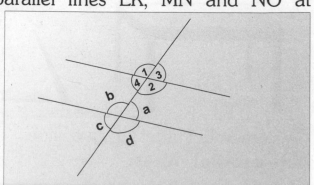

The angles formed by a transversal when it cuts two lines fall into two chief classes. Remember that—

A. 1. The transversal makes eight angles in all. They are ∠1, ∠2, ∠3, ∠4 and ∠5 , ∠6, ∠7, ∠8.

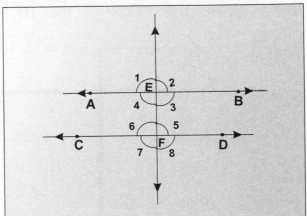

2. ∠1, ∠2, as well ∠7, ∠8 are formed on the *outer sides* of the lines cut by the transversal EF.

So, these four angles are called **exterior angles**.

B. ∠3, ∠4 and ∠5, ∠6 are formed on the *inner sides* of the lines cut by the transversal.

So, these four angles are called **interior angles**.

C. 1. The transversal cuts the lines at E and F.

2. Each of these two points forms a common vertex for four angles.

3. The angles at E are four in number. ∠1 is opposite ∠3 while ∠2 is opposite ∠4.

So, ∠1 and ∠3 are called **vertically opposite angles.** ∠2 and ∠ 4 are also *vertically opposite angles.*

Similarly at the common vertex F, ∠5 and ∠7 are **vertically opposite angles** and ∠6 and ∠8 are also *vertically opposite angles.*

Out of each pair of vertically opposite angles, one angle is an *exterior angle* and the other is an *interior angle*.

DRAWING PARALLEL LINES

Let us now learn **how to draw a line parallel to a given line AB at a given distance** *(say 8 cm.).*

For it, we shall proceed as under :

1. Take the pair of set-squares out of your geometry-box.

2. Adjust the longer straight edge of the longer set-square along the given line AB with the support of a ruler.

3. Press the ruler with your left hand firmly and move the set-square along the edge of the ruler up to the given distance (8 cm.).

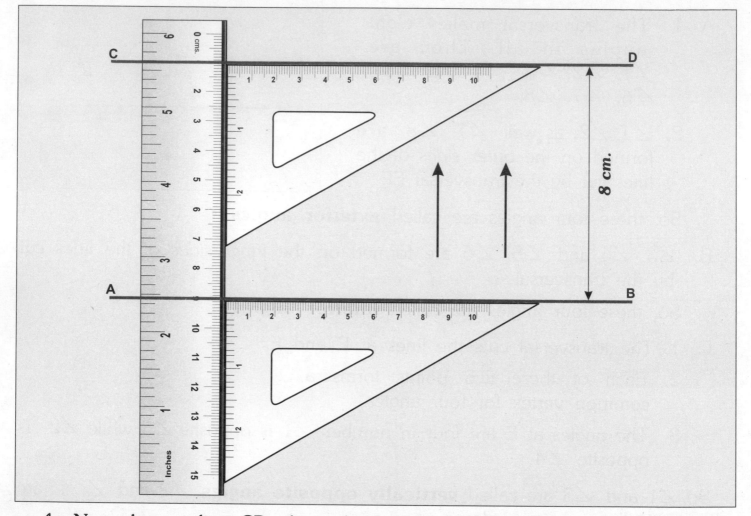

4. Now draw a line CD along the longer straight edge of the set-square.

5. Remove the ruler and the set-square both.

   CD is the required line parallel to AB.

TO DRAW A LINE PARALLEL TO A GIVEN LINE THROUGH A GIVEN POINT

Suppose we are given a line AB and a point P outside it. We are to draw a line CPD parallel to AB through the point P.

For it, we shall proceed as under :

1. Adjust the longer straight edge of the longer set-square along the given line AB with the support of a ruler.

2. Press the ruler firmly with your left hand and move the set-square towards the point P.

3. Let the edge of the set-square touch the point P.

4. Draw a line CPD through the point P along the edge of the set-square.

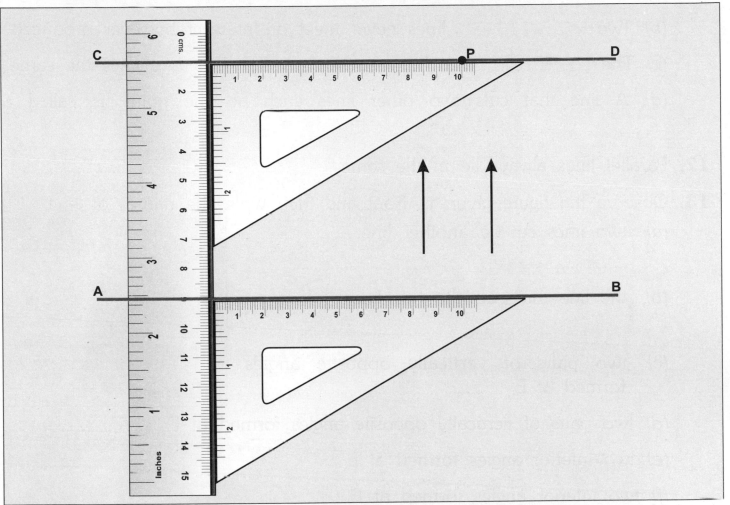

5. Remove the ruler and the set-square.

Line CPD is the required line parallel to AB.

PRACTICE EXERCISES 31

A. Define :

1. Parallel Lines
2. Non-parallel Lines
3. Transversal
4. Parallel Rays
5. Parallel Line-segments
6. Exterior Angles
7. Interior Angles
8. Vertically Opposite Angles
9. Give five examples of parallel lines naming objects around you.
10. Given below are a few figures. Name the pairs of parallel lines in each.

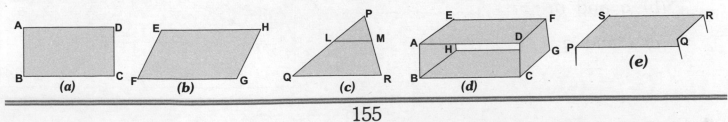

155

11. Fill up each blank :

(a) Two lines that meet or cut each other are called ....

(b) Two .... lines never meet or intersect however produced.

(c) The .... between two parallel lines is always the same.

(d) A line that cuts two other lines each at one point, is called a

....

12. Parallel lines always lie in the same. ....

13. Observe the figure given in front and then write the names of—

(a) two lines cut by another line.

....

(b) the line that cuts the two lines.

....

(c) two pairs of vertically opposite angles formed at E : ...., ...

(d) two pairs of vertically opposite angles formed at F : ...., ...

(e) two interior angles formed at E : ....

(f) two interior angles formed at F : ....

14. Observe the figure given in front and name—

(a) the ray parallel to BC ....

(b) the ray parallel to AB ....

(c) transversal to rays BC and QR ....

(d) transversal to rays AB and PQ ....

15. Observe the adjoining figure and name the transversals to the following lines :

(a) *l* and *m* ....

(b) *q* and *m* ....

(c) *l* and *q* ....

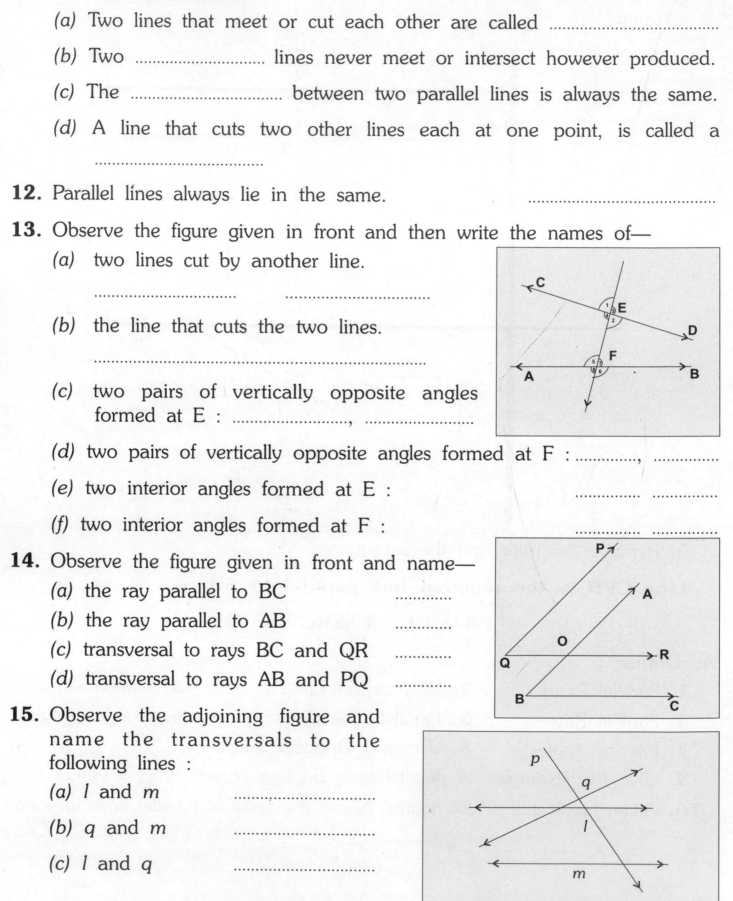

20 KINDS OF ANGLES

KINDS OF ANGLES

We have read about angles in chapter 18. In this chapter, we shall read about various kinds of angles. We already know about the following angles :

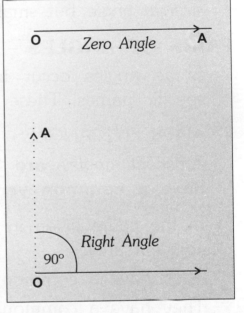

1. ZERO ANGLE

It is the angle which measures 0°.

It is there when any ray is in its initial position. In this position, the ray does not make any angle at all because it does not move or rotate from its position.

2. RIGHT ANGLE

It is the angle that measures 90°.

It is there when any ray rotates to come in the upright position on its initial point.

3. STRAIGHT ANGLE

It is the angle that measures 180° or 2 right angles.

This angle is there when a ray rotates from its initial position to come in line with this position on the opposite side. This angle is so called because it forms a straight line.

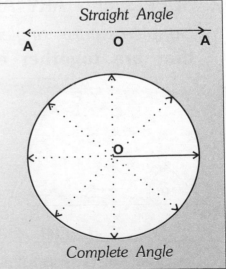

4. COMPLETE ANGLE

It is an angle that measures 360° or 4 right angles.

It is there when a ray rotates to go through a full round and comes to its original position again.

5. ACUTE ANGLE

It is an angle that measures between 0° and 90°.

It is there when an angle is larger than a *zero angle* and smaller than a *right angle*.

6. OBTUSE ANGLE

It is an angle that measures between 90° and 180°.

It is there when an angle is larger than a *right angle* and smaller than a *straight angle*.

7. REFLEX ANGLE

It is an angle that measures between 180° and 360°

It is there when an angle is larger than a *straight angle* but smaller than a *complete angle*.

PAIRS OF ANGLES

Some angles occur in pairs. So, they have been given specific names. These angles are as under :

1. ADJACENT ANGLES

Adjacent angles **are two angles that lie in the same plane and have a common vertex, a common arm but separate interiors.**

In the figure given in front, ∠AOB and ∠AOC are adjacent angles.

They have a common vertex O

They have a common arm AO

2. SUPPLEMENTARY ANGLES

Supplementary angles **are two angles that lie in the same plane that are together equal to 180° or two right angles.**

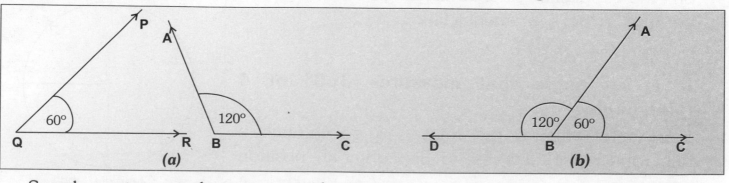

Supplementary angles may stand apart from each other as in figure *(a)*.

But supplementary angle may also be adjacent angles. In this case, their uncommon arms are in the same straight line ; as in figure *(b)* on page 158. So, *supplementary adjacent angles* are also called a **linear pair**.

Remember that—

1. **angles of a linear pair are always supplementary.**

2. **But supplementary angles do not always form a linear pair.**

3. COMPLEMENTARY ANGLES

Complementary angles **are two angles that lie in the same plane and are together equal to 90° or 1 right angle.**

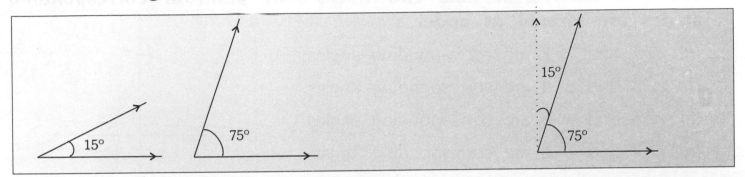

An angle of 75° is the complement of an angle of 15°. Inversely, an angle of 15° is the complement of an angle of 75°.

4. VERTICALLY OPPOSITE ANGLES

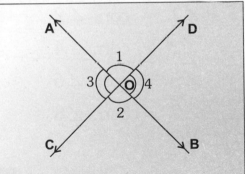

These angles are formed on the opposite sides of a common vertex when two lines intersect.

$\angle 2$ is the vertically opposite angle of $\angle 1$.

$\angle 4$ is the vertically opposite angle of $\angle 3$.

ANGLES MADE BY A TRANSVERSAL WITH TWO LINES

1. ALTERNATE ANGLES

When a transversal cuts two lines, four pairs of alternate angles are formed as under :

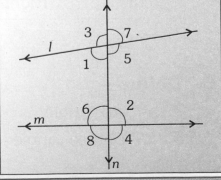

(a) $\angle 1$ and $\angle 2$ are interior alternate angles.

(b) $\angle 3$ and $\angle 4$ are exterior alternate angles.

(c) $\angle 5$ and $\angle 6$ are interior alternate angles.

(d) $\angle 7$ and $\angle 8$ are exterior alternate angles.

Remember that—

If the two lines cut by a transversal **are parallel to each other**, the angles of each alternate pair are **equal** to each other.

$$\angle 1 = \text{alt. } \angle 2$$
$$\angle 3 = \text{alt. } \angle 4$$
$$\angle 5 = \text{alt. } \angle 6$$
$$\angle 7 = \text{alt. } \angle 8$$

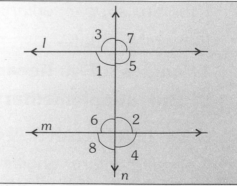

2. CORRESPONDING ANGLES

When a transversal cuts two lines, four pairs of corresponding angles are formed as under :

(a) $\angle 1$ and $\angle 2$ are corresponding angles.

(b) $\angle 3$ and $\angle 4$ are corresponding angles.

(c) $\angle 5$ and $\angle 6$ are corresponding angles.

(d) $\angle 7$ and $\angle 8$ are corresponding angles.

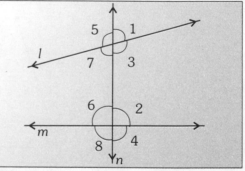

If the two lines cut by a transversal **are parallel to each other**, the angles of each corresponding pair are **equal** to each other ; as—

$$\angle 1 = \text{corr. } \angle 2$$
$$\angle 3 = \text{corr. } \angle 4$$
$$\angle 5 = \text{corr. } \angle 6$$
$$\angle 7 = \text{corr. } \angle 8.$$

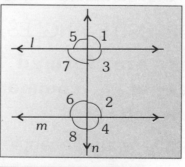

PRACTICE EXERCISES 32

A. Here are measures of some angles. Write each angle in its column.

1. 120°   **2.** 15°   **3.** 180°   **4.** 90°   **5.** 210°   **6.** 360°

Acute	Right	Obtuse	Straight	Reflex	Complete
....	....	....	....	....	....

B. Define—

7. a zero angle   **8.** an acute angle   **9.** a right angle

10. an obtuse angle   **11.** a straight angle **12.** a reflex angle

13. a complete angle   **14.** adjacent angles   **15.** supplementary angles

16. complementary angles   **17.** alternate angles   **18.** corresponding angles

19. vertically opposite angles

C. Given below are figures showing *adjacent angles, complementary angles, supplementary angles, alternate angles, corresponding angles, vertically opposite angles* **and** *adjacent supplementary angles.* **Write below each figure, the angles that it shows.**

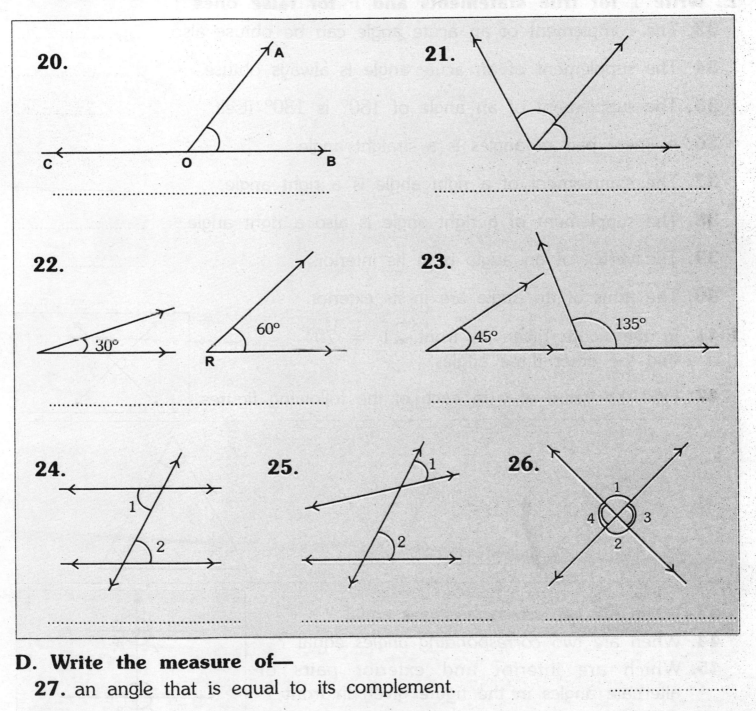

20.

....

21.

....

22.

30°

60°

R

....

23.

45°

135°

....

24.

1

2

....

25.

1

2

....

26.

1

4   3

2

....

D. Write the measure of—

27. an angle that is equal to its complement.   ....

28. an angle that is equal to its supplement.   ....

29. an angle that is twice its supplement. ....

30. an angle that is twice its complement. ....

31. an angle that is 4 times its supplement. ....

32. an angle that is 4 times its complement. ....

E. Write *T* for true statements and *F* for false ones :

33. The complement of an acute angle can be obtuse also. ....

34. The supplement of an acute angle is always obtuse. ....

35. The supplement of an angle of 180° is 180° itself. ....

36. A linear pair of angles is a straight angle. ....

37. The complement of a right angle is a right angle. ....

38. The supplement of a right angle is also a right angle. ....

39. The vertex of an angle is in its interior. ....

40. The arms of an angle are in its exterior. ....

F. 41. In the figure given in front, ∠1 = 70°
find the other three angles.

42. Find the value of *y* in each of the following figures.

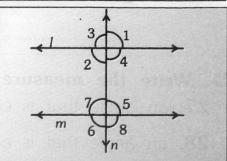

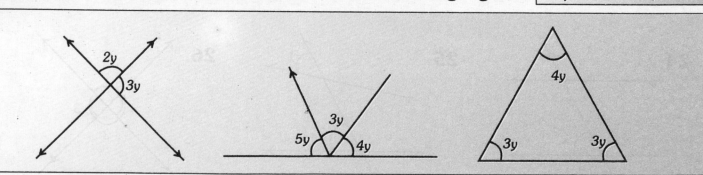

43. When are two *alternate angles* equal ?

44. When are two *corresponding angles* equal ?

45. Which are interior and exterior pairs of
alternate angles in the figure given in front ?

21 TRIANGLES OR TRIGONS

WHAT FORMS A TRIANGLE ?

Let us take three non-collinear points A, B and C. If we join them in pairs, we shall get three line-segments that will be meeting one another at the points A, B, C.

Viewed from another angle, two line-segments taken at a time will form an angle. The vertex of this angle will be at the point common in the two line-segments. In this way, we shall have three **angles**— ∠ **ABC**, ∠ **ACB** and ∠ **BAC**.

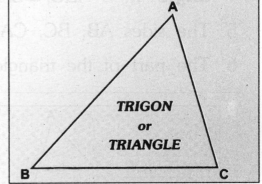

TRIGON
or
TRIANGLE

The arms of these three angles will enclose a figure. This figure will be formed of the **interiors** of these three angles. The interiors will be overlapping one another. Also, the arms of the three angles will form the three sides of the figure enclosed by them. These **sides** will be **AB, BC** and **CA**.

In the light of the above discussion, it is not difficult to understand that the **three-sided** (three-angled) figure mentioned above can be named in two different ways :

(a) If we name it as a figure formed by three angles, we shall call it a **triangle**.

(b) If we name it as a figure bounded by three sides, we shall call it a **trigon**. Just as we call a figure with five sides a **pentagon** and a figure with eight sides an **octagon**.

The symbol used for a triangle or trigon in mathematics is Δ.

A triangle ABC can be named in any of the following three ways—Δ ABC or Δ BCA or Δ CAB.

MORE ABOUT TRIANGLES

The following facts regarding triangles are very important :

1. A triangle has six chief parts—**three sides** and **three angles**. These six parts are called the **six elements** of a triangle.

2. The three points at which the sides of a triangle meet or the three angles are formed, are called its **vertices** or **angular points.** A, B, C of the triangle ABC are its angular points.

3. The side on which a triangle rests is called its **base**. BC is the *base* of △ ABC.

4. The angle opposite to the base of a triangle is called its **vertical angle**. In △ ABC, ∠BAC or ∠A is its vertical angle.

5. The sides AB, BC, CA mark the boundary of △ ABC.

6. The part of the triangle's plane inside its sides is called its **interior.**

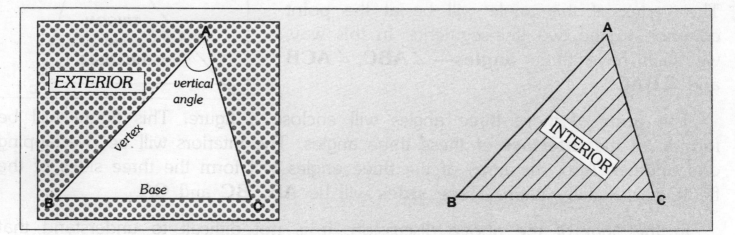

7. The part of the triangle's plane outside its sides is called its **exterior**.

8. If all the three sides of a triangle are of the same length, all its three **angle are also equal**.

9. If two sides of a triangle are equal, **the angles opposite to these equal sides are also equal**.

10. Inversely, if the three angles of a triangle are equal, **all its sides are also equal.**

11. If two angles of a triangle are equal, **the sides opposite to these equal angles are also equal.**

12. Any **two sides of a triangle are together > its third side.**

13. The sum of the angles of a triangle is always **180°**, *i.e.* **two right angles**.

14. If one side of a triangle is produced, the angle formed outside the triangle is called its **exterior angle**.

15. The *exterior angle* of a triangle is always equal to the sum of the two **interior opposite angles**.

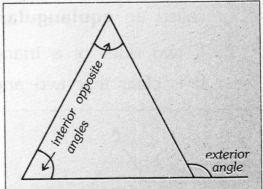

16. The line joining a vertex of a triangle with the middle point of the opposite side is called its **median**.

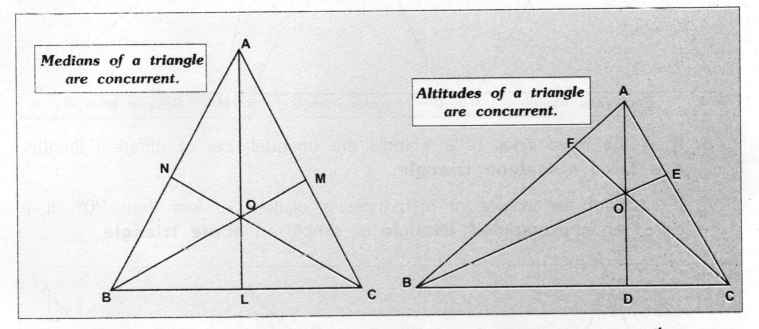

17. All the three medians of a triangle are **concurrent,** *i.e.* they pass through the same point.

18. If a line drawn from a vertex of a triangle is perpendicular to the opposite side, this line is called the **altitude** of the triangle.

19. All the three altitudes of a triangle are also **concurrent,** *i.e.* they pass through the same point.

TYPES OF TRIANGLES

There are several types of triangles. These types have been named keeping in view the sides and angles of triangles :

1. If the three sides of a triangle are of the same length, the triangle is called an **equilateral triangle**.

It is clear that an equilateral triangle has all its angles equal. So, it is called an **equiangular triangle** as well.

2. If two sides of a triangle are equal, it is called an **isosceles triangle**. It is clear that two angles of an isosceles triangle are also equal.

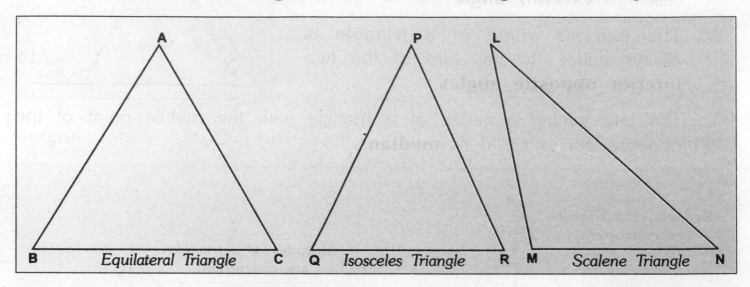

Equilateral Triangle   Isosceles Triangle   Scalene Triangle

3. If all the three sides of a triangle are unequal, *i.e.* of different lengths, it is called a **scalene triangle**.

4. If each of the angles of a triangle is acute, *i.e.* less than 90°, it is called an **acute-angled triangle** or simply an **acute triangle**.

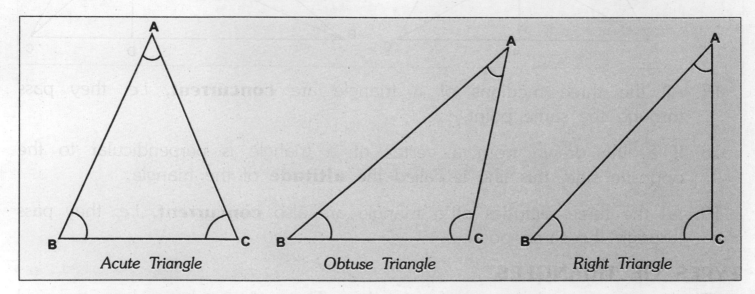

Acute Triangle   Obtuse Triangle   Right Triangle

5. If one of the angle of a triangle is a *right angle*, it is called a **right-angled triangle** or simply a **right triangle**.

6. If one of the angles of a triangle is an *obtuse angle*, it is called an **obtuse-angled triangle** or simply an **obtuse triangle**.

Example 1 : **The angles of a triangle are in the ratio 3:4:5. Determine its angles.**

Solution : Suppose the angles of triangle ABC are $3x°$, $4x°$, $5x°$

∵ The sum of the angles of a $\triangle$ ABC $= 180°$

∴ $\angle 3x° + \angle 4x° + \angle 5°x = 180°$

or $12x° \qquad\qquad\qquad = 180°$

or $12x \qquad\qquad\qquad = 180$ or $x = 15$

∴ The angles of the triangle $= \textbf{45°, 60°, 75°}$ **Ans.**

Example 2 : **An isosceles triangle has one of its equal angles measuring 75°. Find its third angle also.**

Solution : An isosceles $\triangle$ has two of its angles equal.

One of the equal angles $= 75°$

∴ The other equal angle $= 75°$

Now sum of the three angles of a $\triangle = 180°$

Sum of the two equal angles $= 75° + 75° = 150°$

The third angle $\qquad\qquad = 180° - 150° = \textbf{30°Ans.}$

Example 3 : **In a triangle ABC, $2\angle A = \angle 3\angle B = 6\angle C$. Find the measures of angles A, B and C.**

Solution : $2 \angle A = 3 \angle B$ or $\angle A = \dfrac{3}{2} \angle B$

$6 \angle C = 3 \angle B$ or $\angle C = \dfrac{3}{6} \angle B = \dfrac{1}{2} \angle B$

Now $\angle A + \angle B + \angle C = 180°$

or $\dfrac{3}{2} \angle B + \angle B + \dfrac{1}{2} \angle B = 180°$

or $\left(\dfrac{3}{2} + 1 + \dfrac{1}{2}\right) \angle B = 180°$

or $3 \angle B = 180°$ or $\angle B = \textbf{60°}$

$\angle A = \dfrac{3}{2} \angle B = \dfrac{3}{2} \times 60° = \dfrac{180°}{2} = \textbf{90°}$

$\angle C = \dfrac{1}{2} \angle B = \dfrac{1}{2} \times 60° = \dfrac{60°}{2} = \textbf{30°}$

So, $\angle A = \textbf{90°}, \angle B = \textbf{60°}, \angle C = \textbf{30°}$ **Ans.**

Example 4 : In a $\triangle$ ABC, vertical $\angle A = 40°$. The bisectors of angles B and C meet in O. Find $\angle BOC$.

Solution :

In $\triangle$ ABC

$$\angle A + \angle B + \angle C = 180°$$

or $40° + \angle B + \angle C = 180°$ [$\because \angle A = 40°$

or $\angle B + \angle C = 180° - 40° = 140°$

or $\dfrac{1}{2}\angle B + \dfrac{1}{2}\angle C = 140° \div 2 = 70°$

Now in $\triangle$ OBC

$$\angle 1 = \dfrac{1}{2}\angle B \text{ and } \angle 2 = \dfrac{1}{2}\angle C$$

$$\angle 1 + 2 = \dfrac{1}{2}\angle B + \dfrac{1}{2}\angle C = 70°$$

Also, we know that—

$$\angle 1 + \angle 2 + \angle BOC = 180° \quad (\angle s \text{ of a } \triangle)$$

or $70° + \angle BOC = 180° \quad (\angle 1 + \angle 2 = 70°)$

or $\angle BOC = 180° - 70° = \textbf{110° Ans.}$

PRACTICE EXERCISES 33

A. Answer in short :

1. What is a figure with three sides called ? ....

2. What is a figure with three angles called ? ....

3. In which two other ways can we name $\triangle$ ABC ? ....

4. How many vertices are there of a triangle ? ....

5. What is the other word for *vertex* ? ....

6. What do we call the side of $\triangle$ on which it rests ? ....

7. What is the angle opposite the base of a $\triangle$ called ? ....

8. What do the sides of a triangle mark ? ....

9. What do the sides of a triangle enclose ? ....

10. What do the sides of a triangle separate ? ....

11. What is the other name for an equilateral triangle ? ....

12. What is a triangle with two equal sides called ? ....

13. What is the sum of the angles of a triangle equal to ? ....

14. What is an exterior angle of a triangle equal to ? ....

15. How many right angles are there in a right triangle ? ....

16. How many acute angles are these in a right triangle ? ....

17. How many obtuse angles are there in an obtuse triangle ? ....

18. How many elements are there of a triangle ? ....

19. Which symbol is used for a triangle ? ....

B. Define—

20. interior of a triangle	21. a scalene triangle
22. exterior of a triangle	23. exterior angle of a triangle
24. median of a triangle	25. altitude of a triangle
26. an acute triangle	27. a right triangle
28. vertical angle of a triangle	29. an isosceles triangle

C. Fill up each blank :

30. The exterior angle of a triangle .... each of the interior opposite angles.

31. The sum of the angles of a triangle is equal to .... right angles.

32. The elements of a triangle include its three .... and three ....

33. A triangle has .... vertices, ... angles and .... sides.

34. A triangle with all its sides unequal is called a .... triangle.

35. The *medians* and *altitudes* of a triangle are ....

36. A triangle's plane outside its boundary is called its ....

37. A triangle's plane inside its boundary is called its ....

38. The three sides of a triangle mark its ....

39. An exterior angle of a triangle is equal to two .... angles.

40. Any two .... of a triangle are together greater than its ....

41. The angles of a triangle are in the ratio 2 : 3 : 4. Find their measures.

42. Observe the figure given in front closely. Find the sum of $\angle A + \angle B + \angle C + \angle D + \angle E + \angle F$.

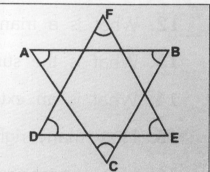

43. If one angle of triangle is equal to the sum of the other two angles, prove that the triangle is right-angled.

44. The acute angles of a right triangle are in the ratio 2 : 3. Find their measures.

45. In a triangle ABC, $3\angle A = 4\angle B = 6\angle C$. Find $\angle A$, $\angle B$ and $\angle C$.

46. If the three sides of a triangle are produced in order. What will be the sum of the measures of the three exterior angles so formed ?

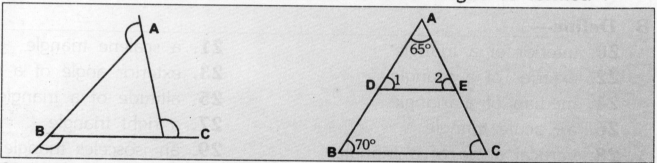

47. Observe the figure given above on the right. There is a triangle ABC with $\angle A = 65°$ and $\angle B = 70°$. DE is drawn parallel to BC. Find the measures of $\angle C$, $\angle 1$ and $\angle 2$ respectively.

48. A right triangle is isosceles also. Find its two acute angles.

49. In a given triangle ABC, $\angle A = 80°$. The bisecters of $\angle B$ and $\angle C$ meet in $\angle P$. Find the measure of $\angle BPC$.

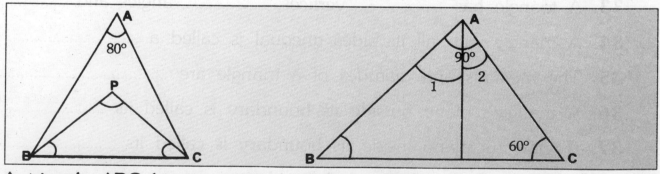

50. A triangle ABC has its vertical angle = 90° and $\angle C = 60°$. Also, AL is drawn perpendicular to BC. Find the measures of $\angle B$, $\angle 1$ and 2.

51. Which of the following sets of sides can enclose a triangle ?

(a) 3 cm, 4 cm, 5 cm   *(b)* 2 cm, 3 cm, 4 cm   *(c)* 6 cm, 7 cm, 8 cm

> *KNOW THESE TERMS :*
> 1. **equidistant**—at an equal distance from two or more points/lines etc.
> 2. **circumference**—boundary-line of a circle
> 3. **concentric circles**—circles that have one and the same centre
> 4. **compasses**—a geometrical instrument used for describing circles

Look around yourself you will see many objects which are circular in shape. The **wheels** of various *vehicles*, **coins, clocks** and **watches**, the **globe**, the **full moon**, the **sun** and all **discs** are like circles in shape.

A *circle* **is a round plane figure whose boundary-line is everywhere equidistant from a fixed point inside it.**

The boundary of a circle is an endless curved line made of points closely set together. Each of these points is equidistant from a fixed point called *centre*. Remember the following facts about circles :

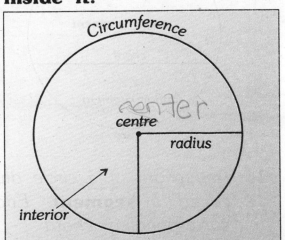

1. *The fixed point mentioned above forms the* **centre** *of the circle.*

2. *The boundary-line of the circle is called its* **circumference**.

3. *The ever-equal distance between the centre and the circumference is called the* **radius** *of the circle.*

4. The part of the circle's plane inside its boundary is called its **interior.**

5. The part of the circle's plane outside its boundary is called its **exterior.**

6. A line-segment passing through the circle's centre and having its end-points on its boundary is called **diameter. Diameter = 2 × radius.**

7. A line-segment having its end-points on the boundary of a circle is called a **chord** of the circle. **Diameter is the largest chord of a circle.**

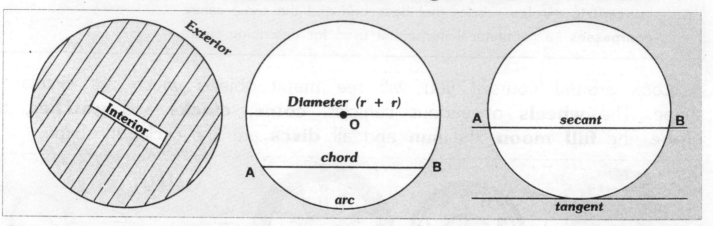

8. A part of the circle's boundary is called an **arc.** It is a curved segment of the circumference.

9. A line passing through a circle's interior and intersecting its boundary at two points is called a **secant.**

10. A line that passes just touching the boundary of a circle at a point is called a **tangent.**

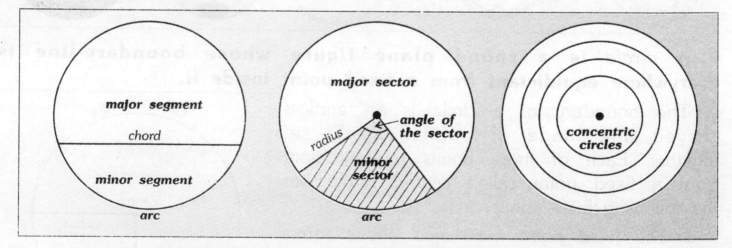

11. Any chord of a circle divides its interior into two parts. Each of them is called a **segment.** Each segment is enclosed by an arc and the corresponding chord.

A segment smaller than a semi-cirlce is called a **minor segment.**

A segment larger than a semi-circle is called a **major segment.**

12. *The part of the interior of a circle cut off by two radii is called a* **sector**. *A sector smaller than half the interior of a circle is called a* **minor sector**. *A sector larger than half the interior of a circle is called a* **major sector**.

13. *A sector is enclosed by two radii and the arc joining their end-points.*

14. *The angle that a sector makes at the centre of the circle is called the* **angle of the sector**.

15. *Two or more circles drawn with one and the same centre are called* **concentric circles**.

HOW TO DRAW A CIRCLE

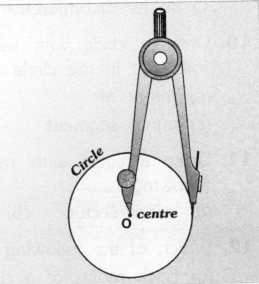

In order to draw a circle, we need a pair of compasses. Take any point *(say O)* to be used as the centre of the required circle. Place the tip of the needle-arm of your compasses on O. Then open the other arm according to the size of the circle you want to draw. Let the pencil touch the paper and turn the pencil-arm of the compasses along the paper. The tip of the pencil will describe a circle.

HOW TO FIND THE CENTRE OF A CIRCLE

1. Take a bangle made of steel or glass. Place it on the paper and hold it firmly with your left hand.

2. Trace the inside boundary of the bangle with a sharp pencil. You will get a circle. Now we are to find the centre of this circle.

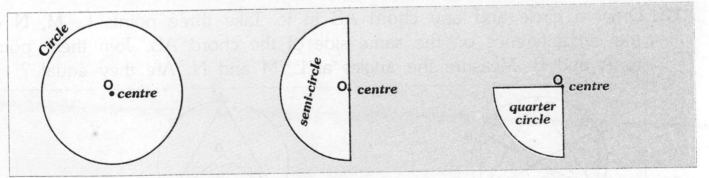

3. Cut the paper along the boundary of the circle described above. You will get a circular piece of paper.

4. Fold this round piece into two semi-circles and get a crease.

5. Again fold the semi-circle into a quarter circle and get another crease.

6. The tip of the quarter circle will mark the centre of the circle.

A. Using your compasses, draw circles with the following radii—

1. 2·5 cm.   **2.** 3·5 cm.   **3.** 4·2 cm.   **4.** 5 cm.

B. Draw circles with the following diameters :

5. 5 cm.   **6.** 7·6 cm.   **7.** 8 cm.   **8.** 6·6 cm.

C. 9. Draw a circle with radius 4 cm. Mark a point P in its interior, a point Q on its circumference and a point R in its exterior.

10. Draw a circle with radius 3·5 cm. Draw a chord AB and mark the following in the circle :

(a) minor arc   (b) major arc

(c) minor segment   (d) major segment

11. Draw a circle with radius 3 cm. Draw its two radii and mark the following :

(a) minor sector   (b) major sector   (c) angles of both the sectors

12. Which of the following statements are true :

(a) Each radius of a circle forms a chord.   (   )

(b) The area between two radii is called a sector.   (   )

(c) Diameter of a circle is its largest chord.   (   )

(d) A segment of a circle is enclosed by an arc and a chord.   (   )

(e) A secant just touches a circle at a point.   (   )

(f) The circumference of a circle is double its radius.   (   )

13. Draw a circle and any chord AB in it. Take three points L, M, N on the circumference on the same side of the chord AB. Join these points to A and B. Measure the angles at L, M and N. Are they equal ?

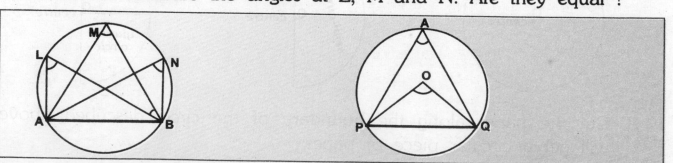

14. Draw a circle and any chord PQ. Join P, Q to the centre O and to any point A on the circumference. Measure ∠POQ and ∠PAQ. What is the ratio between them ?

23 PRACTICAL GEOMETRY—I

KNOW THESE TERMS :
1. **protractor**—a geometrical instrument used to measure and draw angles
2. **set-squares**—two three-side plates each with a right angle. They are used for drawing and testing angles and parallel lines.
3. **compasses**—a geometrical instrument with two legs used for drawing circles, arcs etc.

Practical geometry means drawing various geometrical plane figures using geometrical instruments. In this lesson, we shall learn how to draw angles of various sizes.

A. USING A PROTRACTOR

Example 1 : Draw an angle of 60° using a protractor.

Steps :
1. Draw a ray AB with its initial-point at A.
2. Place the centre of the protractor at A. Adjust its edge so that its zero-mark may coincide with AB.
3. Starting from the side of the B-mark reach the 60° mark on the protractor.
4. Mark a dot just against the 60°-mark.
5. Remove the protractor and join AC.

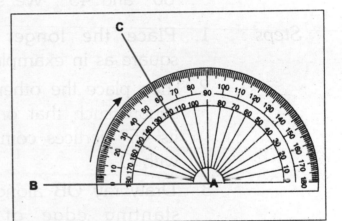

BAC will be equal to 60°.

B. USING SET-SQUARES

There are two set-squares in a geometry-box. One of them has angles of 90°, 30°, 60°. It is the longer set-square.

The other set-square has angles of 90°, 45°, 45°. It is the shorter set-square.

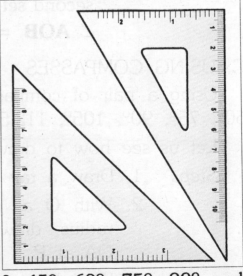

So, using set-squares, we can draw angles of 30°, 45°, 60°, 75°, 90° and 105°. Let us draw an angle of 60° using set-squares.

Steps :

1. Draw a ray OA.

2. Place a ruler along OA.

3. Place the longer set-square such that its 60°-edge falls along the ruler.

4. Move the set-square along the edge of the ruler so that its 60° vertex coincides with point O.

5. Draw ray OB along its slanting edge.

   ∠ **AOB will be equal to 60°.**

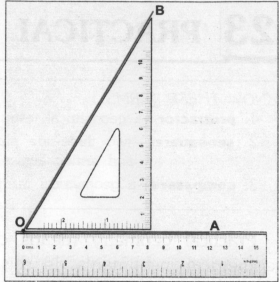

Example 2. Draw an angle of 105° using set-squares.

In order to draw an angle of 105° using set-squares, we shall use both the set-squares to draw adjacent angles of 60° and 45°. We shall proceed as under :

Steps :

1. Place the longer set-square as in example 1.

2. Then place the other set-square such that one of its 45° vertices coincides with O.

3. Draw ray OB along the slanting edge of the second set-square.

   ∠ **AOB = 60° + 45°**

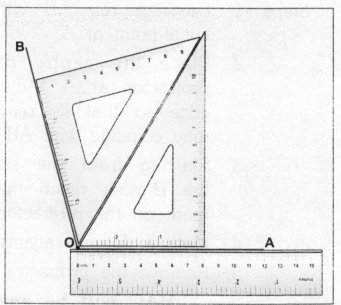

C. USING COMPASSES

Using a pair of compasses and a ruler, we can draw angles of 30°, 45°, 60°, 75°, 90°, 105°, 112·5°, 120°, 150° etc.

Let us see how to draw an angle of 60°.

Steps : 1. Draw a ray OA.

2. With O as centre and a proper radius, draw an arc that meets OA at P.

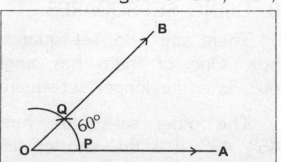

3. With P as centre and the same radius, draw another arc that cuts the previous arc at Q.

4. Join OQ and produce it to make a ray OB
   ∠**AOB is the required angle of 60°.**

Example 3 : Draw an angle of 120° using compasses.

Steps :
1. Draw a ray OA as in the above example.
2. With O as centre and a proper radius, draw a big arc that meets OA at P.
3. With P as centre and the same radius draw an arc that cuts the previous big arc at Q.

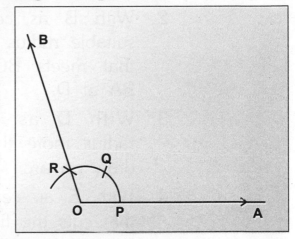

4. Again with Q as center and the same radius, draw another arc that cuts the big arc at R again.
5. Join OR and produce it into ray OB.
   ∠ **AOR is the required angle of 120°.**

Example 4 : Draw an angle of 90° using compasses.

Steps.
1. Draw a ray OA.
2. With O as centre and a proper radius, draw an arc that meets OA at P.
3. With P as centre and the same radius draw an arc that cuts the first arc at Q.

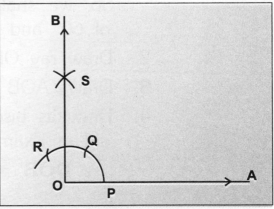

4. Again with Q as centre and the same radius draw another arc that cuts the first arc at R again.
5. With Q and R as centres respectively and the same radius, draw two arcs that cut each other at S.
6. Join OS and produce it to make Ray OB
   ∠**AOB is the required angle.**

BISECTING ANGLES

We can bisect a given angle using compasses and a ruler. Let us see how to do it..

Example 5. Bisect a given angle using compasses.

Steps :

1. Let ∠ ABC be the given angle to be bisected.

2. With B as centre and a suitable radius draw an arc that meets BC at E and BA at D.

3. With D as centre and radius more than half DE, draw an arc.

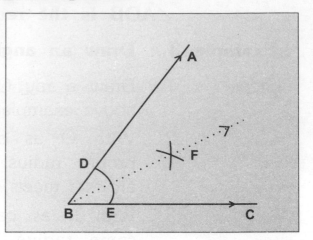

4. With E as centre and the same radius draw another arc that cuts the first arc at F.

5. Join BF and produce it.
   This ray BF is the required bisector.

Example 6. Draw an angle of 30° using compasses.

Steps :

1. We know that 30° = 60° ÷ 2 So, we shall draw an angle of 60° and then bisect it.

2. Draw ray OB.

3. Draw ∠AOB = 60° *(as in Ex. 1)*

4. Draw its bisector OD as you did in Example 5 above.

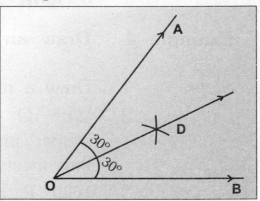

∠ **DOB = 30° and also** ∠ **AOD = 30°.**

Example 7. Draw an angle of 45° using compasses.

Steps :

1. We know that 45° = 90° ÷ 2 So, we shall draw an angle of 90° and then bisect it.

2. Draw a ray BC.
   Draw ∠ABC = 90° *(as in Ex. 4)*

3. Draw BD the bisector of ∠ ABC

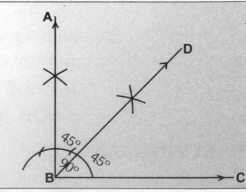

∠ **ABD = 45° and also** ∠ **CBD = 45°.**

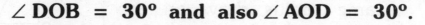

A. Define—

    1. a protractor   **2.** compasses   **3.** set-squares

B. Draw the following angles using your protractor :

    4. 80°   **5.** 110°   **6.** 170°

    Draw the bisector of each of these angles :

C. Construct the following angles using set-squares :

    7. 60°   **8.** 90°   **9.** 105°

    10. 75°   **11.** 120°   **12.** 135°

C. Answers *yes* **or** *no* **:**

    13. We can draw an angle of 1° using a protractor.   ....

    14. We cannot draw a straight angle using a protractor.   ....

    15. Either of the set-squares has a circular edge.   ....

    16. The longer set-square has an angle of 30° also.   ....

    17. The shorter set-square has two equal angles of 45°.   ....

    18. A circle forms an angle of 360°.   ....

D. Measure these angles :

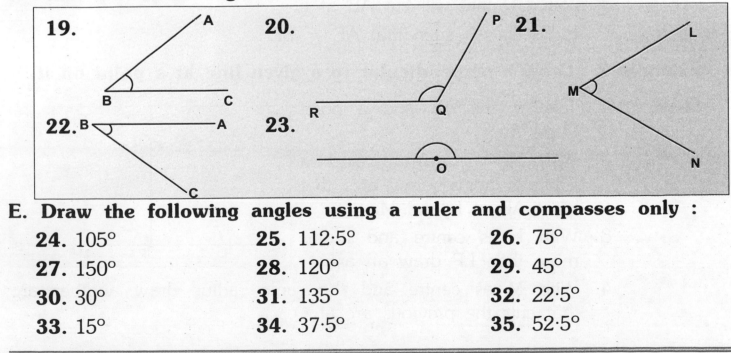

E. Draw the following angles using a ruler and compasses only :

    24. 105°   **25.** 112·5°   **26.** 75°

    27. 150°   **28.** 120°   **29.** 45°

    30. 30°   **31.** 135°   **32.** 22·5°

    33. 15°   **34.** 37·5°   **35.** 52·5°

PRACTICAL GEOMETRY—II

We studied in the previous chapter how to construct angles using protractor, set-squares and compasses. In this chapter, we shall study some more **constructions**.

Example 1. Bisect a given line segment AB.

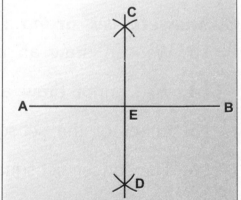

Steps :   1. Draw a line-segment AB = 5 cm.

2. With A as centre and radius more than half AB draw arcs on both sides of AB.

3. With B as centre and the same radius draw arcs on both sides of AB cutting the previous arcs in C and D respectively.

4. Join CD that will cut AB at E.

   E bisects AB such that AE = BE

Example 2 : Draw a perpendicular to a given line at a point on it.

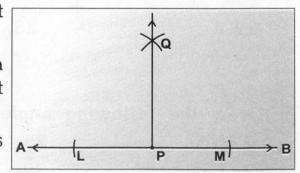

Steps :   1. Take a line AB and a point P on it.

2. With P as centre and a suitable radius, draw arcs that meet AB at L and M.

3. With L as centre and radius more than LP draw an arc.

4. With M as centre and the same radius draw another arc that cuts the previous arc at Q.

5. Join PQ and produce it. **QP is the required perpendicular**, *i.e.* QP perpendicular to AB. Measure the angles QPA and QPB.

Each of them will be equal to 90°.

Example 3. Draw a perpendicular to a given line from a given point outside it.

Steps :

1. We are given a line AB and a point P outside it.

2. With P as centre and a suitable radius draw an arc that cuts AB at C and D.

3. Now, with C as centre and a radius more than half CD draw an arc.

4. Again with D as centre and the same radius, draw another arc that cuts the previous arc at E.

5. Join PE that cuts AB at F.

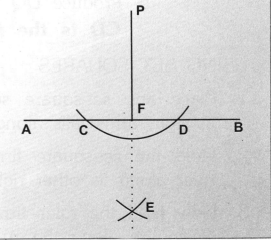

Then PF is the required perpendicular.

Example 4. Draw an angle equal to a given angle.

Steps :

1. We are given an angle ABC.

2. With B as centre and any radius, draw an arc cutting BA at L and BC at M.

3. Now draw any ray QR.

4. With Q as centre and the same radius (as in 2) draw an arc cutting QR at D.

5. With D as centre and radius equal to LM cut the above arc at E.

6. Join QE and produce it into ray QP

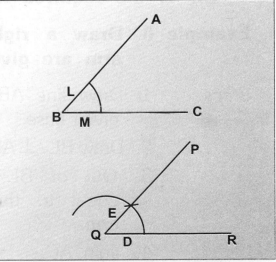

∠PQR will be the required angle equal to ∠ABC.

Example 5. Draw a line parallel to a given line through a given point outside it.

Steps :

1. We have a line AB and a point Q outside.
2. Take any point P on AB.
3. Join PQ.
4. Draw ∠PQD = alternate ∠QPA
5. Produce DQ to C to form line CD

CD is the required line parallel to AB.

USING SET SQUARES

1. Place any set-square such that one of its right arms falls along AB.
2. Hold the set-square firmly and place a ruler along its other right arm.
3. Now hold the ruler firmly and slide the set-square along the ruler towards point Q.
4. When the set square's edge touches point Q, hold it fast and let the ruler go.
5. Draw a line CD along the edge of the set-square through Q.

CD is the required line parallel to AB.

Example 6. Draw a right ∠d triangle whose base and the right arm are given.

Steps :

1. Draw line AB equal to the given *base*.
2. Draw BL ⊥ AB.
3. Out of BL, cut off BC equal to the given right arm.
4. Join AC.

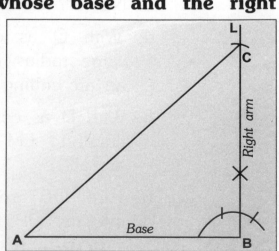

ABC is the required right triangle.

A. 1. Draw a line segment AB = 5 cm. Find its middle point using compasses and a ruler. Measure both the parts of AB. Are they equal ?

2. Draw a line-segment PQ = 7 cm. Draw its right bisector.

3. Draw a line-segment LM = 6 cm. Draw MN perpendicular to LM.

4. Draw a line-segment CD = 6·5 cm. Take any point P on CD. Raise PQ perpendicular to CD.

5. Draw a line segment EF = 5·8 cm. Draw a perpendicular to EF from a given point P outside EF.

6. Draw angle of 75° using a protractor. Now draw an angle equal to it using compasses and a ruler.

7. Construct an angle of 60° using compasses. Bisect it using compasses. Measure its parts. What is their measure ?

8. Draw an angle of 90°. Bisect it using compasses. Measure either part. Is it 45° ?

9. Draw a line-segment PQ. Take a point M outside it. Through M draw LMN parallel to PQ using—

(a) set-squares   (b) compasses

10. Draw a right triangle ABC whose base BC is equal to 3 cm. and the right arm CA = 4 cm. Measure AB.

11. Draw an angle PQR = 60° with QR = 5 cm. and PQ = 4 cm. Draw a line parallel to PQ through R. Also, draw a line parallel to QR through P. Let these lines cut each other at S. Measure PS and RS.

12. Given below are two angles. Draw an angle equal to either angle using compasses in the box.

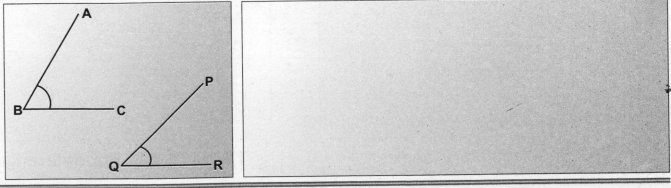

A. Define the following :

1. Point
2. Line
3. Plane
4. Collinear Points
5. Parallel Lines
6. Line Segment
7. A Ray
8. Angle

B. Shown below are some angles. Name each of them :

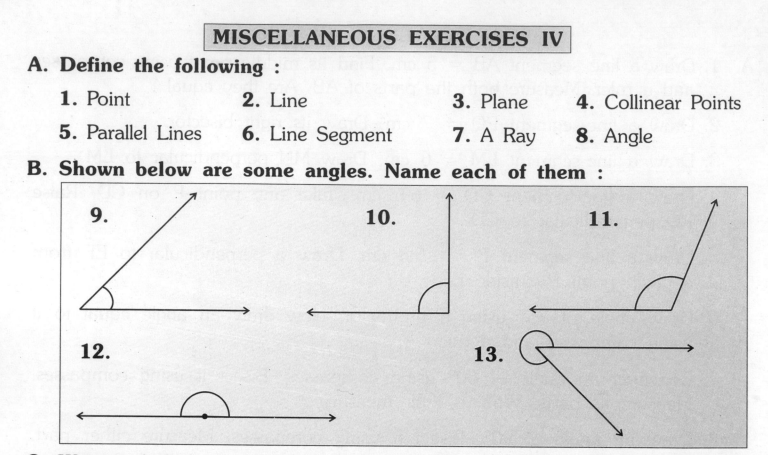

9. 10. 11.

12. 13.

C. Written below are names of some pairs of angles. Draw a diagram for each :

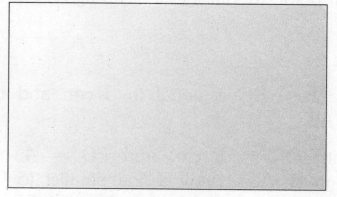

14. Adjacent angles

15. Complementary angles

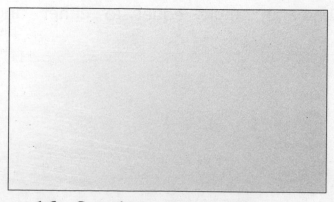

16. Supplementary angles

17. Vertically opposite angles

18. Alternate angles

19. Corresponding angles

D. Answer *yes* **or** *no* :

20. A triangle is another word for a *trigon*. ....

21. A vertex is also called an *angular point*. ....

22. The *interior* of a triangle is outside its sides. ....

23. Two sides of an *isosceles triangle* are equal. ....

24. Equilateral triangles are *equiangular* also. ....

25. An *acute triangle* has one of its angles less than 90°. ....

26. A *right triangle* has all its angles equal to 90°. ....

E. Name the following :

27. The angle opposite the base of a triangle ....

28. The side on which a triangle rests ....

29. An angle between 180° and 360° ....

30. A triangle with all its sides of different lengths ....

31. Perpendicular from a vertex to the opposite side of a triangle ....

32. The line marking the boundary of a circle ....

33. The line joining the centre of a circle with its circumference ....

34. A line that passes just touching a circle ....

35. The instrument used to draw circles ....

36. The instrument used to draw and measure angles ....

F. Using only *a scale* **and** *compasses*, **draw the following angles :**

37. 60°   **38.** 30°   **39.** 90°   **40.** 45°

41. 105°   **42.** 120°   **43.** 150°   **44.** $112\frac{1}{2}°$

G. Draw the following :

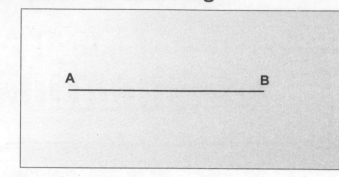

45. Bisector of Line AB.

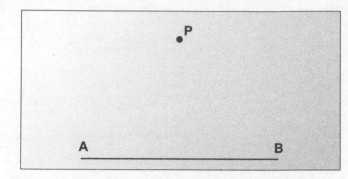

46. Perpendicular from P to AB

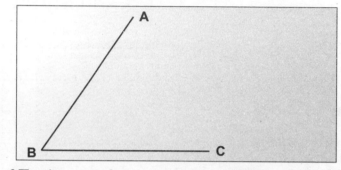

47. An angle equal to ∠ABC

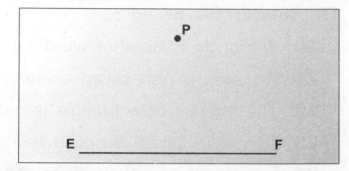

48. PQR parallel to EF through Q

MEMORABLE FACTS

1. A point has **no dimensions**.
2. A line has **only length** as its dimension.
3. **Innumerable lines** can be drawn through a *point*.
4. **Only one line** can be drawn through *two given points*.
5. More than two points lying on a line are said to be **collinear**.
6. Three or more lines passing through the same point are called **concurrent lines**.
7. A line-segment has **two end-points**.
8. A ray has only one end-point called its **initial point**.
9. Two rays starting from the same initial point and making a straight lineare called **opposite rays**.
10. A line cutting two or more other lines each at a point is called a **transversal**.
11. If a transversal cuts two parallel lines, then—
    (a) pairs of **corresponding** angles are equal.
    (b) pairs of **alternate angles** are equal.
    (c) **interior angles on the same side of the transversal** are supplementary.

MENSURATION

Mensuration is a branch of measurement that measures *distance* (length), *surfaces* (areas) and *space* (volumes).

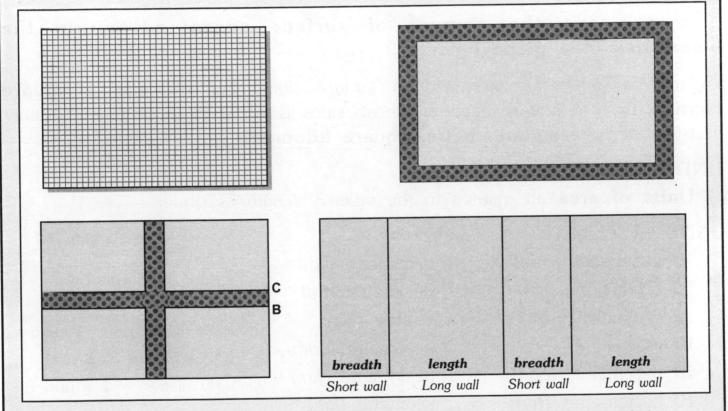

breadth *length* *breadth* *length*
Short wall Long wall Short wall Long wall

1. **Distance/Length** means the measurement between two points.
2. **Surface/Area** means the measurement of the total expanse of a surface.
3. **Space/Volume** means the measurement of the total space occupied by an object.

IN THIS UNIT—
25. Measurement of Area
26. Measurement of Volume

25 MEASUREMENT OF AREA

WHAT IS AREA ?

Area **means the amount of surface contained within the boundaries of a plane figure.**

Area is generally expressed in *square units*. For example, a **square centimetre** is a square each of whose sides is equal to 1 centimetre. Other units of area are **square metre, square kilometre** etc.

UNITS OF AREA

Units of area are related to the *units of length* as under :

UNITS OF LENGTH

10 millimetres *(mm)*	= 1 centimetre *(cm)*
10 centimetres *(cm)*	= 1 decimetre *(dm)*
10 decimetres *(dm)*	= **1 metre (m)**
10 metres *(m)*	= 1 decametre *(dam)*
10 decametres *(dam)*	= 1 hectometre *(hm)*
10 hectometres *(hm)*	= 1 kilometre *(km)*

> **From this table, we get that—**
>
> 1000 millimetres = **1 metre**
> 100 centimetre = **1 metre**
> 1000 metres = **1 kilometre**

UNITS OF AREA

10 mm × 10mm	= 100mm²	= 1cm²
10 cm × 10 cm	= 100 cm²	= 1dm²
10 dm × 10 dm	= 100 dm²	= 1m²
10 m × 10 m	= 100 m²	= 1 dam²
10 dam × 10 dam	= 100 dam²	= 1 hm²
10 hm × 10 hm	= 100 hm²	= 1 km²

1 cm.
1 cm.

10 cm.
10 cm.

From the above table, we get that—

10000 cm² = **1m²** and 1000000 m² = **1 km²**

MEASUREMENT OF AREA

Area of a plane figure can be measured using a **squared paper**. Such a paper is called a **graph paper** also. The area of each square on the squared paper is 1 sq. centimetre.

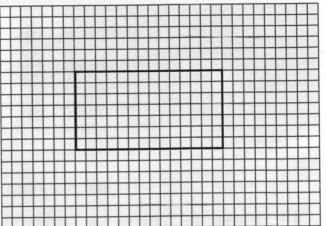

Suppose we want to find out the area of a **rectangle**. For that, we will take the following steps :

1. Trace the given rectangle on a tracing paper.

2. Place the traced rectangle on the squared paper.

3. Observe the squares fully covered by the traced rectangle.

4. Count these squares and multiply them by 1 square centimetre.

5. The product will be the area of the given rectangle.

The area of the rectangle in the front picture is **98 square cm.**

A. IRREGULAR FIGURES

Remember that squared papers are generally used to find out the areas of irregular figures. The diagram in front shows an irregular figure placed on a squared paper. In order to find out its area, proceed as under :

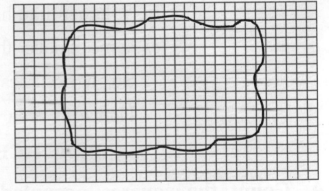

1. Count the full squares covered by the irregular figure.

2. Count the squares that are half the given square or larger than it.

3. Leave off the squares that are smaller than half the given square.

4. Add up the number of full squares to the number of half-squares and those larger than half-squares.

5. Multiply the total number of squares by 1 square centimetre. The product will be the area of the given irregular diagram.

Example 1. The triangle given on page 190 is drawn on a squared paper. Count the number of squares occupied by it and find its area if each square measures 1 sq. centimetre.

Solution : The figure in question occupies

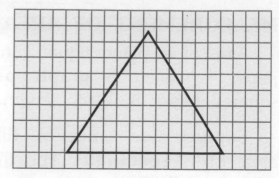

(a) 36 complete squares

(b) 8 larger-than-half squares

(c) 2 half-squares = 1 square

(d) 9 smaller-than-half squares

We shall neglect the smaller-than-half squares and take larger-than-half squares as full squares.

The triangle occupies 36 + 8 + 1 = 45 squares in all

Hence its area = **45 sq. cm.** *Ans.*

Example 2. **Trace a copy of the figure given in front on a squared paper and then find its area.**

Solution : Tracing the figure and placing it on the squared paper, we find—

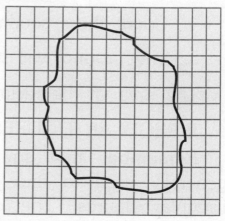

(a) it occupies 59 complete squares

(b) 9 larger-than-half squares

(c) some smaller-than-half squares

So, it occupies 59 + 9 squares

Hence its area = **68 sq. cm.** *Ans.*

PRACTICE EXERCISES 37

A. Count the squares occupied by each figure and find its area.

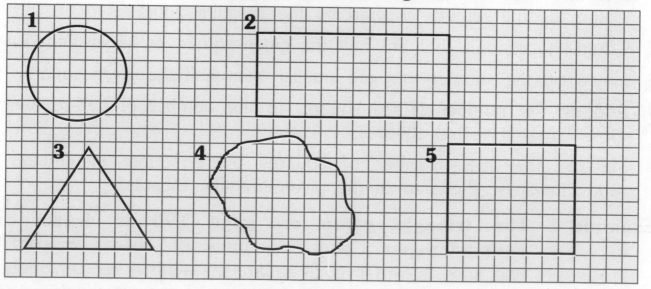

B. Using a centimetre squared paper find the area of each of the following figures :

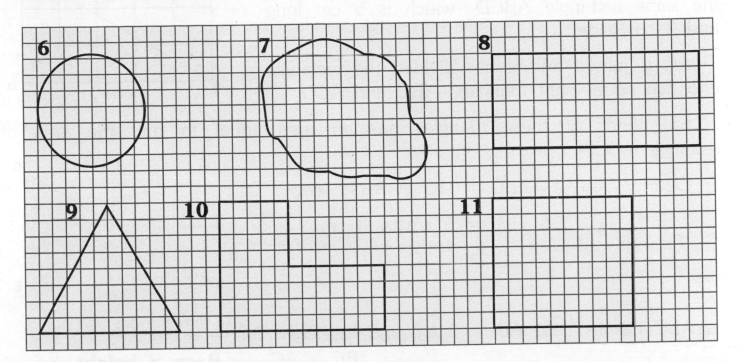

FINDING AREAS OF REGULAR FIGURES

Now we shall study the methods of finding areas of some regular figures—**rectangles, right triangles,** and **squares**.

A. AREA OF A RECTANGLE

Observe the figure given in front. It is a four-sided figure with each of its angles = 90° and opposite sides equal. Such a figure is called a **rectangle**. The length and breadth of a rectangle are unequal. So, it has an oblong shape.

Suppose, the given rectangle ABCD is 5 centimetres long and 3 centimetres wide. If we divide it into five equal parts *lengthwise* and into three equal parts *widthwise,* we shall have 15 equal squares. Each square will have its side equal to 1 cm. So, its area will be **1 square centimetre**.

Clearly, the area of the rectangle = Area of the 15 squares

$$= \textbf{15 sq. cm} = (5 \times 3) \text{ square cm.}$$
$$= 5 \text{ cm} \times 3 \text{ cm.} = \text{Length} \times \text{breadth}$$

So, **the area of a rectangle = Length × breadth**

B. AREA OF A RIGHT TRIANGLE

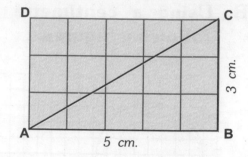

Now observe the figure given in front. It is the same rectangle ABCD which is 5 cm long and 3 cm wide.

AC is joined and it has divided the rectangle into two equal right triangles—ABC and ACD

So, either of these triangles has an area equal to half the area of rectangle ABCD.

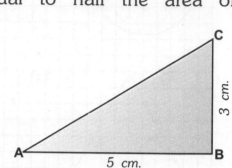

Clearly, area of $\triangle$ABC = (15 ÷ 2) sq. cm.

$$= \frac{5 \text{ cm} \times 3 \text{ cm}}{2}$$

$\triangle$ABC has its base AB = 5 cm and its height BC = 3 cm.

Hence the **area of a rt. triangle** $= \dfrac{BC \times AC}{2} = \dfrac{\textbf{Base} \times \textbf{height}}{\textbf{2}}$

C. AREA OF A SQUARE

A *square* **has all its four sides equal and each of its angles equal to 90º.**

Clearly, a square is a rectangle whose length and breadth are equal.

So, the **area of a square = side × side = (side)²**

PERIMETER

The word—**perimetre**—means *measure of all the sides of a plane figure taken together.* So—

1. **Perimetre of a Rectangle** = Length + breadth + length + breadth

                                      = **2 (length + breadth)**

2. **Perimetre of a square** = sides + side + side + side

                                      = **4 × side**

☞ CAUTION—While finding area or perimeter of a plane regular figure, its dimensions must be expressed in the same unit.

Example 1. **A rectangular field is 30 metres long and 15 metres wide. Find its area as well as perimetre.**

Solution :   Length of the field = 30 m.

Breadth of the field = 15 m.

Area of a rectangle = Length × Breadth

∴ Area of the field = 30 m × 15 m = **450 sq. m.** Ans.

Its perimetre   = 2 (Length + Breadth)

= 2 × (30 + 15)m = **90 metres** Ans.

Example 2. **A rectangular chart is 25 centimetres long and 16 centimetres wide. Find its area.**

Solution :   Length of the chart = 25 cm.

Breadth of the chart = 16 cm.

∴ Its area = 25 cm. × 16 cm. = **400 sq. cm.** Ans.

Example 3. **Find the area and perimeter of a square whose side is 16·4 cm.**

Solution :   The side of the given square = 16·4 cm.

∴ Area of a square = side × side = 16·4 cm. × 16·4 cm.

$$= \left(\frac{164}{10} \times \frac{164}{10}\right) cm^2 = \frac{37696}{100} cm^2$$

$$= \textbf{376·96 cm}^2$$

$$\left. \begin{array}{l} \\ \\ \\ \end{array} \right]$$ *Ans.*

Perimeter = 4 × side

$$= \left(4 \times \frac{164}{10}\right) cm. = \frac{656}{10} cm. = \textbf{65·6 cm.}$$

Example 4. **The area of a rectangular field is 1400 sq. metre. If its length be 40 m, find its breadth and perimeter.**

Solution :   Area of the rectangular field   = 1400 sq. m.

Length of the rectangular field = 40 m.

∴ Its Breadth = Area ÷ Length

= 1400 sq. m. ÷ 40 m. = **35 m.**

∴ Perimeter   = 2 (L + B) = 2 (40 + 35)m = **150 m.** Ans.

Example 5. A black-board is 2 metres long and 1 metre broad. Find the cost of painting it at Rs. 2·5 per sq. meter.

Solution :

Length of the black-board = 2 m.

Breadth of the black-board = 1 m.

∴ Area of the black-board = 2 × 1 = 2 sq. m.

Cost of painting per sq. metre = Rs. 2·5

∴ Total cost = 2 × 2·5 m. = **Rs. 5** *Ans.*

Example 6. A square bed-room has a side equal to 7 metres. Its floor is to be covered with tiles each measuring 35 cm. × 35 cm. If each tile costs 50 paise, find the total cost of tiling the bed-room.

Solution :

Side of the room = 7 m = 700 cm.

Area of the room = 700 cm. × 700 cm. = 490000 sq. cm.

Size of the tile = 35 cm. × 35 cm. = 1225 sq. cm.

∴ Reqd. No. of tiles = $490000 \times \dfrac{1}{1225}$ = 400

∴ Cost of tiling = Rs. $400 \times \dfrac{50}{100}$ = **Rs. 200** *Ans.*

Example 7. The cost of paving the floor of a square room at Rs. 10 per sq. m is Rs. 4000. Find the side of the room.

Solution :

The total cost = Rs. 4000

Cost per sq. m. = Rs. 10

Area of the room = Total Cost ÷ Cost per sq. m.

= Rs. 4000 ÷ Rs. 10 = 400 sq. m.

∴ Side of the room = $\sqrt{400}$ m. = **20 m.** *Ans.*

Example 8. A right triangle has its base = 8 cm. long and its height = 4 cm. Find its area.

Solution :

Base of the triangle = 8 cm.

height of the triangle = 4 cm.

Area of the triangle = (Base × height) ÷ 2

= (8 × 4) ÷ 2 sq. m.

= **16 sq. cm.** *Ans.*

194

A. Find the area of a rectangle whose—

1. length = 30 m	breadth = 12 m	
2. length = 35 m	breadth = 18 m	
3. length = 13 cm.	breadth = 7 cm.	
4. length = 46 cm.	breadth = 17 cm.	
5. length = 34 cm.	breadth = 18 cm.	

B. Find the area of a square whose side is—

6. 9 cm.	**7.** 16 cm.	**8.** 45 cm.
9. 18 cm.	**10.** 38 cm.	**11.** 56 cm.

C. 12. The length and breadth of a rectangular field are 34 metres and 18 metres respectively. Find the area of the field.

13. A room measures 9·68 metres long and 6·2 metres wide. Find its area. Also find how many tiles will be needed to pave it if the size of a tile = 22 cm. × 10 cm.

14. The length of an office is 8 metres while its breadth is 7·5 metres. What will be the cost of paving its floor at the rate of Rs. 8·50 per square metre ?

15. A square garden has its side measuring 65 m 5 dm. Find its area.

16. Find the cost of flooring a square room at Rs. 9 per square metre if its side is 8 metres.

17. The length of a playground is 62·60 metres while its breadth is 25·40 metres. Find the cost of turfing it at Rs. 2·50 per square metre ?

18. A lawn is 30 metres long and 15 metres wide. How long will it take a person to go along its borders and complete its one round at a speed of 2 metres per second ?

19. A rectanglular name-plate made of metal is 45 cm. long and 30 cm. wide. What will it cost if the metal sells at the rate of Rs. 50 per square metre ?

20. A room is 9 metres long and 5 metres wide. How many students can sit in it if each student occupies 75 cm. × 50 cm. floor area ?

PATHS AND CROSS-ROADS

Example 9. A park is 250 metres long and 200 metres wide. A path 4 metres wide has been made inside it all along its boundary. Find the cost of cementing the path at Rs. 8 per square metre.

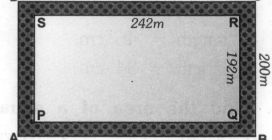

Solution :   Suppose the park is ABCD as shown in front.

Length of the park = 250 m

Width of the park = 200 m

∴ Area of the park = 250 m × 200 m = 50000 sq. m

Width of the path = 4 m

Length of the remaining park PQRS = (250–8)m = 242 m

Breadth of the remaining park PQRS = (200–8)m = 192 m

∴ Area of the remaining park = 242m × 192m = 46464 sq. m

∴ Area of the path = Area of the park – Area of the inner park

= (50,000 sq. m – 46, 464) sq. m

= **3536 sq. m**

∵ Cost of cementing the path = Rs. (3536 × 8) = **Rs. 28288** *Ans.*

Example 10. A room is 12 metres long and 7 metres wide. It has a verandah all round it. If the verandah is 4 metres wide find its area.

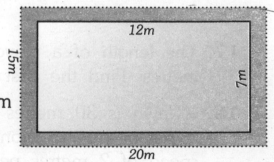

Solution :   Length of the room = 12m

Breadth of the room = 7m

∴ Area of the room = 12m × 7m

= 84 sq. m

Width of the verandah = 4m

∴ Length of the (room + verandah) = 12 + 4 + 4 = 20m

Breadth of the (room + verandah) = 7 + 4 + 4 = 15m

∴ Area of (room + verandah) = 20m × 15m = 300 sq. m

∴ Area of the verandah = 300 sq. m – 84 sq. m

= **216 sq. m** *Ans.*

Example 11. **A field 300 metres long and 200 metres wide has a 10-metre wide path along its bounds outside it. Find its area and cost of levelling it at Rs. 2 per sq. m.**

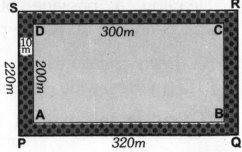

Solution : Suppose the field is ABCD

Including the path, it will take the shape of PQRS

Length of the field ABCD = 300m

Breadth of the field ABCD = 200 m

∴ Area of the field ABCD = 300 m × 200 m = 60000 sq. m

Now, length of the figure PQRS = (300 + 10 + 10)m = 320 m

Breadth of the figure PQRS = (200 + 10 + 10)m = 220 m

∴ Area of figure PQRS = 320 m × 220m = 70400 sq. m

∴ Area of the path = Area of PQRS – Area of ABCD

= 70400 sq. m – 60000 sq. m

= 10400 sq. m

Cost of levelling the path = Rs. (10400 × 2) = **Rs. 20800** *Ans.*

Example 12. **A field 60 m long and 40 m wide has two roads crossing each other in its middle. One of them is parallel to the length and the other parallel to the width. The roads are 2 m wide. Find their area and the cost of levelling them at Rs. 5 per sq. m.**

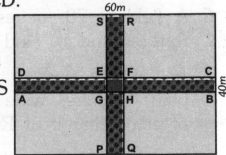

Solution : The road parallel to the length is ABCD.

Its length = 60m and breadth = 2m

Its area = 60m × 2m = **120 sq. m**

∴ The road parallel to the width is PQRS

Its length = 40m and width = 2m

∴ Its area = 40m × 2m = **80 sq. m**

The area of the crossing EFGH = 2 m × 2 m = 4 sq. m

This area of the crossing has been calculated twice.

Total area of the cross-roads = 120 sq. m + 80 sq. m – 4 sq. m

= 200 sq. m – 4 sq. m = **196 sq. m**

Cost of levelling the roads = Rs. 196 × 5 = **Rs. 980** *Ans.*

1. A hall is 20 metres long and 15 metres wide. It is to be carpeted leaving a passage 50 cm. wide along the walls. Find the cost of carpeting it at Rs. 5 per square metre.

2. A lawn measures 36 metres × 20 metres. It is surrounded by a path 1·5 metres wide on its outside. Find the area of the path.

3. Calculate the area of the shaded region in each figure.

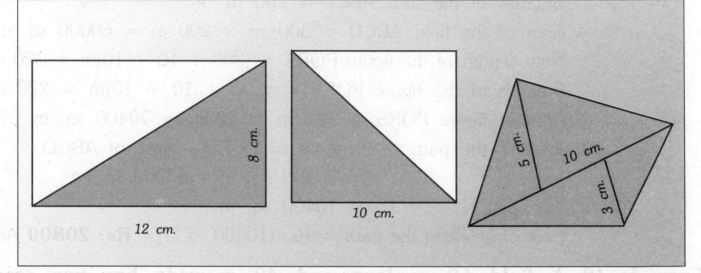

4. A saree is 5·5 metres long and 1·25 metres wide. Its border is 10 cm. wide. This border is to be printed on both its sides. Find the cost of printing this border at Rs. 15 per square metre.

5. A room is 8·5 metres long and 4·5 metres wide. It has a verandah 2 metres wide all around it. Find the area of the verandah.

6. A field is 78 metres long and 38 metres wide. A road 1 metre wide runs around it. Find the area of the road.

7. An oblong park is 250 metres long and 200 metres wide. It has a path 4 metres wide all around it on its inside. What will be the cost of cementing it at Rs. 9·50 per square metre ?

8. A garden is 75 metres long and 35 metres wide. Two paths run in its middle crossing each other. One is parallel to the length while the other is parallel to the width. Find the area of the paths if they are 2 metres wide.

9. A field is 60 metres long and 40 metres wide. It has two 3 m wide cross-roads in its middle. One is parallel to the length and the other is parallel to the breadth. Find the cost of paving the roads at Rs. 2·50 per sq. metre.

AREA OF FOUR WALLS

Take a box made of card-board that is oblong in shape. It is the shape of a rectangular room. Open it carefully and spread it. It will take the following shape :

Clearly, the box has taken the shape of a rectangle.

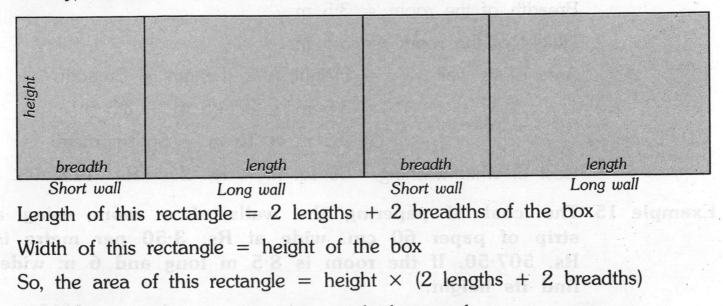

Length of this rectangle = 2 lengths + 2 breadths of the box

Width of this rectangle = height of the box

So, the area of this rectangle = height × (2 lengths + 2 breadths)

Rectangle is in fact the box that we had opened.

Area of the rectangle is equal to the area of the four walls of the box.

And the box was just like a **room**.

So, area of the **four walls of a room** = height × (2 lengths + 2 breadths)

$$= \textbf{Height} \times \textbf{2 (Length + Breadth)}$$

and height of a room = **Area of the four walls ÷ 2 (Length + Breadth)**

Let us solve some examples :

Example 13. A room is 8 metres long, 6 metres wide and 4 metres high. Find the area of its four walls.

Solution :   Length of the room = 8 m

Breadth of the room = 6 m

Height of the room = 4 m

Area of its four walls = Height × 2 (Length + Breadth)

$$= 4 \text{ m} \times 2 (8 \text{ m} + 6 \text{ m})$$

$$= 4 \text{ m} \times 28 \text{ m} = \textbf{112 sq. m } Ans.$$

Example 14. A room is 4·5 metres long, 3·5 metres broad and 3·5 metre in height. What will be the cost of white-washing its walls at Rs. 2 per square metre ?

Solution :

Length of the room = 4·5 m

Breadth of the room = 3·5 m

Height of the room = 3·5 m

Area of its wall = Height × 2 (Length + Breadth)

= 3·5 m × 2 (4·5 m + 3·5 m)

= 3·5 m × 16 m = 56 sq. metre

Cost of white-washing = 56 sq. m × Rs. 2 = **Rs. 112** *Ans.*

Example 15. **The cost of papering the walls of a room using a strip of paper 60 cm. wide at Rs. 3·50 per metre is Rs. 507·50. If the room is 8·5 m long and 6 m. wide, find its height.**

Solution :

Total cost of papering the walls = Rs. $507\frac{1}{2}$ = Rs. $\frac{1015}{2}$

Cost of papering the walls per metre = Rs. $3\frac{1}{2}$ = Rs. $\frac{7}{2}$

Length of the paper strip used = Rs. $\frac{1015}{2}$ ÷ Rs. $\frac{7}{2}$

= Rs. $\frac{1015}{2}$ × Rs. $\frac{2}{7}$

= 145 metres

Width of the paper-strip = 60 cm. = $\frac{60}{100}$ m = $\frac{3}{5}$ m

∴ Area of the four walls = 145 m × $\frac{3}{5}$ m = 87 sq. m

Now, Height = Area of the four walls ÷ 2 (Length + Breadth)

= 87 sq. cm. ÷ 2 (Length + Breadth)

= 87 sq. cm. ÷ 2 (8·5 m + 6 m)

= 87 sq. cm. ÷ 29 m = **3 m** *Ans.*

A. Find the area of the four walls whose—

1. length = 5 m   breadth = 4 m   height = 2·8 m
2. length = 6 m   breadth = 5 m   height = 3 m
3. length = 8·5 m   breadth = 4·5 m   height = 3 m
4. length = 5·5 m   breadth = 2·5 m   height = 3·5 m
5. length = 10 m   breadth = 8 m   height = 4 m
6. length = 8 m   breadth = 7 m   height = 3·5 m

B. Solve :

7. A room is 8 metres long, 6 metres wide and 3·5 metres high. Find the area of its four walls.

8. A hall is 9 metres long 7 metres wide and 4 metres high. Find the area of its four walls. Also find the cost of white-washing its walls at Rs. 1 per square metre.

9. A room is 9·68 metres long, 6·32 metres wide and 4 metres high. Find the area of its four walls. Also find the cost of plastering its walls at Rs. 2 per square metre.

10. A box is 45 cm. long, 35 cm. wide and 30 cm. high. What will be the cost of lining its inside with fine paper that costs 90 paise per metre. This paper is in the form of a strip 10 cm. wide.

11. A room is 7·5 metres long, 4·5 metres wide and 3 metres high. Find the area of its four walls. Also find the cost of plastering its floor, ceiling and four walls at Rs. 12 per square metre leaving 1 square metre for each of the two windows and 2 square metres for a door.

12. An open iron tank 3 metres long, 2·5 metres wide and 4 metres high is to be made. Find the area of the iron sheets that will be used to make it. Find the cost of making it at Rs. 35 per square metre.

13. Find the cost of plastering the four walls and the bed of a swimming pool at the rate of Rs. 20 per square metre if the pool is 25 metres long, 18 metres wide and 4·5 metres deep.

14. A hall is 12 metres long, 10 metres wide and 3·5 metres high. Find the cost of papering its walls with a paper-strip 70 cm. wide if the paper costs Rs. 1·25 per metre.

> *KNOW THESE TERMS :*
> 1. **face**—any of the six plane surfaces of a cube or cuboid
> 2. **edge**—any of the twelve corners of a cube or cuboid
> 3. **vertex**—any of the eight angular points of a cube or cuboid
> 4. **base**—the bottom face of a cube or cuboid
> 5. **roof**—the top face of a cube or cuboid

CUBOID SOLID FIGURES

We have read about plane figures so far. In this chapter, we shall study two types of solid figures—**cubes** and **cuboids**.

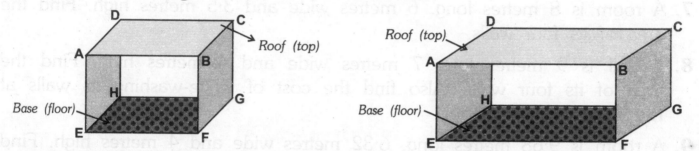

A **cube** is a solid figure that has **six square surfaces**. Its *length, breadth and height/depth are all equal.*

A **cuboid** is a solid figure that has **six rectangular surfaces**. Its *length, breadth and height are all different.*

ELEMENTS OF A CUBE/CUBOID

Three elements of a cube or cuboid are its *surfaces, edges* and *vertices.* They are as under :

1. A cube/cuboid has **six plane surfaces**—(*see the figures given above*)
   They are ABCD, EFGH, AEFB, BCGF, DCGH, AEHD
2. A cube/cubiod has **twelve edges/corners.**
   They are AB, BC, CD, DA, EF, FG, GH, HE, BF, CG, DH, AE
3. A cube/cuboid has **eight vertices/angular points.**
   They are A, B, C, D, E, F, G, H

Remember that the six surfaces of a cube/cuboid are called its **faces.** Clearly, the bottom face is called the **base** while the top face is called the **roof**. The remaining four faces of a cube/cuboid on the sides are called **side faces/lateral faces**.

VOLUME

Volume *means the total space occupied by a solid*. As mentioned above, regular solid figures have three dimensions—**length, breadth** and **height/depth**.

It is clear that the space occupied by a solid is enclosed between its three dimensions. So, it can be calculated by multiplying these three dimensions.

Volume of a cube = side × side × side = (side)^3

Volume of a cuboid = length × breadth × height

Remember that the units of volume are called *cubic units*. They are :

cm^3 or **cubic centimetre**   **m^3** or **cubic metre**

Example 1. Find the volume of a cube whose side is **1·6 cm**.

Solution : ∵ The sides of a cube are equal

∴ Its volume = side × side × side

$$= 1·6 \text{ cm.} × 1·6 \text{ cm.} × 1·6 \text{ cm.}$$

$$= \frac{16}{10} × \frac{16}{10} × \frac{16}{10} \text{ cm}^3 = \frac{4096}{1000} \text{ cm}^3 = \textbf{4·096 cm}^3 \, Ans.$$

Example 2. **Find the volume of a cuboid with length = 3·5 m, breadth = 2 m and height = 1·5 m.**

Solution : Volume of a cuboid = length × breadth × height

$$= 3·5 \text{ m} × 2 \text{ m} × 1·5 \text{ m}$$

$$= \left(\frac{35}{10} × \frac{2}{1} × \frac{15}{10}\right) \text{m}^3 = \frac{105}{10} \text{ m}^3 = \textbf{10·5 m}^3 \, Ans.$$

Example 3. **The volume of a cuboid is 140·608 m³. Find its height if it is 10·4 m long and 2·6 m wide.**

Solution :   Volume of the cuboid = 140·608 m^3

Length of the cuboid = 10·4 metres

Width of the cube = 2·6 metres

∴ Height of the cube $= \dfrac{\text{Volume}}{\text{length × width}} = \dfrac{140·608}{10·4 × 2·6}$ m

$$= \frac{140608}{1000} × \frac{10}{104} × \frac{10}{26} \text{ metres} = \textbf{5·2 metres} \, Ans.$$

Example 4. A rectangular tank is 5m long, 3·5m wide and 1·6m deep. How many litres of water can it hold ?

Solution : Length of the tank = 5 metres
Width of the tank = 3·5 metres
Depth of the tank = 1·6 metres
Volume of the water that can fill it = volume of the tank
= 5 m × 3·5 m × 1·6 m
$$= \left(5 \times \frac{35}{10} \times \frac{16}{10}\right) m^3 = \textbf{28 } \textbf{m}^3 \; Ans.$$

Example 5. The dimensions of a brick are 25 cm. × 10 cm. × 7·5 cm. How much space will 1000 bricks occupy ?

Solution : Length of the brick = 25 cm.
Breadth of the brick = 10 cm.
Height of the brick = 7·5 cm.
∴ Volume of the brick = (25 × 10 × 7·5) cm³ = 1875 cm³
Clearly one brick will occupy 1875 cubic cm. of space.
∴ Space occupied by 1000 bricks = **1875000 cm.** *Ans.*

Example 6. How many bricks will be needed to build a wall 10 metres long, 6 metres high and 25 cm. wide if each brick measures 25 cm. × 10 cm. × 7·5 cm. ?

Solution : Length of the wall = 10 metres = 1000 cm.
Width of the wall = 25 cm.
Height of the wall = 6 m = 600 cm.
∴ Volume of the wall = (1000 × 25 × 600) cm³
Volume of a brick = 25 cm. × 10 cm. × 7·5 cm.
= 1875 cm³
$$\therefore \text{Reqd. No. of bricks} = \frac{1000 \times 25 \times 600 \; cm^3}{1875 \; cm^3} = \textbf{8000} \; Ans.$$

Example 7. A water tank has dimensions 3m × 2m × 1·5m. How many litres of water does it contain ? How many times can a cubical vessel with edge equal to 50 cm. be filled out of the tank ?

Solution : Volume of the tank = 3m × 2m × 1·5m

$$= (300 × 200 × 150) \text{ cm}^3$$

Water contained by the tank $= \dfrac{300 × 200 × 150}{1000}$ litres

$$= \textbf{9000 litres} \ (\because 1 \ litre = 1000 \ cm^3)$$

Volume of the cubical vessel = $(50 × 50 × 50) \text{ cm}^3$

∴ No of times the vessel can be filled out of the tank

$$= \dfrac{300 × 200 × 150}{50 × 50 × 50} = \textbf{72 times} \ Ans.$$

SURFACE-AREA OF A CUBE/CUBOID

We know that a cube/cuboid has six surfaces. So, *the total surface-area of a cube/cuboid is the sum of the areas of these six surfaces.*

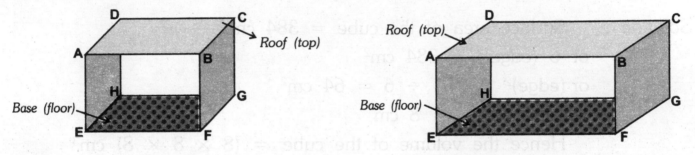

If we take the length, breadth and height of a cube/cuboid as **l, b, h,** then

Area of face ABCD = **l × b**   Area of face EFGH = **l × b**
Area of face AEHD = **b × h**   Area of face BFGC = **b × h**
Area of face AEFB = **l × h**   Area of face CDHG = **l × h**

Total surface-area of the cube/cuboid

$$= (l × b) + (l × b) + (b × h) + (b × h) + (l × h) + (l × h)$$
$$= 2(l × b) + 2(b × h) + 2(l × h)$$
$$= 2 \ lb + 2 \ bh + 2 \ lh = \textbf{2 (lb + bh + lh)}$$
$$= \textbf{2}\big[\textbf{(length × breadth) + (breadth × height) + (length × height)}\big]$$

For a cube, *l = b = h*. So, its surface area = **6 (edge)²**

Example 1. Find the total surface-area of a cube whose edge is 9 cm.

Solution :   Surface-area of a cube   = 6 × (edge)²

$$= 6 × (9)^2 \text{ sq. cm.}$$
$$= (6 × 81) \text{ sq. cm.} = \textbf{486 sq. cm.} \ Ans.$$

Example 2. Find the surface area of a cuboid whose length, breadth and height are 15 cm, 10 cm and 5 cm respectively.

Solution : Length of the cuboid = 15 cm

Breadth of the cuboid = 10 cm

Height of the cuboid = 5 cm

∴ Its surface-area = 2 × (lb + bh + lh)

= 2 × [(15 × 10) + (10 × 5) + (15 × 5)] sq. cm.

= 2 × (150 + 50 + 75) sq. cm.

= 2 × 275 sq. cm. = **550 sq. cm.** Ans.

Example 3. The surface-area of a cube is **384 cm².** Find its volume.

Solution : Surface area of the cube = 384 cm²

or 6 (edge)² = 384 cm²

or (edge)² = 384 ÷ 6 = 64 cm².

∴ edge = $\sqrt{64}$ = 8 cm

Hence the volume of the cube = (8 × 8 × 8) cm³

= **512 cm³** Ans.

Example 4. An iron container is 50 cm long 35 cm. wide and 15 cm high. Find the area of the iron sheet used to make it. Also, find its cost at the rate of 20 paise per square centimetre.

Solution : Length of the tin = 50 cm

Breadth of the tin = 35 cm

Height of the tin = 15 cm

∴ Its surface-area = 2 (lb + bh + lh)

= 2 [(50 ×35) + (35 ×15) + (50 ×15)] sq. cm.

= 2 [1750 + 525 + 750) sq. cm.

= (2 × 3025) sq. cm. = 6050 sq. cm.

Reqd. Cost = $\dfrac{6050 \times 20}{100}$ = **Rs. 1210** Ans.

A. Answer :

1. How many cubic centimetres make a litre ?
2. How many cubic centimetres make a cubic metre ?
3. How is the volume of a cube calculated ?
4. How is the volume of a cuboid calculated ?
5. How many faces does a cube/cuboid have ?
6. What is the bottom face of a cube/cuboid called ?
7. What is the top face of a cube/cuboid called ?
8. How many edges/corners does a cube/cuboid have ?
9. How many angular points (vertices) does a cube/cuboid have ?
10. How many dimensions are there of a cube/cuboid ?

B. Complete the following formulae :

11. Volume of a cuboid = ... × .... × ....
12. Length of a cuboid = Volume ÷ (.................... × ....)
13. Breadth of a cuboid = Volume ÷ (.................... × ....)
14. Height of a cuboid = Volume ÷ (.................... × ....)
15. Volume of a cube = (....................)^3

C. Find the volume of a cuboid whose :

16. length = 12 cm.	breadth = 8 cm.	height = 6 cm.
17. length = 1·2 m	breadth = 30 cm.	height = 12 cm.
18. length = 10 cm.	breadth = 3·2 cm.	height = 4·5 cm.
19. length = 20 cm.	breadth = 15 cm.	height = 12 cm.
20. length = 3·6 m.	breadth = 1·5 m.	height = ·6 m.
21. length = 25 cm.	breadth = 12·5 cm.	height = 7·5 cm.
22. length = 15 cm.	breadth = 9 cm.	height = 6 cm.
23. length = 3 m.	breadth = 2 m.	height = 1·5 m.
24. length = 7 cm.	breadth = 6 cm.	height = 4·5 cm.

D.
25. A rectangular wooden block is made up of 189 cubic centimetres of wood. What is its height if it is 7 cm. long and 6 cm. wide ?
26. Find the volume of a cube whose side is 4·5 cm.
27. A cubic wooden block has an edge 16 cm. in length. How many smaller cubic blocks can be obtained from it if the smaller block has an edge 4 cm. long ?

28. A hall is 12 metres long, 9 metres wide and 3·5 metres high. How many litres of air does it contain ?

29. A wall is 16 m long, 36 cm. wide and 3·5 m high. How many bricks will be needed to build it if each brick is 25 cm. × 10 cm. × 7·5 cm. ?

30. A rectangular water-tank can contain 56000 litres of water. If the base of the tank is 8 metres long and 3·5 metres wide, find its depth.

31. The rainfall on the 27th of July was measured to be 6 cm. How many litres of water fell on a field measuring 3 hectares.

(*1 hectare* = 10000 m² *and 1 litre* = 1000 cm³)

32. The volume of a room is 324 cubic metres. If its floor area is 108 square metres find its height.

33. A field has an area of 56000 square metres. It is to be covered with gravel upto a height of 2 cm. How much gravel is needed for it ?

34. Find the surface-area of a cube whose edge is 5 cm. long.

35. Find the surface-area of a cuboid 16 cm × 9 cm × 6 cm.

36. The surface-area of a cube is 294 sq. centimetres. Find its volume.

37. The dimensions of a tin-box are 56 cm. × 50 cm. × 30 cm. Find the area of the tin-sheet used to make 15 such tins. Find the cost per tin if the tin-sheet sells at 30 paise per square cm.

38. The volume of a cube = 125 cm³. Find its surface-area.

39. Find the cost of painting a cuboidal container from outside at 16 paise per square m., if its dimensions are 13 m × 12 m and 5 m.

40. A water-tank has its dimensions to be 2·5 m × 2 m × 1·5 m. Find the cost of painting it from outside at Rs. 1·50 per square metre.

MISCELLANEOUS EXERCISES V

A. Name—

   1. Three common units of *length* : ....

   2. Three common units of *area* : ....

   3. Three common units of *volume* : ....

B. How many—

   4. square centimetres make a square metre ? ....

   5. square metres make a square kilometre ? ....

6. square metres make a hectare ? ....

7. cubic centimetres make a litre ? ....

C. Complete each relation :

8. Area of a rt. triangle = ... × .... ÷ ....

9. Area of a rectangle = ... × ....

10. Area of a square = ... × ....

11. Volume of a cube = ... × .... × ....

12. Volume of a cuboid = ... × .... × ....

13. Area of the 4 walls of a room = ... × .... (.......... + ...)

D.

14. A rectangular field is 300 m long and 200 m wide. A path runs along its bounds outside it. If the path is 5 metres wide, find its area and the cost of levelling it at Rs. 1·50 per sq. metre.

15. A park is 250 m long and 150 m wide. A path runs along its bounds inside it. If the path is 5 metres wide, find its area and the cost of levelling it at Rs. 1·50 per square metre.

16. A park is 50 metres long and 30 metres wide. Two cross-roads run in its middle parallel to its length and breadth respectively. If the roads are 2 metres wide, find their area and the cost of levelling them at Rs. 1·50 per square metre.

17. The cost of papering the walls of a room with a fine paper-strip 60 cm. wide is Rs. 500. The paper-strip costs Rs. 2·50 per metre. If the room is 8 metres long and 6 metres wide, find its height.

18. A cuboidal water-tank contains 28000 litres of water. Find the depth of the water in it if it has a base area of 28 square metres.

19. A gold lump with a volume of ·5 m³ is hammered into a sheet to cover an area of one hectare. Find the thickness of the gold sheet.

20. What change will occur in the volume of a cube, if the length of its edge is (a) doubled (b) halved

21. Find the area of the four walls of a room 7·5 m long, 4·5 m wide and 3 m high. Find the cost of plastering its floor, ceiling and the four walls from inside only at the rate of Rs. 10 per square metre allowing 2 m² for each of the four windows and 6 sq. metre for either of the two doors.

MEMORABLE FACTS

1. **Length** means the measurement of an object from end to end.

2. **Area** is the measurement of the region occupied by a plane figure.

3. **1 metre** = *100 centimetres* = *1000 millimetres* and **1 kilometre** = 1000 metres.

4. **Perimetre** of a figure is the measure of all its sides taken together.

5. **Area of a Rectangle = Length × Breadth**

6. **Area of a Square = Side × Side**

7. **Area of a Rt. Triangle = (Base × Height) ÷ 2**

8. When a path occurs around a field **outside it**, twice the width of the path is **added** to its length and breadth while finding the area of the bigger field (*field + path*).

9. When a path occurs around a field **inside it**, twice the width of the path is **subtracted** from its length and breadth while finding the area of the smaller field (*field – path*).

10. When two **cross-roads** occur in a field parallel to its length and breadth respectively, the area of the **crossing** of the roads should be taken **once only**.

11. Area of the **four walls of a room = Height × 2 (Length + Breadth)**

12. A **cube/cuboid** has *six plane surfaces* called its **faces**.

13. A **cube/cuboid** has **twelve edges**

14. A **cube/cuboid** has **eight vertices**

15. **Volume of a Cube = Side × Side × Side**

16. **Volume of a Cuboid = Length × Breadth × Height**

17. **Surface area of a Cuboid = 2 [(Length × Breadth) + (Breadth × Height) + (Length × Height)]**

18. **Surface area of a Cube = 6(Edge)²**

Remember that—

1. **Length** is measured in *centimetres, metres, kilometres* etc.

2. **Area** is measured in *sq. centimetres, sq. metres, sq. kilomtres* etc.

3. **Volume** is measured in *cubic centimetres, cubic metres, cubic kilometres* etc.

4. **Volume of liquids** is measured in *litres* and **1 litre = 1000 cubic centimtres**

Statistics *is a set of methods used to collect data and analyse it.*

The word—**statistics**—is used both as a *plural noun* and as a *singular noun.*

(a) In **plural sense**, it points to the *numerical data*

(b) In **singular sense**, it points to the *set of methods* used in statistics.

Statistics helps people solve many problems and take decision about uncertain situations through four basic steps :

1. Defining the Problem
2. Collecting Data
3. Analysing the Data
4. Reaching Inferences (Results)

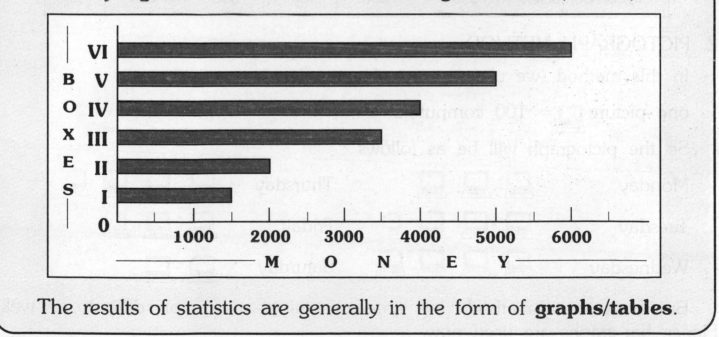

The results of statistics are generally in the form of **graphs/tables**.

IN THIS UNIT—
27. Bar-Graphs

BAR-GRAPHS

As mentioned on page 211, bar-graphs are pictorial pieces used to represent the numerical data.

HOW DO BAR-GRAPHS HELP US ?

Suppose we want to show the production of computers in an electronic workshop for the 6 days of a week. Two methods previously used to do this job were as under :

1. TABLE METHOD

Name of the Day	Mon.	Tues.	Wed.	Thurs.	Friday	Sat.
No. of Computers	300	350	400	350	250	200

2. PICTOGRAPH METHOD

In this method, we use pictures of computers.

one picture ⬚ = 100 computers

So the pictograph will be as follows :

Monday ⬚ ⬚ ⬚	Thursday ⬚ ⬚ ⬚ ⊏
Tuesday ⬚ ⬚ ⬚ ⊏	Friday ⬚ ⬚ ⊏
Wednesday ⬚ ⬚ ⬚ ⬚	Saturday ⬚ ⬚

But both these methods are time-consuming and a bit difficult as well. Hence bar-graphs are used now.

Bar graphs are rectangular columns of uniformly equal width but varying lengths (heights) to represent the varying numerical data.

We may draw a bar-graph vertically or horizontally as is suitable.

We can show the production of computers mentioned in the table and the pictograph through a bar-graph as under vertically as well as horizontally :

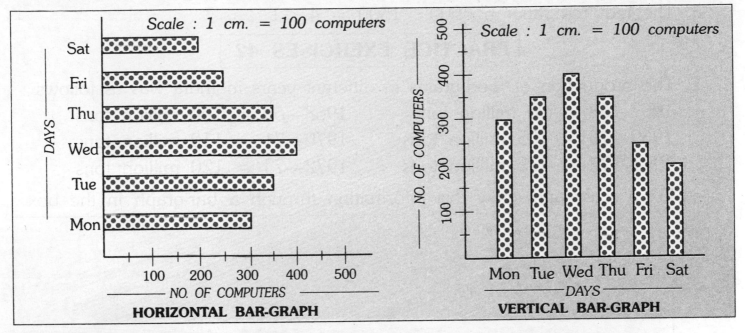

HORIZONTAL BAR-GRAPH

VERTICAL BAR-GRAPH

READING A BAR-GRAPH

Example : Given below is a bar-graph that shows the amounts of money found in six different boxes. Read the graph and answer the questions.

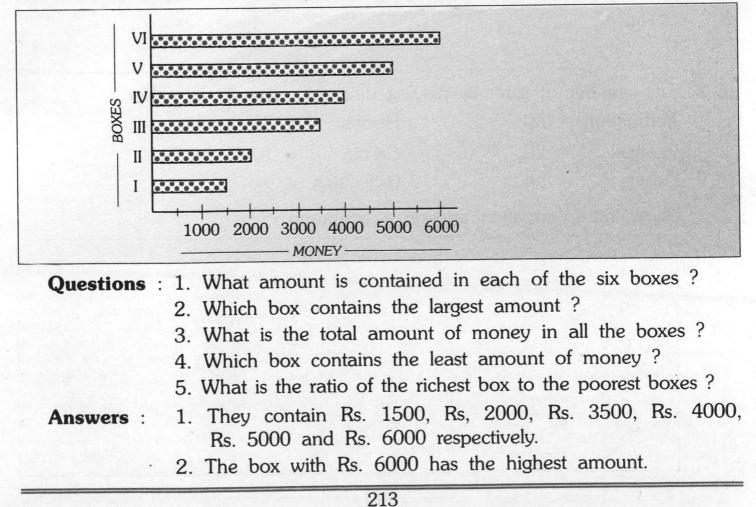

Questions : 1. What amount is contained in each of the six boxes ?

2. Which box contains the largest amount ?

3. What is the total amount of money in all the boxes ?

4. Which box contains the least amount of money ?

5. What is the ratio of the richest box to the poorest boxes ?

Answers : 1. They contain Rs. 1500, Rs, 2000, Rs. 3500, Rs. 4000, Rs. 5000 and Rs. 6000 respectively.

2. The box with Rs. 6000 has the highest amount.

3. The total amount of money in all the boxes is Rs. 22000.
4. The box with Rs. 1500 has the least amount of money.
5. The required ratio = 6000 : 1500 = 4 : 1

PRACTICE EXERCISES 42

1. The production of food-grains in different years in India was as follows :

1967—68 = 95 million tons   1968—69 = 100 million tons
1969—70 = 105 million tons   1970—71 = 110 million tons
1971—72 = 115 million tons   1972—73 = 120 million tons

Fix a scale and show this information through a bar-graph in the box.

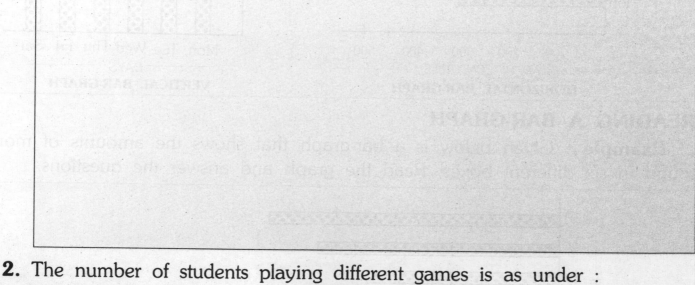

2. The number of students playing different games is as under :

Badminton = 20   Hockey   = 25
Football   = 20   Carom   = 10
Cricket   = 30   Volley-ball = 25

Show this information through a bar-graph.

3. The vehicles passing through a crossing on different days were :

Sunday   = 80   Monday   = 135

Tuesday   = 100   Wednesday = 125

Thursday   = 130   Friday   = 140

Saturday   = 150

Fix a scale and show this information through a bar-graph.

4. Some peaks of the Himalayas have their heights as follows :

1. Mount Everest   = 8848 metres   2. Mount K_2 = 8611 metres

3. Kanchanjangha   = 8598 metres   4. Makalu   = 8481 metres

5. Dhavalgiri   = 8172 metres   6. Cho Oyu   = 8153 metres

Represent these heights in a bar-graph after fixing a proper scale.

5. A class has 60 students in all. They study different subjects as follows :

English = 18   Mathematics = 9

Science = 6   Hindi = 15

Social Studies = 12   Drawing = 14

Draw a bar-graph to represent the data given above.

6. A family spends money on various items every month as under :

House Rent = Rs 500   Food = Rs. 800

Clothes = Rs. 200   Conveyance = Rs. 200

Education = Rs. 300   Miscellaneous = Rs. 200

Represent it through a bar-graph showing a proper scale.

7. The bar-graph given in front shows the number of children in different age-groups. Read it carefully and answer the questions given below.

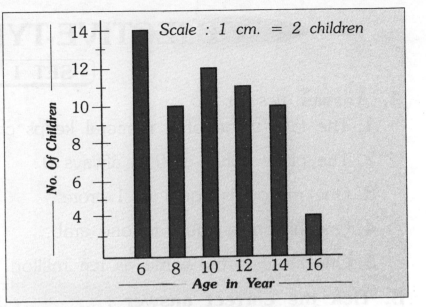

Questions :

1. Which age-group has the largest number of children ?
2. Which are-group has the lowest number of children ?
3. Which two age-groups have the same number of children ?
4. Which age-group has no child at all ?

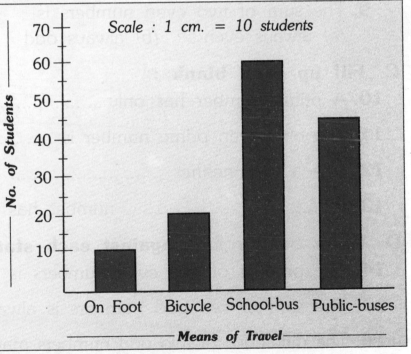

8. The bar-graph shown in front shows the number of students that come to school by different means. Read the graph and answer the questions given below.

Questions :

1. Which is the most popular means of travel ?
2. Which is the least popular means of travel ?
3. How many students cycle to the school ?
4. How many students use the school-bus ?
5. How many students come by public-buses ?
6. How many students come on foot ?

OBJECTIVE-TYPE TESTS

SET I

A. Answer yes or no :

1. The face value of a numeral keeps changing.
2. The place value of 0 is always 0.
3. One million is equal to 1 crore.
4. One billion is equal to one arab.
5. One crore is the same as ten million.

B. Tick the correct answer :

6. The place value of 5 in the numeral 1548 is :
   (a) 5000   (b) 50000   (c) 500   (d) 5
7. 1 is the smallest : (a) whole number (b) natural number (c) integer
8. The smallest 3-digit number is : (a) 999   (b) 100   (c) 101   (d) 909
9. The sum of two even numbers is :
   (a) always even   (b) always odd   (c) may be even or odd

C. Fill up each blank :

10. A prime number has only .... factors.
11. The only even prime number is ....
12. 1 is a digit neither .... nor ....
13. A .... number has more than two factors.

D. Write true or false against each statement :

14. The product of two even numbers is always even.
15. The sum of two odd numbers is always odd.
16. The difference of two odd numbers may be odd or even.

E. Write the correct name of the—

17. person who invented the zero.
18. person who developed the Sieve of Prime Numbers.
19. Arab who wrote a book on numbers in 825 AD.
20. numbers originally used in India.

A. Answer

1. x is older than y. How much older is he ? ....

2. What do C, D and M stand for in Roman notation ? ...., ..., ...

3. Which Roman numeral do these pictures stand for ? (.....) (......)

4. How many lakhs are there in a crore ? ....

B. Tick the correct answer :

5. Is – 5 larger or – 8   (a) – 5   (b) – 8   (c) both are equal

6. Is 7 smaller or – 7   (a) – 7   (b) 7   (c) both are equal

7. Is an arab larger or a billion (a) billion (b) arab (c) both are equal

8. Is 1 a prime or composite number ? (a) prime (b) composite (c) neither

C. What is each of these called ?

9. Divisor x Quotient + Remainder = Dividend   : ....

10. Indian numerals that reached Europe through Arabia   : ....

11. The numeral that exceeds another by only 1   : ....

12. The numeral that is less than another by only 1   : ....

D. Write the technical term for each of the following :

13. The numeral from which another numeral is subtracted : ....

14. The result obtained by multiplying two numerals   : ....

15. The idea of a count formed in the mind   : ....

16. The symbols that are written to express a count   : ....

E. Tick the correct answer :

17. $0 \div 5$ (a) 5   (b) 0   (c) neither of the two

18. $0 + 5$ (a) 5   (b) 0   (c) neither of the two

19. $5 \div 0$ (a) 5   (b) 0   (c) undefined quantity

20. The simplified form of $\dfrac{63}{147}$ is (a) $\dfrac{7}{9}$ (b) $\dfrac{3}{7}$ (c) $\dfrac{9}{7}$

A. Write *true* **or** *false* :

1. A scalene triangle has all its sides equal. ....

2. A right-angled triangle may have two rt. angles. ....

3. A number with 0 in its unit's place is divisible by 5. ....

4. In the term 5xy, 5 is the coefficient. ....

B. Tick the correct answer :

5. The cost of 5 biscuits is Rs. 1·40. What will be the cost of 7 biscuits :

   (a) Rs. 1·60   (b) Rs. 1·96   (c) Rs. 2·24   (d) Rs. 1·70

6. A number divisible by both 2 and 3 is also divisible by :

   (a) 5   (b) 8   (c) 9   (d) 6

7. – 3 is larger than – 7 by :

   (a) 10   (b) 4   (c) 21   (d) 6

8. The number added to – 3 to get – 8 is :

   (a) 5   (b) – 5   (c) 11   (d) – 11

9. The largest number that divides 208 and 272 exactly is :

   (a) 52   (b) 16   (c) 8   (d) 4

10. On dividing a number by 13, the quotient is 7 and remainder is 6. The number is :

    (a) 85   (b) 55   (c) 97   (d) 107

11. The largest number of 4 digits divisible by 5 is :

    (a) 9990   (b) 9995   (c) 9959   (d) 1005

12. Which of the following pairs is a pair of co-primes ?

    (a) 3, 5   (b) 4, 6   (c) 1, 8   (d) neither pair

13. The ratio of gold and copper in a ring is 1 : 24. If the rings weighs 5 grams, find the weights of the copper and the gold :

    (a) ·4 and 4·6 gms.   (b) ·2 and 4·8 gms.   (c) ·5 and 4·5 gms.

14. The angles formed opposite to each other at the point of intersection of two lines are called :

    (a) alternate angles (b) corresponding angles (c) vertically opposite angles

15. The bottom surface of a solid figure is called its :

    (a) floor   (b) base   (c) bottom   (d) ceiling

1. The area of a rectangle is found by multiplying its length by its :

   (a) height   (b) breadth   (c) depth

2. Which digit written in place of the * makes 591*26 divisible by 11 ?

   (a) 7   (b) 3   (c) 4   (d) 5

3. Which least number added to 1046 makes it divisible by 10 ?

   (a) 5   (b) 10   (c) 4   (d) 3

4. A person spends Rs. 1520 a month and saves 20% of his salary. His monthly salary is :

   (a) 1750   (b) 1900   (c) 2000   (d) 1680

5. A clerk was given an increment of 15% in his salary. His new salary is Rs. 3450. What was his old salary ?

   (a) 2800   (b) 3000   (c) 3250   (d) 3300

6. The area of a square is 64 sq. centimetres. Its side is :

   (a) 7·5 cm.   (b) 8 cm.   (c) 10 cm.   (d) 6·8 cm.

7. The S.P. of a bicycle at a loss of 10% is Rs. 2250. Its CP is

   (a) 2500   (b) 2450   (c) 2000   (d) 2600

8. What per cent is 42 of 70 ?

   (a) 35%   (b) 45%   (c) 60%   (d) 37·5%

9. Two lines can intersect at points :

   (a) three   (b) two   (c) only one   (d) four

10. Alternate angles lie on the *side/sides* of a transversal :

   (a) opposite   (b) same   (c) neither

11. Lines drawn through a point can be :

   (a) two only   (b) ten   (c) four   (d) infinite number

12. Tick the correct statements :

   1. A line has two end-points.

   2. A sector of a circle lies between two radii.

   3. A chord divides a circle into two segments.

   4. A tangent cuts a circle at two points.

ANSWERS

A. 1. Seven lakh forty-one thousand eight hundred and one

2. Four crore sixteen lakh twenty-three thousand and five

3. Four crore ninety-five lakh and three.

4. Thirty-four lakh twelve thousand and nine.

5. Twenty-five crore thirty-five lakh nine hundred and two.

6. Eighty-eight crore eight lakh eight thousand, eight hundred and eight.

B. 7. 98,97,53,783   8. 75,08,09,843   9. 39,00,59,011

10. 47,96,26,400   11. 55,78,00,932   12. 93,92,19,009

C. 13. 14,095,603   14. 163,447,809   15. 35,715,912,453

16. 943,476,238   17. Largest = 876,543,210, smallest = 102,345,678.

Eight hundred seventy-six million five hundred forty three thousand two hundred and ten.

One hundred and two million three hundred and forty-five thousand six hundred and seventy-eight.

D. 18. 10   19. 10   20. 1000   21. seven   22. 100000

23. (a) Six crore ninety-four lakh thirty-one thousand two hundred and nine ; Sixty-nine million four hundred thirty-one thousand two hundred and nine.

(b) Sixty-nine crore thirty-seven lakh seventy-one thousand five hundred and two ; Six hundred ninety-three million seven hundred seventy-one thousand five hundred two.

(c) Seventy-six crore fifty-three lakh ninety-four thousand six hundred and seventy-three ; Seven hundred sixty-five million three hundred ninety-four thousand six hundred and seventy-three.

(d) Fifty-five crore sixty-eight lakh thirteen thousand three hundred and sixty-seven ; Five hundred fifty-six million eight hundred and thirteen thousand three hundred and sixty-seven.

(e) Eighty-three crore forty-one lakh seventy-four thousand three hundred and sixty ; Eight hundred thirty-four million one hundred seventy-four thousand three hundred and sixty.

(f) Twenty-four crore ninety-seven lakh thirteen thousand six hundred and eighty-five ; Two hundred forty-nine million seven hundred thirteen thousand six hundred and eighty-five.

24. (a) XIX   (b) CCXLII   (c) MMMCCCLXIX   (d) $\overline{\text{CCCCC}}$LXXV

25. (a) 1076   (b) 1465   (c) 2514   26. 8530764

27. (a) $3 \times 7 + 3 \times 9 = 3(7+9)$ (b) $2 \times 7 + 3 \times 7 = 7(2 +3)$

(c) $4 \times 9 + 4 \times 11 = 4(9 + 11)$ (d) $a \times b + a \times c = a(b + c)$

28. (a) 1   (b) $\frac{7}{9}$ (c) $1\frac{8}{9}$ (d) 4·52

29. 12 days   **30.** 21 days   **31.** 7   **32.** 10780   **33.** 725   **34.** 20 sq. m ; 63 sq. m

35. 3 m   **36.** Rs. 1687·50   **37.** 5000 bricks   **38.** 41 bags

39. (a) *per cent* means on every hundred   (b) 28 % ; 10·5%   **40.** 25%

41. 25% loss   **42.** Rs. 500   **43.** Rs. 2500   **44.** $3\frac{1}{3}$ years

45. (a) two angles that have a common vertex and a common arm

(b) two angles that are formed on opposite sides of a transversal cutting two lines

(c) two angles that are formed on the same side of the two lines cut by a transversal

(d) two angles formed opposite to each other when two lines intersect

(e) two angles whose sum is 180°

(f) two angles whose sum is 90°

46. (a) acute   (b) right   (c) obtuse

(d) supplementary   (e) corresponding   (f) alternate

49. (a) an angle smaller than 90°   (b) an angle larger than 90°

(c) a triangle that has one of its angles larger than 90°

(d) a triangle that has all three different sides

(e) a triangle that has two of its sides equal to each other

(f) a triangle that has all the three sides equal to one another

50. 1. It has its opposite sides equal.   2. It has its opposite angles equal.

3. It has its diagonals cutting at 90°.   4. It has its opposite sides parallel.

There are three chief types of parallelograms—squares, rectangles and rhombuses.

51. 1. They contain Rs. 1500, Rs. 2000, Rs. 3500, Rs. 4000, Rs. 5000 and Rs. 6000

2. The box with Rs. 6000

3. The box with Rs. 1500

4. The total amount is Rs. 22000

PRACTICE EXERCISES 1. (Page 13)

A. 1. 1   **2.** 0   **3.** N   **4.** W   **5.** cannot be said   **6.** cannot be said

B. 7. No   **8.** Yes   **9.** Yes   **10.** No   **11.** 1000   **12.** 9999

C. 13. No   **14.** 1, 2, 3, 4   **15.** 100   **16.** 1000   **17.** Ten   **18.** 100

19. 1   **20.** 2   **21.** 10000   **22.** 999999   **23.** 101

PRACTICE EXERCISES 2. (Page 17)

A. 1. Nothing   **2.** 0   **3.** 0   **4.** 1   **5.** No   **6.** Digits   **7.** Ten   **8.** Ten

B. (a) **9.** 93057   **10.** 832406   **11.** 2808906   **12.** 71502070

13. 451213201   **14.** 5000607809   **15.** 47002308002

(b) **16.** 7303911   **17.** 108072101   **18.** 5057095404   **19.** 32011042612

20. 103412709817

C. **21.** Forty thousand eight hundred and fifty-seven *(same in both)*.

22. *(a)* Fifty-seven lakh two thousand eight hundred and three.

    (b) Five million seven hundred and two thousand eight hundred and three.

23. *(a)* Ninety-four crore thirty-seven lakh twenty thousand six hundred and ninety-five.

    (b) Nine hundred forty-three million, seven hundred twenty thousand six hundred and ninety-five.

24. *(a)* Twelve crore nine lakh five thousand and thirty-four.

    (b) One hundred twenty million, nine hundred five thousand and thirty-four.

25. *(a)* Ninety-two arab seventy five crore fifty-three lakh twenty-five thousand eight hundred and eight.

    (b) Ninety-two billion, seven hundred fifty-five million, three hundred twenty-five thousand, eight hundred and eight.

26. *(a)* Forty-five arab sixty-three crore seventy thousand eight hundred and nineteen.

    (b) Forty-five billion six hundred and thirty million seventy thousand eight hundred and nineteen.

D. **27.** 80000000, 5000000, 300000, 40000, 9000, 200, 10, 9   **28.** 50000 and 50

   29. 6000000 + 900000 + 90000 + 9000 + 900 + 30 + 2   **30.** 754016

E. **31.** 900000   **32.** 738, 783, 387, 378, 873, 837   **33.** 10002

   34. 58653, 637451   **35.** 65579, 758335   **36.** 101   **37.** 111

   38. 99   **39.** 999999, 100000   **40.** 90000

PRACTICE EXERCISES 3. *(Page 21)*

A. **1.** 121   **2.** 159   **3.** 68, 32   **4.** 135, 135   **5.** 175   **6.** 122, 378, 150

B. **7.** even   **8.** even   **9.** Yes   **10.** odd

C. **11.** 500   **12.** 1050   **13.** 2040   **14.** 1940

   15. 2000   **16.** 2300   **17.** 100000   **18.** No

PRACTICE EXERCISES 4. *(Page 23)*

A. **1.** 330   **2.** 1687   **3.** 11637   **4.** 334   **5.** 5940   **6.** 423818

B. **7.** 354252   **8.** 351203   **9.** 12022

C. **10.** 7, 2, 5   **11.** 9, 2, 6, 1   **12.** 3, 0, 5

   13. 5, 8, 2, 2, 4   **14.** 3, 8, 7, 0, 9, 8   **15.** 8, 2, 3, 4, 5, 0, 1

D. **16.** 9899999   **17.** Rs 24372   **18.** 50139   **19.** 4249742

PRACTICE EXERCISES 5. *(Page 26)*

A. **1.** 16378   **2.** 0   **3.** 16   **4.** 1654000   **5.** 14900400

   6. 100   **7.** 30, 7   **8.** 40, 3   **9.** 40, 4   **10.** 6

B. **11.** 187700   **12.** 149600   **13.** 506000   **14.** 8760000   **15.** 295500   **16.** 65500

C. **17.** 13883096 **18.** 48016808 **19.** 40267755 **20.** 14118377 **21.** 4993493 **22.** 142464
D. **23.** 66500 **24.** 46300 **25.** 27900 **26.** 73600 **27.** 3200 **28.** 9780
29. 0 **30.** 0
E. **31.** 999900 **32.** Rs. 654000 **33.** *(a)* 1, 1 *(b)* 0 *(c)* 1

PRACTICE EXERCISES 6. *(Page 30)*

A. **1.** Q = 117, R = 0 **2.** Q = 82 R = 9 **3.** Q = 388, R = 22
4. Q = 241, R = 145 **5.** Q = 22, R = 55 **6.** Q = 495, R = 76
7. Q = 358, R = 208 **8.** Q = 33, R = 257 **9.** Q = 1067, R = 111
10. Q 1116, R = 171 **11.** Q = 234, R = 155 **12.** Q = 6337, R = 704
B. **13.** 4 *(Read 46057)* **14.** 257 **15.** 607926
C. **16.** 725 **17.** 0 **18.** 1 **19.** 1
20. undefined quantity **21.** 22 **22.** 229 **23.** 25
24. 1 **25.** 0 **26.** 9200
D. **27.** yes **28.** yes **29.** No **30.** No
E. **31.** 1 **32.** 1 **33.** 537 **34.** 537
F. **35.** 100 each, 73 **36.** 317 **37.** 35 **38.** 10
39. 99981 **40.** 30

PRACTICE EXERCISES 7. *(Page 33)*

A. **1.** No **2.** Yes **3.** yes **4.** No **5.** Yes **6.** yes
B. **7.** Yes **8.** Yes **9.** No **10.** Yes **11.** No **12.** No
C. **13.** Yes **14.** Yes **15.** Yes **16.** No **17.** Yes **18.** Yes
D. **19.** Yes **20.** Yes **21.** Yes **22.** Yes **23.** Yes **24.** No
E. **25.** Yes **26.** Yes **27.** Yes **28.** Yes **29.** No **30.** Yes
F. **31.** Yes **32.** Yes **33.** No **34.** No **35.** Yes **36.** Yes
G. **37.** Yes **38.** No **39.** Yes **40.** No
H. **41.** divisible by 5 only **42.** divisible by both 5, 10 **43.** divisible by 5 only
44. divisible by both 5, 10 **45.** divisible by both 5, 10 **46.** divisible by both 5, 10
I. **47.** true **48.** untrue **49.** untrue **50.** true **51.** true **52.** true
J. **53.** 14 **54.** 12 **55.** 48

PRACTICE EXERCISES 8. *(page 41)*

A. **1.** two **2.** one set **3.** neither prime nor composite **4.** composite number
5. Greece **6.** 2 **7.** 3 **8.** multiple **9.** common prime factor

C. **14.** $2 \times 2 \times 2 \times 2 \times 3 \times 3$　　**15.** $2 \times 2 \times 2 \times 2 \times 2 \times 2 \times 2 \times 2 \times 2 \times 2$

16. $5 \times 5 \times 5 \times 5 \times 5 \times 5$　　**17.** $2 \times 2 \times 2 \times 13 \times 29$

18. $2 \times 2 \times 2 \times 2 \times 2 \times 2 \times 3 \times 3$　　**19.** $2 \times 3 \times 131$

20. $2 \times 2 \times 3 \times 3 \times 5$　　　　　**21.** $2 \times 2 \times 2 \times 2 \times 2 \times 2 \times 2 \times 2 \times 3$

D. **22.** Yes　　**23.** Yes　　**24.** Yes　　**25.** No　　**26.** Yes

27. No　　**28.** No　　**29.** Yes

E. **30.** 12　　**31.** 1　　**32.** 8　　**33.** 9　　**34.** 125

35. 51　　**36.** 16　　**37.** 36　　**38.** 13　　**39.** 12

40. 36　　**41.** 13　　**42.** 129　　**43.** 24　　**44.** 31 *(Read 155)*

F. **45.** 115　　**46.** 4　　**47.** 145　　**48.** 4　　**49.** 8　　**50.** 747

51. 41　　**52.** 34　　**53.** 301　　**54.** 2665　　**55.** 247　　**56.** 10

G. **57.** 36　　**58.** 15 cm.　　**59.** 852　　**60.** 185　　**61.** By proving that their HCF is 1

62. 7 cm. square, 864 tiles　　**63.** 525, 385　　**64.** D = 479 Q = 83

65. (a) $\dfrac{7}{9}$　　(b) $\dfrac{7}{9}$　　(c) $\dfrac{8}{9}$

66. (a) 1 (b) 1　　**67.** See page 37 *(Remember)*　　**68.** See page 38

PRACTICE EXERCISES 9 (Page 47)

A. **1.** their product　　**2.** L.C.M.　　**3.** No　　**4.** a　　**5.** b　　**6.** a factor

B. **7.** 4　　**8.** 6　　**9.** 6　　**10.** 9　　**11.** 84　　**12.** 72

13. 24　　**14.** 18　　**15.** 30　　**16.** 140　　**17.** 300　　**18.** 126

C. **19.** 12　　**20.** 30　　**21.** 90　　**22.** 180　　**23.** 3780　　**24.** 1008

25. 420　　**26.** 2520　　**27.** 252　　**28.** 600　　**29.** 560　　**30.** 180

D. **31.** 432　　**32.** 450　　**33.** 200　　**34.** 126　　**35.** 180　　**36.** 6720

E. **37.** 220168, 1　　**38.** 9061, 13　　**39.** 2145, 15　　**40.** 3630, 22　　**41.** 936, 78　　**42.** 1848, 14

F. **43.** Rs. 5　　**44.** 39312　　**45.** 5040 km.　　**46.** 11 a.m.　　**47.** 1265　　**48.** 23

49. 3315　　**50.** 145　　**51.** 8700　　**52.** 256　　**53.** 1092 m　　**54.** 857

55. 1663　　**56.** 10507　　**57.** 613　　**58.** 182

PRACTICE EXERCISE 10 (Page 51)

A. **1.** +ve　　**2.** +ve　　**3.** +ve　　**4.** +ve　　**5.** –ve　　**6.** +ve

7. –ve　　**8.** –ve　　**9.** –ve　　**10.** +ve　　**11.** +ve　　**12.** –ve

B. **13.** 5　　**14.** –1　　**15.** 1　　**16.** 0　　**17.** 9　　**18.** 3

C. **19.** 112　　**20.** 11　　**21.** 74　　**22.** 120　　**23.** 457　　**24.** 51

D. **25.** -99　　**26.** –487　　**27.** 1　　**28.** –2　　**29.** –5　　**30.** –526

31. –7　　**32.** –5　　**33.** –701　　**34.** –240　　**35.** –201　　**36.** –20

E. 37. (a) **38.** (b) **39.** (b) **40.** (a)

F. 41. No **42.** Yes **43.** Yes **44.** Yes **45.** Yes **46.** Yes

G. 47. –5 **48.** –9 **49.** –3 **50.** 5

H. 51. –8, –4, –1, 0, 1, 7 **52.** –12, –9, –4, 0, 7, 9

I. 53. 1, 3, **54.** –1, –3

55. –2, –1, 0, 1, 2, **56.** –8, –7, –6, –5,

E. 57. absolute value **58.** natural numbers **59.** whole numbers **60.** integers

PRACTICE EXERCISES 11 (Page 54)

A. 1. Yes **2.** Yes **3.** No **4.** Yes **5.** Yes

B. 6. 0 **7.** 0 **8.** –10 **9.** 2 **10.** 1

11. –13 **12.** –2 **13.** 1 **14.** –2

C. 15. –254 **16.** 8822 **17.** –496 **18.** 133 **19.** 47 **20.** –12326

21. 1754 **22.** –18 **23.** 7 **24.** –1021 **25.** 490 **26.** –608

27. 0 **28.** 1 **29.** –40 **30.** –1416 **31.** –10 **32.** 0

PRACTICE EXERCISES 12 (Page 55)

A. 1. 18 **2.** 15 **3.** –22 **4.** 40 **5.** 600 **6.** –1003.

7. –2695 **8.** –7724 **9.** –17780 **10.** 786 **11.** –595 **12.** –971

13. 1155 **14** –1105 **15.** –5723

B. 16. 6 **17.** –17 **18.** 0 **19.** 18 **20.** –348

21. 309 **22.** 145 **23.** 98 **24.** 77

C. 25. 8 **26.** –15 **27.** No **28.** 114 **29.** 592

30. 17°C **31.** 8265 m **32.** 19 **33.** 1 **34.** 3, 3 **35.** –8

36. 13 **37.** 70 **38.** –4 **39.** 13 **40.** –4

PRACTICE EXERCISES 13 (Page 58)

A. 1. +ve **2.** +ve **3.** –ve **4.** +ve

5. –ve **6.** –ve **7.** –ve **8.** +ve

B. 9. –75 **10.** 750 **11.** 195 **12.** –350 **13.** 440

14. –4320 **15.** 280 **16.** 0 **17.** 11840 **18.** 21840

19. 576 **20.** 630 **21.** –900 **22.** 6600 **23.** 0

24. 18100 **25.** –448

C. 26. first **27.** first **28.** first **29.** first **30.** second

D. 31. Yes **32.** Yes **33.** No

A. **1.** +ve   **2.** –ve   **3.** –ve   **4.** +ve

B. **5.** 6   **6.** 3   **7.** 3   **8.** 3   **9.** –5   **10.** 4

11. 0.   **12.** –6   **13.** 12   **14.** –125   **15.** 81   **16.** –1

17. 9   **18.** –16825   **19.** –144   **20.** 8   **21.** –7   **22.** 7

23. 0   **24.** –9   **25.** 9

C. **26.** –1   **27.** 101   **28.** 0   **29.** –19   **30.** –512   **31.** 657

32. 108   **33.** 20   **34.** –18   **35.** –306   **36.** +ve   **37.** unlike

A. **1.** 2, 8   **2.** –3, 5   **3.** –3, 3   **4.** –a, 7

B. **5.** 3^6 **6.** 7^7 **7.** $(-11)^5$ **8.** 5^8

C. **9.** 900   **10.** 576   **11.** –512   **12.** 1   **13.** 64   **14.** –243

15. 1   **16.** –9261   **17.** 4096   **18.** –3125   **19.** 72   **20.** 81

D. **21.** 1, 4, 9, 16, 25, 36, 49, 64, 81   **22.** 1, 8, 27. 64, 125, 216, 343, 512, 729

23. 4^2, 5^2, 7^2, 9^2, 11^2 **24.** 169, 225, 289, 361, 441, 529, 729, 841

25. 1331, 8000, 15625, 27000, 64000   **26.** 399   **27.** 1072

E. **28.** Yes   **29.** Yes   **30.** Yes

A. **1** 2   **2.** 17   **3.** 133   **4.** $2\frac{1}{2}$ **5.** 52   **6.** 14

7. 4   **8.** 4   **9.** –13   **10.** 13   **11.** 8   **12.** 73

B. **13.** $(9+5)\div7$ **14.** $(7\times4)\div2$ **15.** $50\div\{1+(4+5)\}$

A. **1.** 1   **2.** 0   **3.** unidentified   **4.** 1

5. 2   **6.** composite number   **7.** 1, 2   **8.** H.C.F

B. **9.** ✓   **10.** ✓   **11.** ✓   **12.** ☒   **13.** ☒   **14.** ✓

15. ✓   **16.** ✓   **17.** ✓   **18.** ✓   **19.** ✓   **20.** ✓

C. **21.** 1 onwards   **22.** 0 onwards   **23.** numbers with no common factor except 1

24. two prime numbers with only one composite number between them.

25. the number only 1 less than a given number.

26. the number only 1 larger than a given number.

27. two or more quantities added together.

28. quantity from which another quantity is subtracted.

29. quantity subtracted from a minuend.

30. numeral divided by another numeral.

31. quantity multiplied by another quantity.

32. a numeral that divides another numeral.

33. system of numbers including *natural numbers, 0* and *negative numbers.*

34. natural number above zero   **35.** integers below zero.

36. dividend.   **37.** Bhaaskraachaarya, India   **38.** idea   **39.** numeral.

40. 3   **41.** Eratosthenes   **42.** factor.   **43.** numerical .

44. like.   **45.** –ve.   **46.** base, index

47. (a)
```
   647
 + 289
 -----
   936
```
(b)
```
  5872
− 1393
 -----
  4479
```
(c)
```
  5837
− 1243
 -----
  4594
```

(d)
```
    9837
     308
   78696
    0000
   29511
 -------
 3029796
```

(e)
```
715 ) 153725 ( 215
      1430
      ----
      1072
       715
      ----
      3575
      3575
      ----
         0
```

E. 48. 14024   **49.** 87903000   **50.** 42   **51.** 16

52. (a) $\dfrac{7}{9}$ (b) $\dfrac{5}{8}$ (c) $\dfrac{7}{8}$ **53.** 3771   **54.** 1740

F. 55. 10   **56.** 84.

G. 57. 31, 29, 7, 0, –29, –31

58. 80000000+7000000+600000+10000+2000+400+70+5

59. 5 × 5 × 5 × 5 × 5   **60.** (–1) × (–1) × (–1) × (–1) × (–1) × (–1) × (–1) × (–1) × (–1) × (–1) × (–1) × (–1)   **61.** 11^3 **62.** 2^{10} **63.** 5^6

64. –17   **65.** 86

PRACTICE EXERCISES 17 *(Page 74)*

A. 1. 5 : 7   **2.** 1 : 2   **3.** 3 : 4   **4.** 2 : 3   **5.** 9 : 10

B. 6. 5 : 9   **7.** 9   **8.** 2   **9.** antecedent   **10.** consequent

C. 11. 5 : 4   **12.** 1 : 3   **13.** 1 : 10   **14.** 9 : 7   **15.** 1 : 2

16. 10 : 7   **17.** 4 : 1

D. 18. (a) 1 : 10 (b) 1 : 50 (c) 1 : 5   **19.** (a) 9 : 11 (b) 9 : 20 (c) 11 : 20   **20.** 42, 12

21. Rs. 287, Rs. 328   **22.** Rs. 305, Rs. 549, Rs. 671

23. (a) 5 : 6 > 2 : 3   (b) 3 : 4 > 2 : 3   (c) 17 : 25 > 3 : 5 (d) 4 : 5 > 5 : 8

(e) 7 : 8 > 7 : 10 (f) 15 : 16 > 37 : 40

24. 54   **25** Rs 1100   **26.** $p=3$ **27.** 420, 270

A. **1.** true   **2.** untrue   **3.** true   **4.** true   **5.** true

B. **6.** yes   **7.** no   **8.** yes   **9.** yes

C. **10.** 221   **11.** 168   **12.** 32   **13.** 15   **14.** 64   **15.** 35

D. **16.** 4·5   **17.** $\dfrac{y^2}{x}$ **18.** ·126   **19.** $\dfrac{24}{25}$ **20.** $9\dfrac{1}{3}$ **21.** 49

E. **22.** 56   **23.** 77   **24.** 60   **25.** 16   **26.** 22   **27.** 21

   28. 6   **29.** a^2b^2 **30.** 9

F **31.** When the 1st × 4th = 2nd × 3rd ; as 2 : 3 :: 6 : 9

32. When the 1st × 3rd = 2nd² ; as 25 : 45 and 81

33. The *first* and the *fourth* terms of a proportion are called its *extremes.*

34. The *second* and the *third* terms of a proportion are called its *means.*

35. Product of the *extremes* = Product of the *means.* 2 : 3 :: 6 : 9 in which 2 × 9 = 3 × 6

36. When three quantities are in a continued proportion, the second quantity is called the mean proportional. (16 : 20 :: 20 : 25)   **37.** yes

G. **38.** 168   **39.** Rs 8000   **40.** Rs. 2000   **41.** 1984, 930   **42.** $2\dfrac{2}{3}$ kg

43. $26\dfrac{2}{3}$ m   **44.** 8   **45.** 36   **46.** (a) 180 km   (b) 13·3 cm

A. **1.** Rs. 2   **2.** Rs 40   **3.** 12 days   **4.** 40 paise   **5.** Rs 10

   6. Rs 360   **7.** Rs 20   **8.** 75 days

B. **9.** Rs 315   **10.** Rs 196   **11.** 17 books   **12.** (a) 8 hours   (b) 410 km   **13.** Rs 250

   14. 9 days   **15.** 3 hours   **16.** 60 km   **17.** 51 km/hr   **18.** Rs 6000

   19. Rs 912·50   **20.** 28·5 min.   **21.** Rs 2480   **22.** Rs 21   **23.** 34 km

A. **1.** 43·75%   **2.** 62·5%   **3.** $52\dfrac{8}{21}\%$ **4.** $71\dfrac{3}{7}\%$ **5.** $29\dfrac{7}{17}\%$

   6. 60%   **7.** 35%   **8.** $16\dfrac{2}{3}\%$ **9.** $66\dfrac{2}{3}\%$ **10.** 50%

B. **11.** $\dfrac{8}{25}$, ·32, 8 : 25   **12.** $\dfrac{4}{5}$, ·8, 4 : 5   **13.** $\dfrac{1}{16}$, ·0625, 1 : 16

   14. $\dfrac{1}{3}$, ·33, 1 : 3   **15.** $\dfrac{19}{300}$, ·063, 19 : 300   **16.** $\dfrac{1}{40}$, ·025, 1 : 40

   17. $\dfrac{3}{40}$, ·075, 3 : 40   **18.** $\dfrac{3}{200}$, ·015, 3 : 200   **19.** $\dfrac{3}{160}$, ·01875, 3 : 160

   20. $\dfrac{13}{1000}$, ·013, 13 : 1000

C. **21.** 80% **22.** $66\frac{2}{3}$% **23.** $83\frac{1}{3}$% **24.** 60% **25.** 20%

26. 37·5% **27.** 25% **28.** $16\frac{2}{3}$% **29.** 50% **30.** 40%

D. **31.** ·03 **32.** ·125 **33.** ·3 **34.** ·075 **35.** ·25

36. ·75 **37.** ·07 **38.** ·135 **39.** ·1375 **40.** ·26

E. **41.** 40% **42.** 2% **43.** 2·75% **44.** 6·3% **45.** 56%

46. 8% **47.** 12·5% **48.** ·3% **49.** 70% **50.** 9%

F **51.** Rs 63 **52.** Rs 1·75 **53.** Rs 15·75 **54.** Rs 36·69 **55.** Rs 176

56. Rs.39·19

G **57.** 28·75% **58.** $\frac{50}{151}$% **59.** $2\frac{5}{14}$% **60.** 1·4% **61.** ·8%

62. $11\frac{1}{9}$% **63.** $4\frac{4}{9}$% **64.** $33\frac{1}{3}$% **65.** 5%

H. **66.** 6% **67.** 0·75 **68.** 0·9 **69.** 2·5 **70.** 1·6

71. 90% **72.** $\frac{1}{4}$ **73.** $\frac{1}{8}$ **74.** $1\frac{5}{8}$

I. **75.** 75% **76.** 30% **77.** 40% **78.** $83\frac{1}{3}$% **79.** 37·5% **80.** 50%

81. $41\frac{2}{3}$% **82.** 62·5% **83.** 70% **84.** $66\frac{2}{3}$% **85.** 50% **86.** 43·75%

J. **87.** 308 **88.** Rs. 4600 **89.** 400 **90.** Rs. 2820 **91.** 650

92. $16\frac{2}{3}$% **93.** Rs 7000 **94.** 232000 **95.** 12 marks **96.** 1492800

97. 400 m **98.** Rs. 40,000 **99.** 6 **100.** Rs. 90, Rs. 79·50, Rs. 130·50

PRACTICE EXERCISES 21 (Page 97)

A. **1.** gain = Rs 70 ; gain% = $12\frac{1}{2}$% **2.** gain = Rs 100 ; gain% = 25 %

3. gain = Rs 70 ; gain% = $8\frac{1}{3}$% **4.** gain = Rs 500 ; gain% = $8\frac{1}{3}$%

5. gain = Rs 50 ; gain% = 25% **6.** gain = Rs 100 ; gain% = 4%

B. **7.** loss = Rs 64 ; loss% = 16% **8.** loss = Rs 300 ; loss% = 5 %

9. loss = Rs 4 ; loss% = 16% **10.** loss = Rs 45 ; loss% = $8\frac{1}{3}$%

11. loss = Rs 6 ; loss% = $11\frac{1}{9}$% **12.** loss = Rs 34 ; loss% = 10%

C **13.** Rs. 100 **14.** Rs. 2900 **15.** Rs. 300 **16.** Rs. 317·50

17. Rs. 636 **18.** Rs. 1820 **19.** Rs. 3332 **20.** Rs. 465·50

D. **21.** Rs. 650 **22.** Rs. 96 **23.** Rs. 4250 **24.** Rs.49·50

25. Rs. 645 **26.** Rs. 42 **27.** Rs. 360 **28.** Rs1080

E. **29.** Gain = $\dfrac{\text{Actual Gain} \times 100}{\text{C.P.}}$ Loss% = $\dfrac{\text{Actual Loss} \times 100}{\text{C.P.}}$ **30.** S.P. = $\dfrac{\text{C.P} \times 100 + \text{gain}\%}{100}$

or S.P = $\dfrac{\text{C.P} \times (100 - \text{loss}\%)}{100}$ **31.** C.P. = $\dfrac{100 \times \text{S.P.}}{(100 + \text{gain}\%)}$ or C.P. = $\dfrac{\text{S.P} \times 100}{(100 - \text{loss}\%)}$

F. 32. 10% **33.** $14\frac{2}{7}$% **34.** Rs. 143 **35.** Rs. 60 **36.** 20%

37. Rs. $6\frac{2}{3}$ **38.** Rs. 200 **39.** Rs. 448 **40.** 4 % loss **41.** Rs. 32·50

42. Rs. 250 **43.** 25% **44.** 5 **45.** $\frac{1}{3}$ litre **46.** Rs. 200

47. Rs. 36000 **48.** Rs. 200/quintal **49.** $1\frac{19}{31}$% **50.** 90 paise an *egg*

51. 10% **52.** 5 for a rupee **53.** $33\frac{1}{3}$ % gain

PRACTICE EXERCISES 22 (Page 104)

A. 1. Rs. 42 **2.** Rs.73·15 **3.** Rs. 305 **4.** Rs. 720 **5.** 2016

B. 6. Rs. 9504 **7.** Rs.1853·35 **8.** Rs. 1640·31 **9.** Rs. 225·57 **10.** Rs. 7224

C. 11. Rs. 800 **12.** Rs. 5200 **13.** Rs. 3000 **14.** Rs. 730 **15.** Rs. 3200

D. 16. 3·6 yrs **17.** 2·5 yrs **18.** 8 yrs **19.** 8 yrs **20.** 4 yrs

E. 21. 5% **22.** 6% **23.** 4% **24.** 3% **25.** 3%

F. 26. Rs. 1344 **27.** Rs. 3750, Rs 10,000 **28.** Rs. 4505 **29.** Rs. 8288

30. Rs. 7182 **31.** Rs. 12060 **32.** Rs. 50 **33.** Rs. 6562·60 **34.** Rs. 1020

35. 5% **36.** 20th January **37.** Rs. 2080 **38.** $6\frac{2}{3}$%

MISCELLANEOUS EXERCISES — II (Page 106)

F. 1. $12\frac{1}{2}$% **2.** 142800 **3.** Rs. 50 **4.** Rs. 21000 **5.** Rs. 34·20

6. 8% **7.** Rs. 230 **8.** 8% **9.** 35 days **10.** Rs. 365000

11. Rs. 1080 **12.** Rs. 5060 **13.** Rs. 6250 **14.** $2\frac{1}{2}$ yrs **15.** 25000 m, 5000 m

16. Rs. 2200 **17.** 12 : 7 **18.** Rs. 10·80 **19.** 2·86 **20.** 2667 m.

21. Rs. 18 **22.** 99 h.p. **23.** Rs. 15 **24.** $15\frac{3}{5}$ % **25.** Rs. 250

26. Rs. 21000 **27.** Rs. 6350·65 **28.** 240 days

PRACTICE EXERCISES 23 (Page 114)

A. 1. to 8. *see page 111 and 112*

B. 9. four basic **10.** no **11.** $x - y$ **12.** addition **13.** base, index

14. factors **15.** itself

C. 16. $9 + a$ **17.** $b - c$ **18.** $2x < (y + z)$ **19.** $8 - a$ **20.** $8m - 7$

21. $(a + b) \div 3$ **22.** $\frac{y}{z} + yz$ **23.** $7x = z - y$

D. 24. $a^{10} \div x^{12}$ **25.** (a) $a \times a \times a \times b \times b \times b \times b \times b \times b \times b$

(b) $x \times x \times x \times x \times x \times y \times y \times y \times y \times y \times y$ (c) $l \times l \times l \times l \times m \times m \times m$ **26.** $181 + x$

E. 27. polynomial **28.** monomial **29.** binomial **30.** polynomial

31. monomial **32.** binomial **33.** ploynomial **34.** monomial

F. 35. $2a, -3b, -4c$ **36.** $-5bc, -7ab, 2ab$ **37.** $bz, 4ac, 2ab$ **38.** $3x, -4y$

G **39.** $3z + 2ab + 3xy$ **40.** $7lm + 3mn + 8$ **41.** $4z - 3y - 2x$

. **42.** $5x^2 + 2x + 8$ **43.** $4p^2 - 3pq + 8$

H. **44.** 1   **45.** 2   **46.** -1 **47.** 6   **48.** 9   **49.** a

PRACTICE EXERCISES 24 *(Page 118)*

A. **1.** $9a$ **2.** $8p$ **3.** $13b$ **4.** $2a + 3b$ **5.** $7x + 9y$ **6.** $9xy + y$

7. $4(p + q)$ **8.** $x(2x + 5)$ **9.** $-2x^2$ **10.** ab **11.** $-x^3$ **12.** $6x$

B. **13.** $x^2 + 4x - 1$ **14.** $2x^2 - 11x + 6$ **15.** $7x - y - z$

16. $-5x + 3z$ **17.** $2x^3 + 8x^2 - 4x + 3$ **18.** $6x^3 + 2x^2 - 2x + 13$

19. $4x^2 - 3xy + 3y^2$ **20.** $14x^2 - 13y - 18z^3$ **21.** $p^2 + q^2$

C. **22.** $2pq + 4qr - 7$ **23.** $-5ab + bc + zx$

D. **24.** $3x$ **25.** $3a$ **26.** $13y$ **27.** $5b - 2a$ **28.** $6q - 4p$ **29.** $5y - 11x$

30. $3x^2$ **31.** $-3p^3$ **32.** $17ab$ **33.** $-4xy$ **34.** $20x^2$ **35.** $-ab$

E. **36.** $-6a + b + 5c$ **37.** $11x + 2y + 5z$ **38.** $-2x^3 - 8x^2 + 4x - 3$

39. $-2a + 3b + 5c - 13d$ **40.** $5x^2 + 3xy + 8y^2 - 7$

F. **41.** $x^4 + 7x^3 - 4x^2 + 8x + 7$ **42.** $4x^2 - 4x + 1$

43. $-x + 5y - 4z$ **44.** $x - 2y - 4z$ **45.** $-x^3 + 4x^2 - 9x + 7$ **46.** y

47. $x^4 - 2x^2y^2 + 5y^4$ **48.** $-2x^3 - 7x^2 - 4x - 9$ **49.** $2x^2 - 14x + 12$

PRACTICE EXERCISES 25 *(Page 120)*

A. **1.** $x - y + 2z$ **2.** $4 - 2b + a - 2c$ **3.** $8x - 2y - 3z$

4. $5x^2 - 11xy - 13$ **5.** $6 - 2ab$ **6.** $6x^2 - y + 4z + 7$

7. $8a - 4b - 7$ **8.** $x^4 - 2x^2 + x^2 - 2x + 1$ **9.** $x - 2y + 2z$

10. $5x$ **11.** $-x - 8y$

B. **12.** -1 **13.** -1 **14.** -23 **15.** 15   **16.** -9

17. -106 **18.** 109   **19.** 431   **20.** 8

PRACTICE EXERCISES 26 *(Page 124)*

1. see page 121   **2.** see page 122   **3.** see page 122

4. see page 122   **5.** see page 123   **6.** see page 123

B. **7.** $x - 7 = 14$ **8.** $a \div 3 = 8$ **9.** $5x = 55$

10. $2a - 11 = 11$ **11.** $2x - 15 = 17$ **13.** $(x + 1) + (x + 2) + (x + 3) + (x + 4) = 26$

C **13.** $\frac{2x}{5}$ and 6   **14.** $7x + 8$ and 43   **15.** $36 - y$ and 24

16. $3x - 6$ and 15   **17.** $3x + 20$ and 62   **18.** $9x - 13$ and $11x + 35$

D. **19.** $x = -14$ **20.** $a = 4$ **21.** $x = 5$ **22.** $x = 2$ **23.** $x = 1$

24. $y = 9$ **25.** $x = 16$ **26.** $y = 48$ **27.** $x = 5$

E. **28.** $x = 3$ **29.** $a = -17$ **30.** $y = -4$ **31.** $x = -1$

32. $x = -4$ **33.** $x = 24$ **34.** $a = 9$ **35.** $a = 36$

A. 1. 30, 45   **2.** 9 yrs, 36 yrs   **3.** 16m, 24m   **4.** 28, 36
5. 38m, 76m   **6.** 18 yrs old   **7.** 35, 37   **8.** 12, 14, 16
9. 30 yrs   **10.** 75 coins   **11.** 8m, 12m

MISCELLANEOUS EXERCISES III (Page 127)

A. 1. see page 111   **2.** see page 111   **3.** see page 112   **4.** see page 112
5. see page 112   **6.** see page 112   **7.** see page 123   **8.** see page 116

B. 9. addition, subtraction, multiplication, division.   **10.** vinculum (bar) three types of brackets
11. Left Hand Side, Right Hand Side.

C. 12. $x - a$ **13.** $5 + \dfrac{a}{b}$ **14.** $xy - \dfrac{x}{y}$

D. 15. 9cm, 6cm, 3cm   **16.** $-5a^2 - 11ab + b^2$.   **17.** $11a + 2b + 5c$
18. $6y^2 - 3xy + 1$ **19.** $5x$.   **20.** 23

21. A linear equation has one variable/ variables of the first degree only.
22. (a) same   (b) subtracted   (c) sides   (d) same quantity
23. $a = 2$ **24.** 31, 93   **25.** 18 yrs old   **26.** 43, 45
27. 22, 24, 26   **28.** 18 yrs, 27 yrs   **29.** 1, 19   **30.** 10cm, 30cmpp

PRACTICE EXERCISES 28 (Page 134)

A. 1. points   **2.** unlimited number   **3.** only one   **4.** a line
5. a plane   **6.** a line   **7.** a point   **8.** collinear
9. non-collinear   **10.** a ball   **11.** a table-top   **12.** only one

B. 13. a point is a fine dot like mark.
14. a line is a thread-like thin straight or curved drawing that is endless.
15. a part of a line lying between any two points located on the line .
16. a plane is a flat surface such that the straight line joining any three non-collinear points in it lie wholly inside its bounds.
17. lines drawn such that they never meet however long they are produced on both sides.
18. lines drawn such that they meet when produced in one side.
19. the planes that never meet each other.
20. the planes that meet each other to form a corner/edge.
21. lines passing through the same point.

C. 22. (a) only one   (b) three   **23.** ten   **24.** a brick, a box, the top of a table, a book, a match-box
25. six, three   **26.** (a) c, d ; a, d ; b, c ; a, b   (b) P, Q, R, S   (c) A, R, S, B
   (d) c, d, e   (e) a, b, e
27. (a) AB, CA, AD   (b) D, R, C ; P, O, Q ; A, S, B ; R, O, S ; D, O, B ; A, O, C ; D, P, A ; C, Q, B
   (c) DC, BD, AD, and DRC, SOR
28. Fig 1. (a) *Points* : A, B, C, D, E, F, G, H ; *Lines* : AB, BC, CD, DA, BH, AG, EF, FG, GH, HE, EC, FD
      Planes : ABGH, EFCD, CEHB, ABCD, EFGH, ADFG
     Fig 2. (b) *Points* B, G, P, A, C, H, Q, D, E, R, S, F *Lines* : BGPA, CHQD, ERSP, GHR, PQS, BCE, ADF
     Planes : only one. **29.** *Parallel Planes* : ABCD and, EFGH. *Intresecting Planes* : ABCD and, BCEH.
30. (a) untrue   (b) untrue   (c) true   (d) untrue   (e) true   (f) true

PRACTICE EXERCISES 29 (Page 142)

2. (a) 1200 (b) 860 (c) 506 (d) 90 (e) 106 (f) 580 (g) 276

3. (a) 170 (b) 53 (c) 8630 (d) 127 (e) 46 (f) 67 (g) 1350
(h) 34

5. 3·6cm. **8.** (a) 6 (b) AOL, BOM, CON

PRACTICE EXERCISES 30 (Page 150)

A. **1.** a line has no end-point while a ray has one end-point.

2. a ray has only one end-point but a line-segment has two end-points.

3. The interior of an angle is enclosed by its arms but its exterior is outside then.

4. A vertex is a common point for two non-collinear line-segment but an end-point is a common point for two rays.

B. **5.** see page 144, 145, 148, **12.** OA, OC

13. Dividers, compasses, tongs, forceps

14. Fig 1 : ∠RDQ, ∠DQR, ∠DRQ, ∠SRQ, ∠RQS, ∠RSQ

Fig 2 : ∠AED, ∠EAB, ∠EDC, ∠DCB, ∠CBA

15. ∠1= ∠COB, ∠2 = ∠AOD, ∠3 = ∠BOD, ∠4 = ∠AOC

16. See pages 145, 146

17. The magnitude of an angle means its size. It depends on the amount of rotation of one of its arms from its initial point.

18. By observation, by superimposition, by measurement

PRACTICE EXERCISES 31 (Page 155)

A. **1.** see page 146 **2.** see page 151 **3.** see page 152 **4.** see page 152

5. see page152 **6.** see page 153 **7.** see page 153 **8.** see page 153

9. rails of rail track, edges of table-top, match box, brick, box

10. (a) AD, BC and AB, CD   (b) EF, GH and FG, EH   (c) LM, QR

(d) AD, EF, ; AE, DF ; AD, BC ; DF, GC ; AE, BH ; BH, CG ; BC, GH ; EF, HG

(e) PQ, RS ; PS, QR.   **11.** (a) non-parallel lines   (b) parallel lines

(c) distance   (d) transversal   **12.** plane   **13.** (a) AB, CD   (b) EF

(c) ∠1, ∠2, ∠3, ∠4   (d) ∠5, ∠6, ∠7, ∠8   (e) ∠4, ∠2,   (f) ∠5, ∠7

14. (a) QR   (b) PQ   (c) AB   (d) QR

15. (a) P   (b) P   (c) P

PRACTICE EXERCISES 32 (Page 160)

A. **1.** obtuse **2.** acute **3.** straight **4.** right **5.** reflex **6.** complete

B. **7.** See page 157 **8.** See page 158 **9.** See page 157 **10.** See page 158

11. See page 157 **12.** See page 158 **13.** See page 157 **14.** See page 158

15. see page 158   **16.** see page 159   **17.** see page 159   **18.** see page 158
19. see page 157

C. **20.** acute   **21.** adjacent   **22.** a complementary   **23.** supplementary

24. alternate   **25.** corresponding   **26.** vertically opposite angles

D. **27.** 45°   **28.** 90°   **29.** 120°   **30.** 60°   **31.** 144°   **32.** 72°

E. **33.** F   **34.** T   **35.** F   **36.** T   **37.** F   **38.** T

39. F   **40.** F   **41.** $\angle 2 = 70°$, $\angle 4 = 110°$, $\angle 3 = 110°$

42. $y = 36°$, $y = 15°$, $y = 18°$

43. When they are on the opposite side of a transversal cutting two parallel lines.

44. When they are on the same side of a transversal on the two parallel lines cut by the transversal.

45. $\angle 2$, $\angle 5$ and $\angle 4$, $\angle 7$ are two pairs of internal alternate angles

$\angle 3$, $\angle 8$ and $\angle 1$, $\angle 6$ are two pairs of exterior alternate angles

PRACTICE EXERCISES 33 (Page 168)

A. **1.** trigon   **2.** triangle   **3.** $\triangle$ BCA, $\triangle$ CAB   **4.** three

5. angular point   **6.** base   **7.** vertical angle   **8.** its boundary

9. its interior   **10.** its interior and exterior   **11.** equiangular triangle

12. isosceles triangle   **13.** 180°   **14.** sum of the two interior opposite angles.

15. one   **16.** two   **17.** one   **18.** six   **19.** $\triangle$

B. **20.** see page 166   **21.** see page 168   **22.** see page 168

23. see page 167   **24.** see page 167   **25.** see page 167

26. see page 168   **27.** see page 168   **28.** see page 166

29. see page 168

C. **30.** is greater than   **31.** two r.t. angles   **32.** sides, angles

33. three, three, three   **34.** scalene   **35.** concurrent

36. exterior   **37.** interior   **38.** boundary

39. interior opposite   **40.** sides, third side

D. **41.** 40°, 60°, 80°   **42.** 4 rt. $\angle$s   **44.** 36°, 54°

45. $\angle A = 80°$, $\angle B = 60°$, $\angle C = 40°$ **46.** 4 rt. $\angle$s

47. $\angle C = 45°$, $\angle 1 = 70°$, $\angle 2 = 45°$ **48.** 45° each

49. 130°   **50.** $\angle B = 30°$, $\angle 1 = 60°$, $\angle 2 = 30°$ **51.** a, b, c all are possible $\triangle$5.

PRACTICE EXERCISES 34 (Page 174)

9.   **10.**   **11.**

236

12. (a) false   (b) true   (c) true   (d) true   (e) false   (f) false

13. Yes, they are all equal.   **14.** ∠POR = 2 ∠PAQ

PRACTICE EXERCISES 35 (Page 179)

A.   **1.** see page 177   **2.** see page 177   **3.** see page 177

C.   **13.** Yes   **14.** Yes   **15.** No

     16. Yes   **17.** Yes   **18.** Yes

MISCELLANEOUS EXERCISES IV (Page 184)

A.   **1.** see page 130   **2.** see page 130   **3.** see page 131   **4.** see page 133

     5. see page 151   **6.** see page 137   **7.** see page 144   **8.** see page 144

B.   **9.** acute   **10.** right   **11.** obtuse   **12.** straight   **13.** reflex

D. **20.** yes   **21.** yes   **22.** No   **23.** yes   **24.** yes

     25. No   **26.** No

E. **27.** vertical angle   **28.** base   **29.** reflex angle   **30.** scalene triangle   **31.** altitude

    32. circumference   **33.** radius   **34.** tangent   **35.** compasses   **36.** protractor

PRACTICE EXERCISES 37 (Page 190)

A.   **1.** 28 sq. cm.   **2.** 72 sq. cm.   **3.** 30 sq. cm.   **4.** 51 sq. cm.   **5.** 64 sq. cm.

B.   **6.** 39 sq. cm.   **7.** 70 sq. cm.   **8.** 90 sq. cm.   **9.** 68 sq. cm.   **10.** 64 sq. cm.   **11.** 80 sq. cm.

PRACTICE EXERCISES 38 (Page 195)

A.   **1.** 360 sq. m   **2.** 630 sq. m   **3.** 91 sq. cm.   **4.** 782 sq. cm.   **5.** 612 sq. cm.

B.   **6.** 81 sq. cm.   **7.** 256 sq. cm.   **8.** 2025 sq. cm.

     9. 324 sq. cm.   **10.** 1444 sq. cm.   **11.** 3136 sq. cm.

C.   **12.** 612 sq. m   **13.** 60·016 sq. m, 2728 tiles   **14.** Rs. 510

     15. 4290·25 sq. m   **16.** Rs. 576   **17.** Rs. 3975, 10P

     18. 45 seconds   **19.** Rs. 6·75   **20.** 120 students

PRACTICE EXERCISES 39 (Page 198)

    1. Rs. 1330   **2.** 177 sq. m.   **3.** 48 cm^2. ; 50 cm^2 ; 40 cm^2

    4. Rs. 16·5   **5.** 68 sq. m   **6.** 236 sq. m

    7. Rs. 33592   **8.** 216 sq. m.   **9.** Rs. 727·50

A.   **1.** 50·4 sq. m   **2.** 66 sq. m   **3.** 78 sq. m

       4. 56 sq. m   **5.** 144 sq. m   **6.** 105 sq. m

B.   **7.** 98 sq. m   **8.** 128 sq. m, Rs. 128   **9.** 128 sq. m, Rs. 256

     10. Rs. 5·7375   **11.** 72 sq. m, Rs. 1626   **12.** 51·5 sq. m, Rs. 1802·50

     13. Rs. 16740   **14.** Rs. 275

A.   **1.** 1000   **2.** 10, 00000   **3.** (side)^3 **4.** L × B × H   **5.** six

       6. base   **7.** roof   **8.** 12   **9.** 8   **10.** three

B.   **11.** length × breadth × height   **12.** breadth × height   **13.** length × height

     14. length × breadth (area)   **15.** side × side × side

C.   **16.** 576 cm^3 **17.** 43200 cm^3 **18.** 144 cm^3 **19.** 3600 cm^3

     20. 3·24 m^3 **21.** 2343·75 cm^3 **22.** 810 cm^3 **23.** 9 cu. cm.

     24. 189 cu. cm.   **25.** 4·5 cm.   **26.** 91·125 cm^3 **27.** 64 blocks

     28. 378000 litres   **29.** 10752 bricks   **30.** 2 metres   **31.** 1800000 litres

     32. 3 metres   **33.** 1120 cu. m.   **34.** 150 sq. cm.   **35.** 588 sq. cm.

     36. 343 cu. cm.   **37.** 17·94 sq. m., Rs. 5980   **38.** 150 sq. cm.   **39.** Rs. 179·84

     40. Rs. 35·25

A.   **1.** cm. m, km.   **2.** cm^2, m^2, km^2,   **3.** cm^3, m^3, km^3,

B.   **4.** 10000 cm^2 **5.** 1000000 sq. m   **6.** 10,000 sq. m   **7.** 1000 cm^3

C.   **8.** $\frac{1}{2}$ × base × height   **9.** length × breadth   **10.** (side)^2 **11.** (side)^3

     12. length × base × height/depth   **13.** 2(length + breadth) × height

D.   **14.** 5100 sq. m, Rs. 7650   **15.** 3900 sq. m, Rs. 5850   **16.** 156 sq. m, Rs. 234

     17. $2\frac{1}{2}$ metres   **18.** 1 metre   **19.** 1·25

     20. *(a)* eight times   *(b)* one-eight   **21.** Rs. 1195

     7. 6 years ; 16 years ; 8, 14 years ; none

     8. school-bus ; on foot ; 20 students ; 60 students ; 45 students ; 10 students

SET 1

A. **1.** No   **2.** yes   **3.** No
4. yes   **5.** yes

B. **6.** *(c)*   **7.** *(b)*   **8.** *(b)*   **9.** *(a)*

C. **10.** two   **11.** 2   **12.** prime, composite
13. composite

D. **14.** yes   **15.** no   **16.** no

E. **17.** Bhaaskaraachaarya   **18.** Eratosthenes
19. Al Khwarizmi   **20.** Brahma Sankhyaayen

SET II

A. **1.** x–y   **2.** 100, 500, 1000   **3.** 5, 10   **4.** 100 lakhs

B. **5.** *(a)*   **6.** *(a)*   **7.** *(c)*   **8.** *(c)*

C. **9.** fundamental Theorem of Arithmetic   **10.** Hindse
11. consecutive successor   **12.** consecutive predecessor

D. **13.** minuend   **14.** product
15. number   **16.** numerals

E. **17.** *(b)*   **18.** *(a)*
19. *(c)*   **20.** *(b)*

SET III

A. **1.** false   **2.** false   **3.** true   **4.** true

B. **5.** *(b)*   **6.** *(d)*   **7.** *(b)*   **8.** *(b)*
9. *(b)*   **10.** *(c)*   **11.** *(b)*   **12.** *(a)*
13. *(b)*   **14.** *(c)*   **15.** *(b)*

SET IV

1. *(b)*   **2.** *(c)*   **3.** *(c)*   **4.** *(b)*
5. *(b)*   **6.** *(b)*   **7.** *(a)*   **8.** *(c)*
9. *(c*   **10.** *(a)*   **11.** *(d)*   **12.** ✗, ✓, ✓, ✗

GRADED MATHEMATICS
(Parts 0, 1-8)

Hello ! I am Swaminathan, the Head of the department of Mathematics in a renowned public school. I have seen numerous books on mathematics for primary and middle classes written by big hands. I often felt that they lacked the needful. But since I saw the series—**Graded Mathematics**—published by Dreamland Publications, I have been convinced that these are quite up to the mark. They present the subject-matter in an easy-to-follow style just matching the calibre of the pupils of the respective classes. One outstanding feature of these books is the ample practice which is conspicuously lacking in most of the other books. With these books, the students will neither feel bored nor will they fear this high-scoring subject.

Price Rs. 50

Price Rs. 80

Price Rs. 80

Price Rs. 80

Price Rs. 80

Price Rs. 80

Price Rs. 80

Price Rs. 80

Price Rs. 80